Food Lovers'
Guide to
Massachusetts

HELP US KEEP THIS GUIDE UP TO DATE

Every effort has been made by the authors and editors to make this guide as accurate and useful as possible. However, many things can change after a guide is published—establishments close, phone numbers change, facilities come under new management, etc.

We would love to hear from you concerning your experiences with this guide and how you feel it could be improved and kept up to date. While we may not be able to respond to all comments and suggestions, we'll take them to heart and we'll also make certain to share them with the authors. Please send your comments and suggestions to the following address:

Globe Pequot Press
Reader Response/Editorial Department
P.O. Box 480
Guilford, CT 06437

Or you may e-mail us at

editorial@GlobePequot.com

Thanks for your input, and happy travels!

FOOD LOVERS' SERIES

Food Lovers' Guide to Massachusetts

Second Edition

*Best Local Specialties,
Markets, Recipes, Restaurants,
and Events*

Patricia Harris and David Lyon

gpp

Guilford, Connecticut

To buy books in quantity for corporate use
or incentives, call **(800) 962–0973**
or e-mail **premiums@GlobePequot.com**.

Project editor: Jessica Haberman
Layout artist: Melissa Evarts
Text design: Nancy Freeborn
Maps: Rusty Nelson © Morris Book Publishing, LLC
Illustrations © Jill Butler, with additional illustrations by Carleen Moira Powell

ISSN 1544-7405
ISBN 978-0-7627-5308-6

Printed in the United States of America

10 9 8 7 6 5 4 3 2 1

The prices and rates listed in this guidebook were confirmed at press time. We recommend, however, that you call establishments to obtain current information before traveling.

To our friends who plan their vacations
around their restaurant reservations

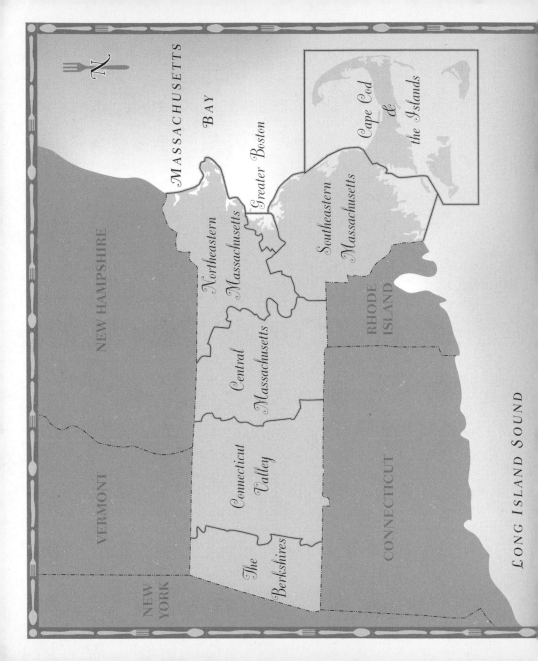

Contents

Acknowledgments

To the Massachusetts farmers, fishermen, chefs, bakers, candy-makers, winemakers, brewmasters, and restaurateurs who gave us good reason to write this book in the first place.

To Laura Strom, who conceived this series, and to editors Cary Hull and Heather Carreiro, who brought the first and second editions, respectively, to fruition.

Many thanks to the following individuals and establishments for graciously providing recipes. Most recipes were adapted for home cooks, and these individuals and companies are not responsible for any inadvertent errors or omissions.

Apple Pizza: Michael Collins, Mike and Tony's Pizza at the Green Emporium; Apple Pie with Dried Apricots and Pineapple: Eileen Maher Kronauer, *Apple of Your Pie*; Berkshire Apple Pancake: Red Lion Inn; Blueberry Bread Pudding: Cecile Collier, Twigs Cafe, Tower

Hill Botanic Garden; Burgundy Pie: Eileen Blake; Cape Cod Crab Cakes: Chatham Fish & Lobster; Chocolate Stout Cake: Barrington Brewery & Restaurant; Cranberry Apple Chutney: Nashoba Valley Winery; Easy Vanilla Wafers: Baldwin & Sons; French Breakfast Puffs: Cottage Street Bakery; Grist Mill Corn Bread: Jenney Grist Mill; Guido's Gazpacho: Guido's Quality Fruit & Produce; Honey Pumpkin Tea Bread: Dunbar Tea Shop; Individual Molten Chocolate Cakes: Delphin Gomes, Cambridge School of Culinary Arts; Jordan Marsh Blueberry Muffins: Jordan Marsh Company; Kale Soup: Bob Gaspar, Gaspar's Sausage Company; Lemon Blackberry Pound Cake: Eunice Feller, Bread & Chocolate Bakery Cafe; Mulled Cider: Clarkdale Fruit Farms; Net Result Baked Cod: Beth Larsen, The Net Result; New England Lobster Bake: Peter Davis, Henrietta's Table, Charles Hotel; Pasta with Tomato Sauce, Broccoli, and Goat Cheese: Westfield Farm; Pilgrim Breakfast Fish Cakes: Mark Santos; Pork Tenderloin with Maple Glaze: North Hadley Sugar Shack; Rice, Lobster, and Cucumber Salad: Chrissi Pappas, Ipswich Shellfish Fish Market; Roasted Garlic: Jeremy Barker-Plotkin, Simple Gifts Farm; Roast Turkey with Rosemary-Scented Stuffing: Kerry Downey Romaniello, Westport Rivers Winery; Scallion-Crusted Cod with Mango Salsa: Ming Tsai, Blue Ginger; Stonehedge's Maple Syrup Crème Brûlée: David Bressler, Left Bank, Stonehedge Inn & Spa; Tuna-Apple Pita Pockets: Ron Williams, Atkins Farms Country Market; Verrill Farm Corn and Tomato Tart: Verrill Farm; Wilted Spinach Salad with Dried Cranberries, Pecans, and Feta: Cape Cod Cranberry Growers' Association.

Introduction

On some level, you don't need this book. All you have to do is follow your nose. As we traveled the breadth of Massachusetts doing research, we often found ourselves transfixed by an aroma in a shop, a scent in the air. Seeking one of the large farm stands in the central part of the state, we put down the map, opened the car windows, and navigated by the sharp smell of freshly harvested onions. Sure enough, when we arrived minutes later, workers were packing them in fifty-pound sacks for shipping. One glorious late August day, we crested a hill and followed our noses to the succulent harvest of freshly picked peaches, heaped in baskets like little globs of sweet sunshine. We burst into bakeries from the winter cold to be assaulted by the heavenly scents of yeast dough and cinnamon. We walked into candy stores where chocolate filled the air.

Again and again we followed our noses—into the fresh salty-sea smell of a fishmonger, the pungent spice of ginger and cardamom in an Indian grocery, the sour promise of fermenting malt in a brewery, the delicate waft of vanilla at an extract maker. The tart scent of cider apples, the astonishing perfume of raspberries, the high and bright notes of roasting coffee beans, the smell of sweet timothy in the dairy barns—they're all part of the scentscape of Massachusetts.

People who raise, harvest, catch, and prepare food are some of the nicest and, we think, noblest people in the world. They share a connection to the deepest and finest impulses of humankind—to nourish, to succor, to share, to provide, to make whole and happy, to satisfy. And they love to talk about what they do and gladly answer questions: What's your favorite? How do you make that? Where does that come from? How long have you grown that and what do you do with it?

These conversations often became windows into our neighbors' foodways and, in a very real sense, into what matters most to them. The Polish lady in Whately, describing how she makes pierogi, spoke with an awed reverence for the rich soil her husband tilled and the sweet, giant cabbages that sprang from it. The transplanted Irishman coaxed us to wait until his loaf of brown soda bread cooled so we could taste his smoked fish the right way. The Taiwan-born farm stand merchant patiently explained how to cook bitter melon, reminiscing about a dish his mother used to make—and which he clearly missed.

We wrote this book to help you make some of those same kinds of connections—to the land, to the people, to all the good things about the foods, foodways, and foodmakers of Massachusetts. In the six years since the book's first edition, the concept of "eating local" has gone from a radical proposal to unquestioned wisdom—something approaching record time for a cultural revolution. When we did the initial research for this book, we were surprised by the depth and intensity of the flavors of our own state. If anything, its riches have grown. Now you can make those same discoveries.

Just follow your nose.

This guide is organized into seven chapters, moving from the hilltop orchards and dairy farms of the west to the fishing villages of the east: the Berkshires, the Connecticut Valley, Central Massachusetts, Northeastern Massachusetts, Greater Boston, Southeastern Massachusetts, and Cape Cod and the Islands. Each chapter includes a map of the region, which can help you plan day trips to do your own exploring. Each chapter contains most of the following categories.

Made or Grown Here

This section identifies local producers of everything from pickles to chowders and growers of everything from mush-rooms to bison. Most of them sell their products directly to consumers, either at a factory or farm store, through the mail, or on the Internet. Those products you can't buy directly have extensive local distribution; they're worth seeking out at farm stands, grocery stores, and gourmet shops. Among Massachusetts's local producers, you'll find two nationally celebrated makers of blue cheeses, packers of specialty Polish and Portuguese sausages, and some of the nation's leading specialty coffee roasters.

Specialty Stores & Markets

This section of each chapter is devoted, to a great extent, to places where you can get all the wonderful raw ingre-dients to prepare a great meal and the shops where you can purchase the kitchen hardware to turn provender into repast. It also includes the pastry shops, bread bakeries, and ethnic markets that make life a little more pleasant. And because the Bay State has both an insatiable sweet tooth and a long confectionery tradition, this is where you'll find the artisanal candymakers.

Farmers' Markets

Many Massachusetts farms have been in the same families for generations, and farmers' markets are essential venues for meeting the people behind your dinner. Farmers selling at the markets often feel they must offer something special, something you cannot get from the local grocery store. That may be an heirloom fruit or vegetable, an unusual ethnic varietal, or the assurance that the food you buy is free of chemicals. Because farmers' markets continue to proliferate, it's always a good idea to double-check times and locations. Where available, we have included Web sites where you can verify those details.

Farm Stands

Farm stands can range from a card table and a hand-lettered sign at the end of a driveway to a year-round store that offers honey, jam, pickles, breads, and flowers in addition to fresh fruits and vegetables. In many cases, you can even pick your own produce. Because the harvest is always unpredictable, it's wise to call ahead.

A special case among farm stands are the maple sugarhouses, active when the rest of agriculture is dormant. The sugaring season typically begins in late February, reaches its peak in March, and may linger into April. All members of the Massachusetts Maple Producers Association (www.massmaple.org) welcome visitors when they are boiling off sap to make syrup, though not all offer tours of the facilities. Conditions can vary from hillside to hillside and one producer may be boiling off while another has yet to stoke the fires. Be sure to dress appropriately for wet spring conditions.

Fishmongers

In some parts of Massachusetts, the biggest local harvest comes from the ocean rather than the fields. We've been very selective in listing fishmongers who either catch their own fish or who have close relationships with local fishermen. The off-shore catch is landed at just a few ports, and most fishmongers are buying from the same boats. But when it comes to shellfish, lobster, and the inshore catch (such as flounder), every shop will differ.

Food Happenings

Massachusetts loves to celebrate, and the calendar is riddled with fairs, festivals, cook-offs, and other culinary events. You'll find the details in this section, from the salty Bourne Scallop Fest in Buzzards Bay to tart Cider Days in the hill towns west of the Connecticut River Valley.

Learn to Cook

Whether you're interested in a career as a professional chef or just want to polish your skills at frosting cakes, there are classes available at adult education centers and culinary schools to suit almost every need. They range from afternoon or evening cooking demonstrations to formal hands-on instruction in a restaurant-like environment.

Landmark Eateries

There are so many great places to eat in Massachusetts! Of the handful we've selected, some are quite literally landmarks— places with so much local character that life in a town or neighborhood seems to revolve around them. Others are leaders in the battle for sustainable farming and fisheries and are champions of local flavor. What they all have in common is food made with care and joy and taste—an experience you shouldn't miss.

RESTAURANT PRICE KEY

$ = inexpensive; most entrees under $15

$$ = moderate; most entrees $15 to $25

$$$ = reasonable; most entrees $25 to $35

$$$$ = expensive; most entrees more than $35

Brewpubs & Microbreweries

Massachusetts is home to several superb microbreweries whose products more closely resemble English ales than the pilsner-style beers popular in most other regions of the United States. The microbrews are usually available both in bottles and on tap at better establishments. The state's brewpubs tend to be a more diverse lot, representing the specialized tastes and interests of their resident brewmasters, and properly so. Now that brewpubs are no longer a fad, all that's left behind is good beer.

Wine Trail

People have been making wine in Massachusetts at least since the first colonists found wild grapes in the forest. But serious winemaking with European *vinifera* varietals is closer to three decades than three centuries old, and in recent years fruit winemakers have emerged as forces to be reckoned with. Good science and smart horticulture have combined to vault some Massachusetts wines into the country's elite ranks. To help you explore Massachusetts wine country, this section of the chapter includes established wineries that have tasting rooms and welcome visitors.

Recipes

Throughout this book you'll find recipes that reflect, we think, some of the flavor of the state. As much as possible, these recipes draw on the local bounty or reflect local tastes and traditions. We are grateful to the chefs and growers who provided them. The recipes have been adapted for home kitchens and their presentation has been standardized. Any errors are our inadvertent introductions rather than the fault of our sources. As Cambridge's most famous chef always chirped, "Bon appétit!"

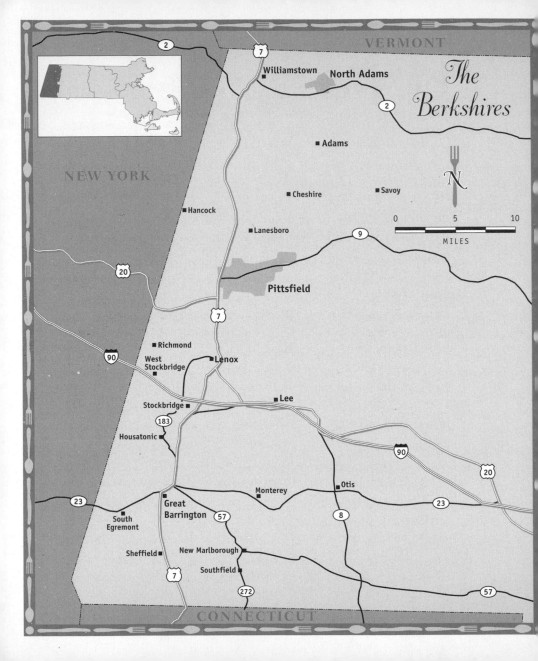

The Berkshires

To much of the world, the Berkshires are a summer place where the Boston Symphony Orchestra plays on the broad lawns of Tanglewood, Shakespeare & Company electrifies audiences with the evergreen plays of the Bard, and Manhattanites carry on a rarified social life in castlelike cottages and oh-so-quaint antique shops. Long, rolling vistas greet the eye—verdant valleys interrupted by the piney Berkshire Hills and the bald-top majesty of Mount Greylock. From Independence Day until Labor Day, the region becomes an idyll of performing arts in a country setting.

But even during the summer hubbub, you need only turn off traffic-clogged Route 7 to within minutes find yourself on a Berkshire back road where every third house, it seems, has set up a card table with the fruits and vegetables that mark the miniseasons of summer—from peas and strawberries through blackberries and peaches. While the cellists are tuning up and the actors are running throat exercises, Berkshire farmers and gardeners are weeding and hoeing, thinning and harvesting. When the hot-weather idyll ends and the summer folk go back to the city, the land remains and the work goes on. Above all, Berkshire County is an intensely agricultural region of small holdings where farmers cultivate bramble and tree fruits, gather maple sap for syrup, and raise livestock.

The urban sophisticates and the country farmers have a common ground in their love of good food, and that's led to the creation of Berkshire Grown, one of the state's most active and effective agricultural support groups. The organization brings together chefs, farmers, retailers, and the interested public in an effort to promote local agriculture and maintain the highest standards for good eating. Shop or dine anywhere the Berkshire Grown emblem is displayed and you'll know you're dealing with people who care where your food came from and how it's been treated—a comforting thought.

Made or Grown Here

Barrington Coffee Roasting Company, 955 South Main St., Great Barrington, MA 01230; (413) 528-0998 or (800) 528-0998; www.barringtoncoffee.com. Barrington Coffee's owners, Barth Anderson and Gregg Charbonneau, and staff are true java junkies, lovingly hand-roasting single-origin coffees by color and aroma to accentuate the special characteristics of each crop—the delicate blueberry note in Ethiopian Harrar, bright toasted peanut in Indian Mysore, the hint of nutmeg in Kauai. Ten or fifteen additional seconds of roasting can make a radical difference in the flavor, so while roasting "seems like a scientific process," says roaster Christine Stanton, "we have an artistic approach." Barrington Coffee has been up and running since 1993, and you might have tasted some of its products in places like the Red Lion Inn or the Honest Coffee Shop, both in Stockbridge. Coffee is available in whole-bean bags in select regional markets (including Guido's), at the headquarters, by mail order and online, and at Charbonneau's coffee shop, **Lenox Coffee** (52 Main St., Lenox; 413-637-1606).

Berkshire Blue, P.O. Box 2021, Lenox, MA 01240; (413) 445-5935; www.berkshireblue.com. Two years after Michael Miller left his job as publisher of the Pulitzer Prize–winning *Berkshire Eagle,* he found a new vocation that demands an equal degree of single-mindedness: making one of the country's finest blue cheeses. Having studied with a farmstead cheesemaker in England, Miller set up his own operation in 1997. He buys raw milk, mostly from High Lawn Farm in Lee, and makes Berkshire Blue by hand every step of the way, ensuring both a personal style and a striking consistency from wheel to wheel. The entire process takes nine weeks, from warm milk to the cool blue-veined cheese that won a gold medal in the 2002 American Cheese Society competition and comparable accolades in competitions worldwide ever since. Miller says he prefers Berkshire Blue with a small glass of port and some walnuts and port-soaked raisins on the side. The cheesemaking facility is not open to the public, but Berkshire Blue is available at select stores in the Berkshires and many natural food and cheese shops throughout the state.

Guido's Gazpacho

This chilled summer vegetable soup is a great way to enjoy the Berkshires' produce in a bowl.

1 zucchini, diced
1 yellow squash, diced
1 each red, yellow, green, and orange pepper, diced
1 large Vidalia onion, diced
1 small red onion, diced
2 stalks celery, diced
1 English cucumber, diced
½ cup chopped fresh cilantro
2 tablespoons chopped basil
Juice of 1 lime
Juice of 1 lemon
⅛ teaspoon ground cumin
1 quart tomato or vegetable juice
1 tablespoon Worcestershire sauce
1 tablespoon balsamic vinegar
1 teaspoon Spike seasoning
⅛ teaspoon ground white pepper
2 cloves garlic, minced

Combine all ingredients in a large bowl. Allow to marinate for 2 to 3 hours in the refrigerator. Serve with a dollop of plain yogurt or sour cream.

Serves 6–8

Guido's Quality Fruit & Produce
1020 South St.
Pittsfield, MA 01201
(413) 442-9912

760 South Main St.
Great Barrington, MA 01230
(413) 528-9255

www.guidosfreshmarketplace.com

Berkshire Mountain Bakery, 367 Park St. (Route 183), Housatonic, MA 01236; (413) 274-3412; www.berkshiremountain bakery.com. Richard Bourdon has been fermenting and baking amazing sourdough loaves from Housatonic for a quarter century and fortunately shows no signs of letting up. In addition to traditional European whole wheat sourdoughs, Bourdon and his staff of more than a dozen bakers also make spelt breads, pizza dough, and even wholesome sprouted grain cookies. For the broadest choice, visit the bakery; some breads are also available in area markets or through the Web site.

The Good Shepherd Farm, 142 Griffin Hill Rd., Savoy, MA 01256; (413) 743-7916. Located well out in the sticks, near the Windsor State Forest, Good Shepherd suddenly appears out of the woods as a broad expanse of fenced mountain meadows where Pat and Tom Sadin's herd of registered Romney sheep graze. The Sadins have been raising sheep and selling lamb since the late 1980s. Unlike imported lamb, which can be up to two years old, Good Shepherd lambs are slaughtered at six to eight months, ensuring maximum tenderness and mild flavor. "They eat only grass, their mothers' milk, and our own hay," Pat says. Good Shepherd takes orders in August, on a first-come, first-served basis, for pickup of freezer packages in October. The Sadins also sell yarn, tanned sheepskins, hand-knit wool hats, and brown and white fleece for hand spinners. Call ahead before visiting, as the farm is well off the beaten path.

High Lawn Farm, 535 Summer St., Lee, MA 01238; (413) 243-0672; www.highlawnfarm.com. The last remaining self-contained dairy farm in the Berkshires has been in continuous production since before 1900, and some of the 180-plus Jersey milkers can trace their lineage back to the original herd. Typical of Jersey milk, High Lawn tests out much higher in calcium and protein than milk from conventional dairies and has a smoother, richer flavor. Most of the milk is distributed through home delivery, but you can buy High Lawn products in a few grocery stores and at farmers' markets in the southern Berkshires. Regardless, it's worth making the trip to the 1,300-acre farm, which stands atop high meadows just outside of Lee. The milking parlor is state of the art, but the architecture of the main barn has a curiously antique Alpine feel. The octagonal cupola and clock tower were designed by a nineteenth-century Austrian architect who must have been homesick. The farm "store," open weekdays and Saturday morning, is nothing more than a refrigerator in the main office. In addition to milk, cream, and butter, the store also stocks Berkshire Blue cheese and Andahuaylan White, a gourmet rendition of *queso blanco* made locally from High Lawn milk using a century-old family recipe from Peru.

Rawson Brook Farm, New Marlborough Rd., Monterey, MA 01245; (413) 528-2138. Visitors are welcome to drop in at Susan Sellew's goat farm and cheese operation at 5:00 p.m. any evening from mid-April to mid-November to watch her milk her herd of fifty droopy-eared Nubian, white Sanaan, and French and American Alpine goats. The farm produces plain Monterey Chèvre and several versions with added herbs. The most popular contains chives and garlic. Each goat yields about a gallon of milk per day, which is enough to make one pound of cheese. Between mid-March and early January, Sellew produces 350–400 pounds per week, keeping back some stock in the freezer to have a supply throughout the year. The cheeses are available at some Berkshire markets as well as at the farm.

Specialty Stores & Markets

Catherine's Chocolate Shop, 260 Stockbridge Rd., Great Barrington, MA 01230; (800) 345-2462. Stop by Catherine's on your way to a play or a concert for a four-ounce "Theater Box" of assorted chocolates. You might want to return later for some of the homemade fudge, nineteen flavors of truffles, or chocolate-dipped fruit. The Sinico family makes a sumptuous "butterkrunch" using a recipe from Cathleen Sinico's great-uncle. This signature confection consists of butter, sugar, cashews, and "other natural ingredients" cooked to 300°F, rolled on a cool marble slab, covered with dark chocolate, and coated in crushed cashews.

Easy Vanilla Wafers

Baldwin & Sons is justifiably proud of its vanilla extract, and this recipe for a classic cookie shows off the vanilla at its finest. Jackie Moffatt recommends draping the cookies over a wooden dowel or the handle of a wooden spoon immediately after removing them from the cookie sheet to give them a pretty curved shape.

¼ cup (½ stick) unsalted butter, room temperature
⅓ cup Vanilla Sugar (recipe follows)

¼ cup egg whites
⅓ cup unbleached all-purpose flour
Pinch of salt

1. Preheat oven to 400°F. Generously butter a large heavy cookie sheet.
2. Beat butter and Vanilla Sugar in a medium bowl until light and fluffy. Beat in egg whites. Gradually mix in flour and salt (batter will be soft).
3. Drop batter by level teaspoonfuls onto prepared cookie sheets, spacing cookies 3 inches apart.
4. Bake until cookie edges are golden brown and centers of cookies are still pale, about 7 minutes. Transfer cookies to racks and cool completely.

Makes about 36 cookies.

Vanilla Sugar

Jackie Moffatt adds that this sugar is also good for sweetening whipped cream.

2 cups sugar

1 vanilla bean, cut into small pieces

Process sugar and vanilla bean in food processor until vanilla bean is very finely minced. Strain sugar to remove any large pieces of vanilla bean. Store sugar in airtight container.

Makes 2 cups.

Charles H. Baldwin & Sons
1 Center St.
West Stockbridge, MA 01266
(413) 232-7785
www.baldwinextracts.com

Charles H. Baldwin & Sons, 1 Center St., West Stockbridge, MA 01266; (413) 232-7785; www.baldwinextracts.com. Five generations of Baldwins have been making flavor extracts in tiny West Stockbridge since 1888. The street-level shop is jammed with baking supplies, spices, country store candy, and Baldwin products, including semi-exhausted vanilla beans useful mostly for potpourri. The vanilla extract is made in the basement, according to Jackie Moffatt, whose husband, Earl Baldwin Moffatt, represents that fifth generation. "Everything else is made up here," she says, referring to the shop's back room, where anise, lemon, orange, spearmint, peppermint, and almond extracts are produced. For the company's signature vanilla, Baldwin uses Bourbon vanilla beans from Madagascar and ages the extract in hundred-year-old oak barrels to produce a dark, rich flavor. The small shop also produces its own Worcestershire sauce from a recipe that Earl and Jackie found wadded up in Earl's grandfather's rolltop desk. Many locals favor Baldwin's Table Syrup, a maple blend developed in the 1920s as a tasty but less expensive alternative to pure maple syrup. Products are also available by mail order.

The Cook's Resource/Different Drummer's Kitchen, 374 Pittsfield Rd., Lenox, MA 01240; (413) 637-0606. You might feel that you need your passport when you walk into this roadside store where you can buy a tortilla press and taco-shell pans; the complete Joyce Chen line of woks and Chinese cooking utensils; Emile Henry custard

cups, quiche pans, and terrines; enameled cast-iron Le Creuset pots and pans; or stainless steel and copper pots from Germany, England, and even the good old USA. While some of the goods are upscale enough to make you think about a home equity loan, there are also dozens of inexpensive but essential trifles, like cutters for making filled linzer cookies. There are also carriers for every size of picnic, ranging from retro baskets to the Picnic Backpack to wheeled picnic luggage to daypacks designed for a bottle of wine, two glasses, a box of crackers, and a small wheel of Brie.

Guido's Quality Fruit & Produce, 1020 South St., Pittsfield, MA 01201; (413) 442-9912. Also 760 South Main St., Great Barrington, MA 01230; (413) 528-9255; www.guidosfreshmarketplace.com. Guido's resembles a farm stand on steroids—lots of local produce as well as the culinary essentials you'd find in a supermarket. Guido's gathers the best seasonal produce from the farms of the Berkshires (and adjacent New York) into one place where you can stand paralyzed by the choices of exquisite foodstuffs. Look here for such local treats as Berkshire Blue and Monterey Chèvre cheeses, Barrington Coffee, Country Hen organic eggs, and Prima Pasta (made at Guido's).

The Monterey Store, 448 Main Rd., Monterey, MA 01245; (413) 528-4437; www.montereystore.com. This building has been the hill town's village store since 1780, but the current incarnation is a long way from an old-timey country store. It is part grocery, part coffee shop with lunch sandwiches (and free Wi-Fi), and sometimes coffeehouse for local acoustic performers. When the weather permits, the store has a Saturday afternoon outdoor barbecue with hamburgers, hot dogs, Italian sausages, and ribs slathered in a chipotle sauce. Bread and pies are baked fresh on the premises daily, and you can always pick up some Rawson Brook goat cheese along with other artisanal products.

Otis Poultry Farm, 1570 North Main Rd., Otis, MA 01253; (413) 269-4438; www.otispoultryfarm. com. If you find the road, you can't miss the store: It's a huge red building with two giant white chickens holding a sign that reads WELCOME TO OTIS POULTRY FARM out front. Another sign proclaims, WE HAVE 23,000 EMPLOYEES WHO PRODUCE CUSTOM-LAID EGGS. The organic eggs begin at extra-large (white or brown) and keep going through jumbo (white or brown). You can even buy double yolks. Otis also sells fresh free-range chicken, frozen soup chickens, chicken croquettes, nuggets, hot wings, tenders, and turkey and chicken potpies (with and without vegetables). Some other products include fresh peanut butter, jellies and preserves, salad dressing, mustard, spreading cheeses, and fudge. Otis sells produce from Guido's and wine, and the staff makes sandwiches (from bread baked on the premises) at a deli counter. The farm prides itself on being the "home of the famous chicken gicken fertilizer—your garden's best friend."

Berkshire Apple Pancake

The Red Lion Inn in Stockbridge has been hosting travelers just about since tourism was invented. This breakfast favorite takes advantage of two of the Berkshires' greatest local treasures: its wonderful apples and its golden maple syrup.

3 apples, peeled and cored
Lemon juice
3 eggs, beaten
3 cups all-purpose flour
1½ tablespoons baking powder
¾ teaspoon salt
5 tablespoons sugar

2 cups milk
¾ teaspoon vanilla extract
¾ teaspoon ground cinnamon
5 tablespoons unsalted butter
¼ cup firmly packed light brown sugar
Warm pure maple syrup, for serving

1. Preheat oven to 450°F.
2. Coarsely chop 2½ of the apples. Slice the remaining ½ apple into thin spirals for garnish. Brush the spirals with lemon juice to prevent them from darkening and set aside.

Rubiner's Cheesemongers & Grocers, 264 Main St., Great Barrington, MA 01230; (413) 528-0488. When chefs from as far away as Napa, California, want a special cheese, they call Matt Rubiner. When the *Wall Street Journal* wants a pithy quote on American farmstead cheese, they

3. Mix together the eggs, flour, baking powder, salt, sugar, milk, vanilla, cinnamon, and chopped apples in a large mixing bowl. Stir until well combined, although the batter will remain lumpy.

4. Melt the butter in a 10-inch cast-iron skillet. Pour the batter into the skillet and arrange the reserved apple spirals on top.

5. Bake the pancake for 15 minutes. Reduce oven temperature to 350°F and bake for 40 minutes more, or until a toothpick inserted in the center comes out clean. Remove the skillet from the oven and let pancake stand for 5 minutes.

6. Sprinkle the brown sugar over the top of the pancake, cut it into wedges, and serve with maple syrup.

Serves 6

Red Lion Inn
30 Main St., P.O. Box 954
Stockbridge, MA 01262
(413) 298-5545
www.redlioninn.com

call Matt Rubiner. When hungry folk in Great Barrington get a hankering for cheese (or cured meats and fish), they visit Rubiner's or pop into **Rubi's Cafe** in the back for salads, cheese and meat boards, and sandwiches—including a divinely simple grilled cheese with sliced cornichons. The shop carries spectacular artisanal and farmstead cheeses from all over the world.

Southfield Store, 163 Main St., Southfield, MA 01259; (413) 229-5050; www.southfieldstore.com. The hamlet of Southfield is so small that many maps don't even show it, but bargain hunters always seem to find their way to the Buggywhip Antique Center, a building that actually made buggy whips well into the final quarter of the twentieth century. When Tim Newman opened the Southfield Store in 2004, just a few minutes' mosey from the old buggy whip factory, he transformed the old general store into a cafe and coffee bar with seating for thirty people, while still keeping the grocery business and a selection of gourmet cheeses, cured meats, and beer and wine. Breakfast and lunch are available, and dinner is served on Friday nights in the summer. Call for hours, which can be erratic from December through April.

The Store at Five Corners, Routes 7 and 43, Williamstown, MA 01267; (413) 458-3176; www.5-corners.com. This intersection has been a focal point of the region for centuries, and the store claims to be the oldest continuously operating business in the country. It's been a tavern, a stagecoach stop, a gas station, a tearoom, a general store, and now a "country gourmet" shop with an unbelievable variety of olive oils, vinegars, jams, jellies, maple syrup, barbecue sauces, grilling rubs, spices, mustards, and cookbooks, as well as an excellent wine selection. The deli makes good sandwiches and offers, among other things, maple-barbecued chicken, potato and pesto salads, and slices of apple, peach, and raspberry pie.

Tunnel City Coffee Roasters, 100 Spring St., Williamstown, MA 01267; (413) 458-5010. Tunnel City roasts its own coffees on the premises, including exotic varieties such as Ethiopian Longberry Harrar. But what sets the shop apart is a vast array of French and Viennese pastries that range from delicate raspberry-filled butter cookies to a drop-dead-beautiful tall chocolate cake filled with alternating layers of raspberry cream and vanilla buttercream.

Wohrle's Food Warehouse, 1619 East St., Pittsfield, MA 01202; (413) 445-5700. No one ever said Wohrle's hot dogs and sausages were gourmet fare, but this food warehouse has been stuffing casings since 1921, and their franks are the dog of choice for roasting on a stick at a state park grill. There's a definite ethnic twist to the sausages, which include bratwurst, kielbasa links, kielbasa rings, sweet and hot Italian sausages, and breakfast patties and links. This is also the place to pick up food-service-size canned foods for a giant family reunion—a gallon jar of maraschino cherries, an eight-pound can of Hershey's chocolate syrup, or fifty-ounce cans of Campbell's soups.

Farmers' Markets

Berkshire Grown—an organization of farmers, chefs, and retailers—keeps an excellent calendar of food-related events, from tastings at farmers' markets to crop-specific festivals and celebrations. See the Web site: www.berkshiregrown.org.

Art of the Tanglewood Picnic

When the Tanglewood Music Festival put on its first outdoor concerts in 1937, inopportune rainstorms drenched the patrons, leading the Boston Symphony Orchestra to construct the open auditorium with overhead roof now known as The Shed. But the real pleasure of Tanglewood is braving the elements to spread a blanket with a sumptuous picnic repast on the grassy lawn.

When preparing a picnic, keep in mind that it's a significant hike from the parking lot to the lawn and don't burden yourself with more than you'll want to carry. That said, we've seen a few ostentatious souls who bring canopies, chairs, and full china and crystal service and begin with iced bowls of caviar. (It's enough to make you go ask if you could borrow a particular brand of pseudo-French mustard.)

If you lack the time, patience, or skill to assemble your own picnic from several different sources, here are two sterling suppliers of complete Tanglewood picnics:

The Gateways Inn & Restaurant will pack up a four-course menu of salad, appetizer, entree, and dessert in Chinese takeout containers, set either in a formal picnic basket with china and cloth napkins or in a paper shopping bag.  Featured items change often, but might include prosciutto and sautéed peaches, grilled shrimp salad with avocado, grilled organic steak with tomato-onion jam and housemade orzo, as well as brownies, cookies, chocolate cake, or a fruit pie.

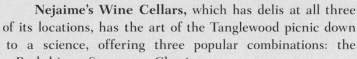

Nejaime's Wine Cellars, which has delis at all three of its locations, has the art of the Tanglewood picnic down to a science, offering three popular combinations: the Berkshire Summer Classic (hummus, tabouli salad, roasted salmon, stuffed grape leaves, Sicilian olive mix, and a baguette), French Country (Brie, chicken liver pâté with truffles, smoked chicken breast, pasta salad, roasted eggplant, and a fruit pie), and Tuscan Table (Piave wedges, Tuscan potato salad, curried chicken, Italian olive mix, dry Italian sopressata, and tiramisu). Nejaime's also has a superb wine selection. If you remember to bring a corkscrew, you'll meet lots of absent-minded people at Tanglewood who didn't.

The Gateways Inn & Restaurant

51 Walker St.
Lenox, MA 01240
(413) 637-2532
www.gatewaysinn.com

Nejaime's Wine Cellars

3 Elm St.
Stockbridge, MA 01262
(800) 946-3987

Other locations:

60 Main St.
Lenox, MA 01240
(800) 946-3978

444 Pittsfield/Lenox Rd.
Lenox, MA 01240
(800) 946-3988

www.nejaimeswine.com

Grow It, See It, Taste It

The display gardens of the Berkshire Botanical Gardens are designed to inspire home gardeners. While the majority of the 3,000 species and varieties planted in this country setting are ornamental plants, a few of the gardens focus on culinary herbs. Taking a stroll past the beds of rosemary and thyme or lavender and borage might inspire you to lay out your own kitchen garden. The visitor center, open daily from May through October, not only sells gardening books, greeting cards, and tools, but it also carries a wonderfully old-fashioned line of herb products made by the Herb Associates. Many members of this volunteer group are septuagenarians or older, and they use herbs from the gardens to make jellies, flavored vinegars, salad dressings, and mustards.

Berkshire Botanical Gardens
5 West Stockbridge Rd.
Stockbridge, MA 01262
(413) 298-3926
www.berkshirebotanical.org

Adams Farmers' Market, 60 Columbia St., Adams. Friday from noon to 6:00 p.m., mid-May through October.

Berkshire Area Farmers' Market, Old State Rd., Lanesboro. Wednesday and Saturday, 8:00 a.m. to 2:00 p.m., May through October.

Great Barrington Farmers' Market, 44 Castle St., Great Barrington. Saturday from 9:00 a.m. to 1:00 p.m., early May through October.

Lee Farmers' Market, Lee Post Office, Lee. Friday from 10:00 a.m. to 1:00 p.m., early May through early October.

Lenox Farmers' Market, 55 Pittsfield Rd., Lenox. Friday from 2:00 to 6:00 p.m., May through mid-October.

North Adams Farmers' Market, 77 Holden St., North Adams. Saturday from 8:00 a.m. to noon, mid-July through October.

Otis Farmers' Market, 2000 East Otis Rd., Otis. Saturday from 9:00 a.m. to 1:00 p.m., May through October.

Sheffield Farmers' Market, Old Parish Church, 340 South Main St., Sheffield. Friday from 3:30 to 6:30 p.m., early May to early October.

Williamstown Farmers' Market, south end of Spring St., Williamstown. Saturday from 8:00 a.m. to noon, late May through October.

Bartlett's Orchard, 575 Swamp Rd., Richmond, MA 01254; (413) 698-2559; www.bartlettsorchard.com. Ron and Rick Bartlett grow eighteen varieties of apples on the premises (including some experimental types such as Stars and Stripes) and make natural apple cider that's sterilized with ultraviolet light, instead of the traditional heat pasteurization, to preserve the cider's natural flavors. The farm store also offers a huge variety of produce—local whenever possible—including the Bartletts' own old-fashioned tomatoes: Mountain Spring, Pik Rite, Jet Star, Prime Time, Market Pride, Brandywine, and Sun Gold cherry tomatoes. During corn season, they pick several times a day to ensure absolute freshness. Open daily year-round.

Cricket Creek Farm, 1255 Oblong Rd., Williamstown, MA 01267; (413) 458-5888; www.cricketcreekfarm.com. This historic small farm milks Jersey and Brown Swiss cows and makes Italian-style cheeses: a live culture mozzarella; a semisoft aged raw-milk farm cheese called Maggie's Round; and a semisoft, buttery aged cheese called Tobasi, made only during the season when the cows are out to pasture. The farm store carries all three, along with certified raw milk, bread and cookies, free-range eggs, grass-fed beef, and whey-fed pork. In season you'll also find fresh vegetables and fruit, along with honey and maple syrup.

IOKA Valley Farm, 3475 Route 43, Hancock, MA 01237; (413) 738-5915; iokavalleyfarm.com. Don and Judy Leab's 600-acre farm in the sweeping valley near Jiminy Peak Ski Resort used to be a dairy operation, but Don converted the old milking parlor into a state-of-the-art facility for canning the maple syrup that he still boils down the old-fashioned way over a wood fire. The Leabs serve pancake meals on weekends from mid-February through early April, offering a choice of three pancakes, waffles, or French toast along with homemade applesauce, corn muffins, coffee, and juice. The farm is open on weekends through most of the year, selling its maple products (syrup, maple cream, maple butter, maple sugar, maple lollipops) and offering pick-your-own strawberries in late June and early July and pick-your-own pumpkins from September to Halloween. The Leabs are also dedicated to teaching the public "about where their food comes from," as Don puts it, so they provide farm education tours for school groups and maintain a petting zoo called "Uncle Don's Barn Yard," with a miniature horse, a donkey, sheep, goats, and llamas. The farm also raises (and sells) all-natural hormone-free beef. Open weekends during maple season and from late June through Halloween.

Lakeview Orchard, 94 Old Cheshire Rd., Lanesboro, MA 01237; (413) 448-6009; www.lakevieworchard.com. Lakeview has a long season of sweet fruits that begins in July with red and black raspberries, continues with sweet cherries and plums, segues into peaches and blueberries, and ends in the fall with apples. You can pick your own raspberries and cherries in July, apples from mid-August into October, and tomatoes in September—or buy them in the store, along with shallots, Walla Walla onions, sweet cider pressed on site, and honey from the farm's own hives. "What we grow—or the neighboring farm grows—is what we sell," says Judy Jurczak. Baked goods include chocolate and pumpkin whoopie pies (a local favorite, for which everyone has a secret recipe), fruit turnovers, and delicious cider donuts that roll off an ingenious cooker called the "Donut Robot." Open Fridays in May and June. Open Tuesday through Sunday (as well as Monday holidays) from early July through late October.

Mountain View Farm, Old Cheshire Rd., Lanesboro, MA 01237; (413) 445-7642. The southeast-facing hillside above the Cheshire Reservoir moderates Mountain View's microclimate to provide the extra warmth and sun needed for bounteous tomato harvests. The season opens in late June with pick-your-own strawberries and continues with tomatoes. Bring your own containers, if you like. Open daily June through October.

Taft Farms, Route 183 and Division St., Great Barrington, MA 01230; (413) 528-1515 or (800) 528-1015; www.taftfarms.com. Dan and Martha Tawczynski and their sons Keith and Paul offer more than 400 produce items at the store, along with freshly laid

Shaker Your Plate

From 1783 to 1960, members of the United Society of Believers in Christ's Second Appearing occupied a model farm community just west of Pittsfield. The Shakers, as they were better known, were widely hailed for their agriculture and animal husbandry, and the museum of Hancock Shaker Village carries on the tradition in a reduced way. Food lovers tend to be fascinated by the heirloom vegetable and herb gardens and by the heritage breeds of livestock. But, as the old saying goes, the proof is in the pudding. On five weekends from October through December, the village offers Shaker Suppers. They begin at 6:30 p.m. with hors d'oeuvres and specialty ciders served in the historic kitchen by hosts in mid-nineteenth-century costume. A candlelight buffet dinner in the Believers' Dining Room follows, then a program of Shaker music. The menu varies through the fall, but it's all drawn from *The Best of Shaker Cooking*, written by the founder of Hancock Shaker Village, Amy Bess Miller. In keeping with Shaker tradition, you should take only what you will eat—and be sure to eat it all. That's called "shakering your plate."

The village is open from late May to mid-October, 10:00 a.m. to 5:00 p.m.; mid-April to late May and mid-October to mid-November, until 4:00 p.m.; mid-November to mid-April by guided tour only (1:00 p.m. weekdays, noon and 2:00 p.m. weekends). Call or visit the Web site for details on Shaker Suppers.

Hancock Shaker Village

1843 West Housatonic St.
(Routes 20 and 41)
Pittsfield, MA 01201
(413) 443-0188
www.hancockshakervillage.org

organic eggs. Although Taft Farms field-grown produce is not certified organic (if you want to learn the complex politics of relatively meaningless USDA certification, just ask), the Tawczynskis are local leaders in promoting organic practices, alternative planting techniques, and soil building to eliminate the need to spray or dust. Taft bakes its own pies, cakes, cookies, and breads and makes soups with homegrown produce. You'll also find their own applesauce, chowchow, and a line of jams, jellies, and preserves. In addition to the farm's own products, the store stocks maple syrup, jams and jellies, breads and cookies, fresh pasta, and local eggs and milk from other Berkshires producers. Pick your own strawberries in June and pumpkins in September and October. Open daily all year.

Turner Farm Maple Syrup, 11 Phillips Rd., South Egremont, MA 01258; (413) 528-5710. Paul and Carla Turner sell syrup, maple sugar, maple candy, and even salad dressings at their Sugar House in season and by mail order the rest of the year. They also offer tours of their dairy farm by appointment. Note that Turner Farm straddles the state line and extends into Hillsdale, New York.

Whitney's Farm Stand, Route 8, Cheshire, MA 01225; (413) 442-4749; www.whitneysfarm.com. Just a short distance north of the Berkshire Mall, the Whitney family has been selling produce and landscaping plants since 1940. Eric and Michelle Whitney's farm offers pick-your-own blueberries and pumpkins, while the store has a broad range of produce, both local and from distributors, including the farm's own sweet corn. Like most area farm stands, the store makes every effort to provide local products, whether it's the cheeses from farmstead cheesemakers, coffee from Barrington Coffee Roasting, or frozen potpies from Otis Poultry. The large deli makes excellent sandwiches and sells cookies and other sweets baked on the premises. Kids enjoy the small petting zoo with pigs, goats, and various poultry. Open daily from Easter through late December.

Windy Hill Farm, Route 7, Great Barrington, MA 01230; (413) 298-3217. Located on the Great Barrington–Stockbridge town line, Windy Hill's retail operation is devoted principally to landscaping and bedding plants, with great masses of petunias and impatiens in the spring and equally vast collections of chrysanthemums starting in August. The garden center also sells a wide variety of landscape decorations—birdbaths, cast-concrete garden animals, and the like. But from mid-August through late October, the hillside behind the garden center is one of the most convenient pick-your-own apple orchards around. All trees are on dwarf stock, obviating the need for ladders. Open daily August through October.

***August*: Adams Agricultural Fair,** Bowe Field, off Route 8, Old Columbia St., Adams, MA 01220; (413) 743-2148; www.adamsfair. com. One of the most rural of the Massachusetts agricultural fairs, the Adams Fair is known for its rabbit and poultry competitions and its demonstrations of sheepdog herding skills. That's not to say that it lacks the whole panoply of pies, pickles, and produce or any of the more colorful accoutrements of country fairs—hot rods, chain-saw sculpture, tractor pulls, and country music. You can see it all while walking around with handheld country-fair food.

***August*: Tanglewood Wine & Food Classic,** Tanglewood grounds, 297 West St., Lenox, MA 01240; (508) 228-1128; www. bso.org. Tanglewood has always been associated with great pic-nics, but for one weekend it turns to the pleasures of the complete table with wine and food seminars, meet-the-chef and meet-the-winemaker events, a gala dinner and wine auction, and the Saturday "Great Tasting" with hourly cooking demos.

***September*: Hancock Shaker Village Country Fair,** 1843 West Housatonic St. (Routes 20 and 41), Pittsfield, MA 01201; (413) 443-0188; www.hancockshakervillage.org. A deliberate throwback to New England's agricultural heyday of the mid-nineteenth century, this old-time country fair features the largest exhibit of heritage breed livestock in the Northeast. Heirloom vegetables and fruits are offered for sale, and your mouth will no doubt water at the pie-judging contest. Some of the top practitioners of traditional crafts demonstrate blacksmithing, woodworking, basket-making, and other country skills. Don't miss the museum's impressive display of heirloom quilts.

Landmark Eateries

Blantyre, 16 Blantyre Rd., Lenox, MA 01240; (413) 637-3556; www.blantyre.com; $$$$. This stunning nineteenth-century property, modeled on a Scottish country estate, puts on a lavish spread fit for the robber barons who first made the Berkshires their rustic hideaway a century ago. The dining room of the main house remains an open space during the day, undergoing a complete transformation in the late afternoon as tables are brought out, dressed in rich linens, and set with sterling, cut crystal, and fine china— with different matched settings at each table. As the dinner hour approaches, the harpist begins playing and candles are lit. Both Blantyre guests and those who come only for dinner are welcomed for before-dinner drinks and canapés in the music room or outside on the covered terrace. Your order is taken, and when your first course is ready, you are escorted to your table. If you're rushing out for an evening performance, you can postpone the cheese and dessert courses until your return. The fixed-price menu, which changes with the season, is as luxurious as the property. You might start with a few seared scallops or Hudson Valley foie gras with a potato confit, move on to a sumptuous roast loin of venison served with cranberry risotto, and wrap up with a small plate of cheeses and a nougat ice cream served with roasted peaches and figs. The wine list is deep and broad, emphasizing Bordeaux and Burgundy but spiced by the addition of some memorable New World wines. Diners are expected to dress for dinner, with jacket and tie *de rigueur* for gentlemen. Open nightly for dinner, but limited to house guests only on Mondays and Tuesdays during the winter.

Gould Farm Roadside Store & Cafe, Route 23, Monterey, MA 01245; (413) 528-2633; www.gouldfarm.org; $. Since 1913, Gould Farm has offered a therapeutic refuge for persons with psychiatric disabilities, and for more than two decades the Roadside Store & Cafe has been one of the cottage industries that help support the community. The few shelves of the "store" carry the farm's own beef, homemade breads, cheddar-type cheese, eggs, and mint tea. The cafe is a classic roadside stop that serves bounteous breakfasts, including huge pancakes with the farm's own maple syrup. In fact, the majority of the food is made with Gould Farm products, which include organic vegetables and herbs, dairy items, meat, maple syrup, and cheeses. Open Thursday through Tuesday year-round for breakfast and lunch.

Jae's Spice, 297 North St., Pittsfield, MA 01201; (413) 443-1234; $$$. This fresh and exciting restaurant combines the pan-Asian vision of restaurateur Jae Chung with the inventive talents of executive chef Douglas Luf, one of the co-founders of the Berkshire Grown network. If all those super-healthy vegetable-laden dishes begin to seem *too* healthy for a good time, you can always order Luf's decadent lobster macaroni and cheese. Open daily for lunch and dinner.

Old Inn on the Green, 134 Hartsville–New Marlborough Rd., New Marlborough, MA 01230; (413) 229-7924; www.oldinn.com; $$–$$$. This circa-1760 stagecoach inn doesn't exactly overdo the electric lights—the dining rooms are lit entirely by romantic candlelight, which is only a problem for scrutinizing the menu. Chef and co-owner Peter Platt is a big booster of local farms, so his highly seasonal menus tend to reflect the Berkshire harvest. While the weekend fixed-price dinner is a rather formal affair of multiple courses, Platt offers a la carte meals and bargain midweek three-course fixed-price menus. A Wednesday night $25 special might start with a French lentil soup with bits of corncob-smoked ham, move on to braised lamb shank, and finish up with a triple-fudge chocolate brownie. The facility is also an inn, with cozy historic rooms and modernized suites in the original inn building and equally ancient Thayer House next door on the village green.

Pappa Charlie's Deli, 28 Spring St., Williamstown, MA 01267; (413) 458-5969; $. If it will fit between two pieces of bread, Pappa Charlie's probably makes it—and has named it after a celebrity or someone locally famous. Most sandwiches carry the names of actors or directors who've appeared with the Williamstown Theatre Festival. Walk up to the counter (there's no table service) to order and pick up, and ogle the play and movie posters while you wait. There's no linking the names with the contents—or else most sandwiches would be ham on wry. In general, they are the midday meals ordered by their namesakes. The Joanne Woodward, for example, consists of whole wheat bread slathered with peanut butter and jam, sprinkled with raisins, and overlaid with banana slices. The Blythe Danner is tuna fish, sprouts, tomatoes, Swiss cheese, avocado, and mayonnaise on whole wheat bread. The Richard Dreyfuss at least sounds like a real deli sandwich: hot pastrami, melted provolone, coleslaw, and Russian dressing. (Say, isn't that a version of a Reuben?) The younger generation is also represented. Order a Gwyneth Paltrow and you'll get eggplant parmigiana with a salad on the side. Open daily.

Red Lion Inn, 30 Main St., Stockbridge, MA 01262; (413) 298-5545; www.redlioninn.com; $$–$$$$. The chefs of this historic inn, which serves food in both a cozy tavern and formal dining rooms, were among the founders of the Berkshire Grown network that began promoting local food years before Slow Food got up off its Italian couch and started agitating in America. Current chef Brian Alberg continues the good work, offering a range of menu choices from traditional New England country fare to contemporary New American dishes—all of them leaning heavily on local farms and orchards. Alberg has also introduced "sustainable menus," on which virtually everything comes from suppliers in the Berkshires or a short distance over the state line in New York. The Sunday and Monday night dinners are entirely sustainable, and guests have several sustainable choices on every morning's breakfast menu. As a general rule, the inn tries to buy each year's top 4-H steer at the Big E in Springfield as one of its beef choices for the fall and winter.

Brewpubs & Microbreweries

Barrington Brewery & Restaurant, 420 Stockbridge Rd., Great Barrington, MA 01230; (413) 528-8282; www.barringtonbrewery.net; $. Although brewmaster Andrew Mankin had been an enthusiastic homebrewer for a dozen years, he apprenticed at the Vaux Brewery in Sunderland, England, before going pro here in 1995. Not surprisingly, the signature Barrington Brown Ale achieves a rich, nutty, English style—a nice middle ground between the Hopland Pale Ale (very lively with Pacific Northwest hops) and the dark and creamy, deeply roasted Black Bear Stout. Mankin also makes three to four additional seasonal beers. Sampler flights of six small beers are available. The midday menu emphasizes burgers, sandwiches, and sausages. In fact, the best lunch is probably the sausage on a roll—choice of bratwurst, bauernwurst, or kielbasa—steamed in beer and

Chocolate Stout Cake

We all know how well red wine and chocolate go together, but who would have guessed that deep, dark beer would meld so nicely with rich cocoa to make a robust, moist, chocolate-covered cake? This recipe replicates the three-layer version at Barrington Brewery & Restaurant in Great Barrington, the most popular dessert on the menu.

Cake

2 cups stout (such as Guinness)

2 cups (4 sticks) unsalted butter

1½ cups sweetened cocoa powder (preferably Dutch-process)

4 cups all-purpose flour

4 cups sugar

1 tablespoon baking soda

1½ teaspoons salt

4 large eggs

1⅓ cups sour cream

Icing

2 cups whipping cream

1 pound bittersweet (not unsweetened) or semisweet chocolate, chopped

For the cake:

1. Preheat oven to 350°F. Butter three 8-inch round cake pans with 2-inch-high sides. Line with parchment paper. Butter paper.
2. Bring stout and butter to a simmer in a large heavy saucepan over medium heat. Add cocoa powder and whisk until mixture is smooth. Cool slightly.
3. Whisk flour, sugar, baking soda, and salt in a large bowl to blend.
4. Using electric mixer, beat eggs and sour cream in another large bowl to blend.

5. Add stout-chocolate mixture to egg mixture and beat just to combine. Add flour mixture and beat briefly on slow speed. Using rubber spatula, fold batter until completely combined.
6. Divide batter equally among prepared pans. Bake cakes until tester inserted into center of cakes comes out clean, about 35 minutes. Turn cakes out onto a rack and cool completely.

For the icing:

1. Bring cream to a simmer in a medium heavy saucepan. Remove from heat.
2. Add chopped chocolate and whisk until melted and smooth. Refrigerate until icing is spreadable, stirring frequently, about 2 hours.
3. Place one cake layer on plate. Spread ⅔ cup icing over.
4. Top with second cake layer. Spread ⅔ cup icing over.
5. Top with third cake layer. Spread remaining icing over top and sides of cake.

Serves 8–12

Barrington Brewery & Restaurant
420 Stockbridge Rd.
Great Barrington, MA 01230
(413) 528-8282
www.barringtonbrewery.net

served with sauerkraut. After 5:00 p.m. the restaurant offers more substantial plates of steak, chicken, and pastas—not to mention its dreamy Chocolate Stout Cake. Open daily for lunch and dinner.

Pittsfield Brew Works, 34 Depot St., Pittsfield, MA 01201; (413) 997-3506; www.pittsfieldbrew works.com. Christine Bump and Bill Heaton met in a brewery in Pennsylvania and discovered this Depot Street space and its idle five-barrel brewing system on a road trip through New England. They are skilled craft brewers who adjust their offerings for the season, making a thirst-quenching golden ale touched with a kiss of Czech hops in the summer, and a huge barley wine with deep English and German malts and East Kent Golding hops to stave off the chill of winter. Their lightly toasted Irish red is a malt-lover's delight. Chris and Bill also serve some good pub fare, including a cheddar ale fondue and mussels steamed in beer. If you need a counterpoint to the malt, opt for a pulled pork sandwich or the classic English pub dish of bangers (sausages) and mash.

Wine Trail

Furnace Brook Winery/Hilltop Orchards, 508 Canaan Rd. (Route 295), Richmond, MA 01254; (413) 698-3301; www.furnace brookwinery.com. Some of the trees in John Vittori's orchards date back a full century and include heir-loom apples rarely seen even at specialist orchards, including Wealthy and Milton. Vittori began contracting with a New York winery in 1994 to produce Johnny Mash hard cider from his apples, and in 1999  he acquired a winery license and the equipment to make his own wines and hard ciders. In addition to the American/British-style Johnny Mash (made from a blend of Golden Russet, Northern Spy, and McIntosh apples), Vittori also produces Furnace Brook Cidre, a Normandy-style cider (containing Golden Russet, Ida Red, and Kingston Black apples) that's aged in oak. The Special Reserve spends about four months in medium-toast French oak barrels before bottling; the standard cider the same time in American oak. Both are bottled as sparkling ciders (6.7 percent and 6 percent alcohol, respectively). Furnace Brook also produces varietal wines from grapes mostly grown on Long Island. The ciders and wines are available at the retail store and at Nejaime's Wine Cellars around Berkshire County. The retail store, which offers tastings of all the Furnace Brook wines and ciders, also has a bakery and cafe. From June through October you can buy wines and ciders by the glass to enjoy with panini on the terrace. Hilltop Orchards also offers pick-your-own apples, pears, and plums. The retail store is open year-round Friday through Sunday, 11:00 a.m. to 5:00 p.m.

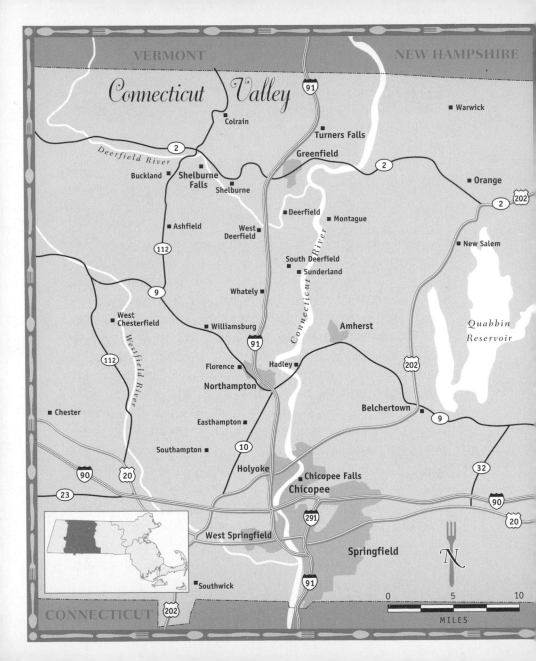

Connecticut Valley

If representatives from the culinary subcultures of the Connecticut River Valley all sat down to a barbecue, the menu might be tofu kielbasa with a side of organic sauerkraut, washed down by a micro-brewed beer spiked with fair-trade coffee, and followed by a pint of super-premium maple ice cream with rainforest nuts smooshed in.

Preposterous fusions aside, the people of the Connecticut Valley cultivate diversity as surely as they grow pumpkins next to bitter melons, asparagus a field away from lemongrass, and Silesian cabbage cheek by jowl with bok choy. The bottomlands along the Connecticut River are some of the richest agricultural soils in the Northeast and arguably some of the most beautiful.

Despite the presence of industrial Springfield, the Connecticut River flows through a largely bucolic valley populated with small towns. Northampton, Amherst, and South Hadley are the homes of Smith, Amherst, Hampshire, and Mount Holyoke Colleges as well as the behemoth flagship campus of the University of Massachusetts. These institutions provide the yeast of youth and the leavening effects of urban sophistication to an otherwise rural countryside.

Yet at the same time that urban exiles tool around the valley in their Volvos, the villages in the Berkshire foothills west of the valley still echo with the cannon shots of the 1960s cultural revolution and Polish-American farmers along the river hold fast to their Old World traditions. Where else can you get a pierogi and a kielbasa sandwich when you stop to buy sweet corn?

All this cultural diversity makes the Connecticut Valley a fascinating place for food lovers. The extraordinary vegetables of the Sunderland, Whately, and Hadley truck farms dominate the summer menus of haute-cuisine restaurants and highway diners alike—and they're often for sale at makeshift stands on the side of the road. You'll find farm boys and frat boys side by side at the bar, quaffing IPAs and bitters and chowing down on quesadillas stuffed with black beans and goat cheese. Even old-timers who once thought nothing of tucking into nightly meals of steak and potatoes entertain the idea of tofu burgers. (To the utter amazement of most of the rest of Massachusetts, tofu is considered an acceptable, even delectable, source of protein in much of the Connecticut Valley.)

The penchant for polemics so characteristic of the Five College Area necessarily makes eating a political act. Local farming is promoted by a group that calls itself Community Involved in Sustaining Agriculture (CISA). But we have to agree: Real food should come from one's own backyard whenever possible, and CISA identifies the farmers of Franklin, Hampshire, and Hampden Counties as "Local Heroes." It offers a comprehensive list of farm stands, farmers' markets, and community-supported farms, as well as an agricultural calendar of events and a detailed farm products list. The guide can be downloaded from the CISA Web site (www.buylocalfood.com) and is available in hotels, B&Bs, and tourist information centers. Take a look, hit the road, and bon appétit!

Made or Grown Here

Austin Brothers Valley Farm, 270 West St., Belchertown, MA 01007; (413) 688-6843; www.austinsfarm.com. The Austins raise their cattle naturally, letting them graze on green pasture much of the year and on the farm's own hay and silage through the winter. The beef are finished on grain for four months to boost marbling and flavor, then dry-aged for fourteen to twenty-one days after slaughter. The results are both economical—buying direct is actually cheaper than buying a poorer grade at a supermarket—and delicious. Family members also sell at some farmers' markets, and a stand at the farm is open Tuesday, Wednesday, and Friday through Sunday. Call for hours, as they change with the season. In late summer and fall, the farm also has sweet corn, pumpkins, fresh eggs, and (by special order) pies.

Chase Hill Farm, 74 Chase Hill Rd., Warwick, MA 01378; (978) 544-6327. Chase Hill's farmstead cheeses are carried in gourmet shops, delis, and some grocery stores in the Connecticut Valley. The cheesemakers achieve a full, rich flavor by using raw milk produced by their own herd of grass-fed cows. They make Colby, cheddar, and Camembert-style wheels in small lots, then age them sixty days before sale.

Chicopee Provision Company, 19 Sitarz St., Chicopee, MA 01014; (800) 924-6328; www.bluesealkielbasa.com. Since 1920 this specialist in Polish sausages has absorbed smaller meat packers to emerge as the premier maker of kielbasa in western New England—and even claims to hold the record for manufacturing the world's largest kielbasa (600 pounds). It also produces a full line of hot dogs, sweet and hot sausages, and luncheon meats that are sold in grocery stores and delis throughout New England under the Blue Seal brand.

Hager Brothers, 11 Merrifield Lane, Colrain, MA 01340; (413) 624-3993. The Hagers tap thousands of trees and have one of the most highly developed marketing operations of the Connecticut Valley maple producers, packaging syrup in several grades and sizes that range from half pints to five-gallon containers. Maple cream, maple candy, and granulated maple sugar are also available in bulk or small packages. On-site store open year-round Monday through Saturday.

Hillman Farm, 305 Wilson Rd., Colrain, MA 01340; (413) 624-3646; www.hillmanfarm.com. Cows are hardly the only milk animals in the Connecticut Valley. Up in the hill towns west of Greenfield, Carolyn and Joe Hillman milk a herd of Alpine goats and fashion

small wheels—five to ten pounds—of Gouda-style aged goat cheese. Firmer and more strongly flavored than the soft chèvre style usually associated with American goat cheeses, these Hillman Farm cheeses have a distinct, nutty flavor. Available in limited quantities from some area health food stores and gourmet shops, the full-flavor, natural-rind cheeses come in two grades: Hilltown (aged two to five months) and the firmer Harvest Goat Cheese (aged four to six months). The Hillmans also produce a range of fresh chèvres. For cheese fans who like something a little more intense than the fresh goat's milk cheese, the Hillmans make a gold-medal-winning cheese called Lottie Garris. Its savory flavor comes from two to three months of aging, which produces a crust that ranges from tacky to dry.

Millie's Pierogi, 129 Broadway, Chicopee Falls, MA 01020; (413) 594-4991 or (800) 743-7641; www.milliespierogi.com. You'll find Millie's pierogi in the fresh-meat cases of many grocers in Massachusetts, Connecticut, and Rhode Island, and you might even get the chance to sample the goods at some of the larger harvest fairs, including the Eastern States Exposition. If you get hooked, Millie's will ship a minimum of six dozen directly to your home. All the pierogi are hand-pinched, which produces a thinner dough than machines can, and then precooked before freezing. Essentially a substantial cross between a turnover and a dumpling, the pierogi are filled with plain cabbage, potato and cheese, prunes, or potato and cheese with kielbasa.

GRADING MAPLE SYRUP

Many maple producers will let you sample their various grades when you visit their sugar shacks. Standards for maple syrup vary slightly from state to state, but Massachusetts recognizes four grades, which are established on the basis of color and season.

Grade A Light Amber is the most delicate of all the maple syrups. Sometimes called Fancy Grade or, in Canada, No. 1 Extra Light, this grade is pale and mild. Made early in the season when the weather is still cold, Grade A Light Amber is the best for maple candy and maple cream.

Grade A Medium Amber is the most popular table syrup. It is a bit darker and has a more pronounced maple flavor. It is usually produced at midseason when the weather begins to warm.

Grade A Dark Amber, as the name suggests, is even darker and has a robust maple flavor. It is usually produced later in the season as the days get longer and warmer. It is good for sweetening yogurt or oatmeal.

Grade B Syrup is very dark and has a strong maple flavor and a caramel tang. Sometimes called cooking syrup, it is particularly good for baking and for flavoring puddings and custards. Hard-core maple fans sometimes favor Grade B as a table syrup. It is also used as a flavoring agent in syrup blends that combine maple and corn syrups. It is usually made from sap tapped at the end of the season.

New England Wild Edibles, 65 Foundry Village Rd., Colrain, MA 01340; (413) 624-5188; www.newedibles .com. Around the hill country of Franklin County, Paul Legreze is simply "the mushroom man." He grows shiitakes on birch logs and forages for oyster and morel mushrooms (and wild ramps) in season. His 'rooms are sold at Green Fields in Greenfield and several Whole Foods Markets. Contact him directly to purchase in quantity, but don't be surprised if he's out of town when you call in the spring—he makes regular trips to Manhattan to provide chefs with morels.

Real Pickles, P.O. Box 40, Montague, MA 01351; no phone; www .realpickles.com. There's a preachy earnestness about this company, which points out that its cucumbers, dill, garlic, and cabbage are entirely organic and purchased from family farms in the Northeast. But the proof is in the pickle, and these lacto-fermented, unpasteurized pickles and sauerkraut are the real thing—sort of like eating a real Brandywine after years of subsisting on supermarket cardboard tomatoes. Moreover, they're good for you. Predictably, the pickles can be hard to find outside food co-ops and health food stores, but they're worth seeking out. If all else fails, check McCusker's Market in Shelburne Falls or Atkins Farms Country Market in Amherst.

The Black Sheep, 79 Main St., Amherst, MA 01002; (413) 253-3442; www.blacksheepdeli.com. The tempting treats of this deli begin with wonderful breads—whole wheat, anadama, rye, six-grain, pumpernickel raisin, oatmeal, etc.—which serve as the base for both traditional and unusual sandwiches. Not only can you order whitefish salad or kippered salmon filling, but you can also get the "East Meets West" of roasted tofu, carrots, red onions, roasted garlic sauce, and peanut hoisin sauce on a baguette or the "Valley Girl" of smoked turkey, Brie, honey-cup mustard, lettuce, and tomato on a baguette. If you have a dinner party in the offing, stop by for a selection of such appetizers as shrimp satay and crab-stuffed mushrooms, and such entrees as grilled lemon-ginger chicken and roasted salmon. Five lasagnas (roasted vegetables and herbs, roasted chicken and basil pesto, classic beef, four cheese, and butternut squash) each serve ten people. Cakes are high and luscious and include ever-popular carrot cake with cream cheese frosting, Black Forest cake, a lemon-curd white cake, and frosted gingerbread. Pies tend to be seasonal but often include peach, apple, blueberry, pumpkin, and, in late summer, pear mango.

The Cook's Resource/Different Drummer's Kitchen, 34 Bridge St., Northampton, MA 01060; (413) 586-7978. Not quite as overwhelming as the Lenox store, this trimmed-down version of the one-stop kitchen hardware shop will set you up to make your own pressed terrines (in French terrine pans), stir-fries (in authentic

woks), and tortillas (in your very own press). This version of the small chain emphasizes hand tools over large electric appliances and king's-ransom pots and pans.

Elmer's Store, 396 Main St., Ashfield, MA 01330; (413) 628-4003; www.elmersstore.com. This clapboard building in the center of Ashfield village has been the town store off and on since 1835, but it's unlikely that it was ever the community epicenter that it's become since Nan Parati bought the place in 2005 and actually *asked* everyone in town what they wanted in a store. They wanted breakfast, for one, and Elmer's serves some of the best breakfasts in the Connecticut River Valley and adjoining hill towns. They wanted the crumbly cheddar cheese from a wheel under glass that had been a fixture at Elmer's since the 1930s. They got that, too. And they wanted a community center of sorts where people could post notices or hang out and talk over a fresh cup of coffee. Check. Organic food and basic groceries round out the mix—but Nan Parati's smile is also key.

Frigo's Gourmet Foods, 90 William St., Springfield, MA 01105; (877) 413-7446; www.frigofoods.com. This stalwart of Springfield's South End Italian neighborhood was launched in 1950 by current owner Joe Frigo's grandfather, an immigrant from the Asiago region in northern Italy. Nonno was a cheesemaker, and though the family sold off the cheese company years ago, cheese is one of the deli's specialties. Joe still sells Asiago made under the Frigo name—but he ages most of it for many months in his cavernous chilled cheese cellar. Custom butchery is another store specialty, but the big business during the day is at lunch, when cops and office workers alike stop at the shop across from the Mt. Carmel church for sandwiches or hot entrees like spinach lasagna and chicken Florentine. You can order some of the store's specialty products through its Web site, but if you want the nutty aged Asiago, you'll have to buy it in person.

Green Fields Market, 144 Main St., Greenfield, MA 01301; (413) 773-9567; www.greenfieldsmarket.com. This natural foods co-op serving the northern Connecticut Valley community bakes its own breads on a rotating schedule (including an organic rosemary sourdough bread) and offers a striking variety of ready-to-heat meals and grain and vegetable salads prepared on the premises. Attesting to a strong commitment to sustainable agriculture, Green Fields carries many products from local farms, orchards, small dairies, and beekeepers, as well as a full line of locally manufactured soybean-based meat substitutes.

La Fiorentina, 883 Main St., Springfield, MA 01103; (413) 732-3151. Also 25 Armory St., Northampton, MA 01060; (413) 586-7693; www.lafiorentinapastry.com. Established in Springfield in 1946, La Fiorentina calls itself the "home of the rum cake," but it's even better known among aficionados of sfogliatelle for making some of the best this side of the Atlantic. "We make a couple thousand every week," says Anna Daniele, who runs the bakery with her husband, Leo. It's a laborious process that begins on Tuesday (the dough has to rest overnight between steps) and finally culminates with the custard-filled, clam-shaped pastries going on sale on Friday. By Sunday they're all gone. Indeed, La Fiorentina is the home of Italian pastries of all sorts, including whipped cream cakes, ricotta cakes, and delicate sugar cookies spiked with a little anise seed. The Northampton outlet tends to emphasize cookies and small pastries (all the better to go with the excellent espresso bar), while the Springfield original also sells fennel bagels, Italian corn bread, and other breads. It is also one of the valley's premier makers of classic wedding cakes.

Lamson and Goodnow Manufacturing Company, 45 Conway St., Shelburne Falls, MA 01370; (413) 625-0201; www.lamsonsharp. com. Established in 1837, during the early days of the Industrial Revolution, Lamson and Goodnow is the oldest continuous producer of cutlery in the United States. Some of the craftsmen who produce knives for such catalog retailers as Sur La Table, Williams-Sonoma, and Crate & Barrel are descendents of the artisans who worked at the company when it first opened. The factory store just above the falls on the Buckland side of Shelburne Falls has informative displays showing the difference between forged and stamped knives (they make both, but the forged knives last longer, cut better, and cost more). Both types are for sale. Forged knives are sold at a 25 percent discount; stamped knives at 30 percent. If you can't resist one of the sets of five to sixteen knives, you'll get an additional discount. Lamson and Goodnow also produces barbecue tools, spatulas, spreaders, and other stovetop utensils, some of which are available in both right- and left-handed versions.

McCusker's Market, 3 State St., Shelburne Falls, MA 01370; (413) 625-9411. There are those in the Connecticut Valley who hold that Shelburne Falls is as much a state of mind as a real place. The village's only real food store provides an instant scan of that peculiar local psyche. Large bins of culinary herbs and local produce share floor space with patent-medicine herbal remedies. The deli counter has several vegetarian entrees and sandwiches and separates dairy from nondairy sweets. Despite the countercultural hoopla, this is a great place to buy local organic vegetables, apples, cider, cheese, and breads.

Pekarski's Sausage, Route 116 (Conway Rd.), South Deerfield, MA 01373; (413) 665-4537. You might sniff out Pekarski's before you see it on the twisting road between South Deerfield and Conway. Last time we were in, the woman at the counter asked, almost rhetorically, "Can you smell it? We're smoking pork loins." They also smoke hocks, spareribs, hams, kielbasa, and bacon on the premises, and they make unsmoked kielbasa, cheese kielbasa, bratwurst, breakfast sausage, Canadian bacon, and Italian sausages that run the gamut from sweet to hot to extra-hot. Despite the vegetarian bent of this end of the Connecticut Valley, Pekarski's is always busy. Some products are also available at area farm stands, grocers, and gourmet shops.

RAO's Coffee Roasting Company, 17 Kellogg Ave., Amherst, MA 01002; (413) 253-9441; www.raoscoffee.com. On a Sunday morning in nice weather, the line at RAO's sometimes extends out the door, as Amherstites descend on their local roaster for tall skinny lattes and big fat pastries to devour at leisure over the *Times.* Actually, RAO's tends to be extremely busy on all days in all seasons. Subscribing to the East Coast philosophy of medium and overall lighter roasts, RAO's offers a full line of world coffees. Its special passion, though, is reserved for Central American and South American beans.

Richardson's Candy Kitchen, 500 Greenfield Rd. (Routes 5 and 10), Deerfield, MA 01342; (413) 772-0443; www.richardsons candy.com. One of the classic small New England candymakers, Richardson's is known for certain specialties, including Dixies (turtles entirely enrobed in chocolate), Hedgehogs (similar to turtles but made with crisped rice), and wintergreen mints, offered both as chocolate patties and as dipped creams. Barbara Woodward, who operates Richardson's with her daughter,

Kathie Williams, says that when it comes to the pink wintergreen, "People do or don't like it. There's not much middle ground." The shop has a few seasonal specialties as well. During the three weeks of local strawberry season, a farmer custom-picks berries with intact stems for Richardson's. Barbara and Kathie dip the berries first in fondant, then in chocolate. The strawberries are sold only on the day they are picked, and it's worth making a special trip to the shop during June for one of the most perfect pairings of fruit and chocolate. If you miss the strawberries, you can cool off with a frozen banana dipped in a mixture of dark and milk chocolates. In October, try chocolate-covered caramel apples. And during November and December, Richardson's makes pecan logs—nougat dipped in caramel and rolled in pecans. No chocolate? "No," says Barbara. "It's a relief."

Table & Vine, 1119 Riverdale Rd. (Route 5), West Springfield, MA 01089; (413) 736-4694; www.tableandvine.com. Despite the homey name, Table & Vine is a branch of the Big Y grocery chain, but don't let that deter you from checking out one of New England's most

extensive displays of wine and spirits—more than 4,000 selections in all. Table & Vine is especially strong on small wineries of northern Italy, southern France, and Spain, where some of the best bargains are currently available. In addition, the shop stocks literally hundreds of cognacs, Armagnacs, single-malt whiskeys, and imported lagers and ales. The food side

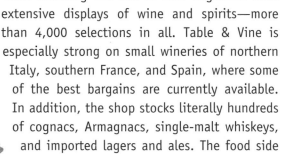

specializes in USDA prime meats (the restaurant grade usually not available to consumers) and carries a gourmet cornucopia of cheeses, pâtés, terrines, fresh foie gras, chocolates, olives, pastas, sauces, oils, vinegars, teas, coffees, and cookies.

Viva Fresh Pasta Co., 249 Main St., Northampton, MA 01060; (413) 586-5875; www.vivafreshpasta.com. The founders got started making pasta on  Martha's Vineyard in 1985 but moved to Northampton a year later, where another partner helped them open a small bistro in downtown NoHo to showcase their pastas and sauces. Retail cases right inside the door offer tortellini (cheese, spinach, roasted pepper, tricolor, and wild mushroom), ravioli (artichoke heart, cheese and spinach, low-fat spinach and mushroom, wild mushroom and walnut, vegetable, and sun-dried tomato and sweet potato), and a range of sauces to put on them (Alfredo, Asiago with almonds, creamy Cajun, Indonesian satay, olive and herb, pesto, puttanesca, romesco, sun-dried tomato and mozzarella, tomato, and roasted red pepper). Of course, if you'd rather taste before you buy, you can sit down to lunch or dinner in the two-floor restaurant or, during warm weather, at the handful of outdoor tables.

Wheatberry, 321 Main St., Amherst, MA 01002; (413) 253-1411; www.wheatberry.org. Amherst has an embarrassment of riches when it comes to bread bakeries, but Wheatberry opened in 2007 because Ben and Adrie Lester's customers at the farmers' market wanted a place to buy their organic breads every day. The couple dropped their wholesale business and opened the bakery cafe, where they also serve earthy luncheon entrees, fair-trade coffee, and teas and tisanes, some from herbs grown in their home town of Shutesbury.

Williamsburg General Store, Main St. (Route 9), Williamsburg, MA 01096; (413) 268-3036; www.wgstore.com. Hardly the unsophisticated, old-fashioned country store it pretends to be, Williamsburg General Store is crammed with crafts, country-decor knickknacks, pottery, and greeting cards. Look past all that to the bulk spices, the local honey, and the store's own jellies, preserves, fruit butters, and "good and evil" pickles with garlic. The real draw here is the bakery, where you can purchase roasted garlic, three-cheese, or cheddar breads, or indulge in cinnamon pecan buns, pumpkin cream-cheese pie, or chocolate raspberry cream-cheese coffee cake.

Farmers' Markets

Community Involved in Sustaining Agriculture (CISA) not only provides listings of Connecticut Valley farms, farm stands, and farm products, but also keeps tabs on the many farmers' markets in Franklin, Hampshire, and Hampden Counties. See the Web site: www.buylocalfood.com.

Amherst Farmers' Market, Spring St. parking lot, Amherst Center. Saturday from 7:00 a.m. to 1:30 p.m., May through October.

Chicopee Farmers' Market, Chicopee and Perrault Streets, Chicopee. Wednesday from 11:00 a.m. to 3:30 p.m., early July to mid-September.

Easthampton Farmers' Market, Union Plaza, Easthampton. Tuesday from 2:30 to 6:30 p.m., early May to October.

Florence Farmers' Market, Florence Civic Center, Florence. Wednesday from 2:00 to 6:00 p.m., May to October.

Greenfield Farmers' Market, Court Square, Greenfield. Saturday from 8:00 a.m. to 12:30 p.m., late April to late October.

Holyoke Farmers' Market, High St. between Suffolk St. and City Hall, Holyoke. Thursday from 11:30 a.m. to 5:00 p.m., May to October.

Northampton Farmers' Market, Gothic St., downtown Northampton. Saturday from 7:00 a.m. to 12:30 p.m., May to early November.

Orange Farmers' Market, Butterfield Park, East River St., Orange. Thursday from 3:00 to 6:00 p.m., late May to mid-October.

Springfield Cooperative Farmers' Market, Avocado St., Springfield. Saturday from 7:00 to 11:00 a.m., early May to late October.

Springfield Farmers' Market, Tower Square Park, Springfield. Wednesday from 10:00 a.m. to 3:00 p.m., June through September.

Springfield Farmers' Market at the X, 475 Sumner Ave., Springfield. Tuesdays from 1:00 to 6:00 p.m., early May to late October.

Turners Falls Farmers' Market, Peskeomskut Park at 6th St. and Avenue A, Turners Falls. Wednesday from 3:00 to 6:00 p.m., May through October.

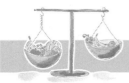

Farm Stands

Apex Orchards, Peckville Rd., Shelburne, MA 01370; (413) 625-2744; www.apexorchards.com. The sweeping hilltop view is a bonus when you come here to pick McIntosh, Gala, Paula Red, and other apples, all growing on compact trees. Owner Timothy Smith, one of the area's most active beekeepers, packs his own extraordinarily spicy honey under the Shelburne Honey Company label. You'll find both clear and creamed honey, as well as a particularly well-rounded cider vinegar. Open daily August through April.

Atkins Farms Country Market, 1150 West St., Amherst, MA 01002; (413) 253-9528; www.atkinsfarms.com. Atkins has been

Tuna-Apple Pita Pockets

At midday on a weekend, it can be a ten-minute wait to order a "quick" lunch at the Atkins Farms Country Market deli counter, but that doesn't faze local shoppers. Chef Ron Williams provides this fall favorite, best made with fresh local apples.

1 medium McIntosh apple
1 stalk celery, cut in ¼-inch slices
1 teaspoon lemon juice
1 small onion, chopped
8 ounces canned tuna
1 teaspoon dill weed
½ cup mayonnaise (Hellmann's recommended)
4 whole pita pockets
4 Boston lettuce leaves

1. Core apple and chop in medium bowl. Add celery and sprinkle with lemon juice. Add onion.
2. Drain tuna. Add to bowl with dill weed and mayonnaise. Mix well.
3. Cut one edge off of pitas, and place a lettuce leaf in each. Stuff with tuna mixture.

Serves 4

Atkins Farms Country Market
1150 West St.
Amherst, MA 01002
(413) 253-9528
www.atkinsfarms.com

farming this acreage near the Belchertown border since 1887 and sells its own apples, peaches, and pears at a supersize farm stand. (You can also pick your own apples and peaches.) You'll need one of the full-size shopping carts to stock up on produce from many other local farms, as well as Atkins' own maple syrup, jellies, fruit butters, preserves, marmalades, applesauce, and mixes (buttermilk and apple cinnamon pancakes, for example, and maple pecan and apple cinnamon scones). The bakery breads include raisin, wheat, garlic, pesto, honey oatmeal, and cheddar cheese, as well as English muffins. They're made with unbleached, unbromated flour—the next best thing to whole grain from a nutritional standpoint. Even harder to resist are the sweets, especially the dense, moist apple cider doughnuts and the apple squares with cream cheese frosting. Atkins' bakers also create wedding cakes with a month's advance notice. Open daily year-round.

Boisvert Farm and North Hadley Sugar Shack, 181 River Dr. (Route 47), Hadley, MA 01035; (413) 585-8820; www.north hadleysugarshack.com. Even if your kids don't like vegetables, they will love this busy farm stand with its own "animal village" of pigs, goats, sheep, and chickens. A sign beckons (and warns), PLEASE ENTER . . . WE LIKE TO BE BRUSHED. WE LIKE TO PLAY . . . BUT DON'T CHASE US. NO FEEDING ALLOWED. WE WANT TO STAY HEALTHY. During March and April, the sugar shack serves daily pancake breakfasts, continuing on weekends into May. From June through October, there's a weekend stand with hot dogs and hamburgers, and maple soft-serve ice cream is always available.

Oh, yes, the stand sells all varieties of local produce as well as the farm's own honey, maple syrup, and mixes for blueberry muffins, peach cobbler, peach crisp, apple crisp, carrot cake, and pumpkin bread. Open mid-February through December.

Clarkdale Fruit Farms, 303 Upper Rd., West Deerfield, MA 01342; (413) 772-6797. Reached off the Route 2 traffic circle in Greenfield, Clarkdale grows thirty-five apple varieties. The farm stand also sells pears, peaches, and cider, as well as deeply discounted McIntosh drops. Open daily from mid-August through December, weekends through February.

Cold Spring Orchard, 391 Sabin St., Belchertown, MA 01007; (413) 323-6647; www.coldspringorchard.com. This research facility for agricultural scientists at the University of Massachusetts at Amherst grows more than a hundred varieties of apples to test new varietals and to find more environmentally friendly ways to grow them. A pioneer in integrated pest management (the use of pest traps and other devices to reduce and better target spraying), Cold Spring Orchard offers pick-your-own opportunities for eighteen varieties of apples, which range from such antiques as Baldwin and Golden Russet to standards (McIntosh, Golden Delicious) to new varieties. Among the recently developed apples showing promise for this region are Akane, a cross between Jonathan and Worcester Pearmin, and Ginger Gold, a spicy-sweet natural sport that appears to have both Golden Delicious and Pippin in its ancestry. Profits

Mulled Cider

Everyone loves the aroma (and flavor) of mulled cider. The key to successful mulling is extremely low heat, to keep from cooking the little bits of apple pulp still present in good fresh cider. This version comes from Clarkdale Fruit Farms in West Deerfield.

½ gallon fresh apple cider
3–4 cinnamon sticks
2 teaspoons whole cloves
2 teaspoons allspice
1–2 tablespoons orange juice concentrate (optional)
1–2 tablespoons honey (optional)

1. Pour ½ gallon or more of apple cider into a large steel or enamel saucepan. Simmer for 1 hour over very low heat, stirring occasionally. Do not let cider boil!
2. Just before serving, add cinnamon, cloves, allspice, and orange juice concentrate and honey (if using).

Makes 8 cups

Clarkdale Fruit Farms

303 Upper Rd.
West Deerfield, MA 01342
(413) 772-6797

from the farm are plowed back into further research. As you drive down Sabin Street from Route 9, you'll pass a number of orchards that have benefited from the efforts at Cold Spring. Open daily August through November.

Gould's Sugarhouse, Mohawk Trail, Shelburne, MA 01370; (413) 625-6170. The willful rusticity of Gould's farm store and restaurant makes it a classic bit of Americana. From its prime spot on the Mohawk Trail, Gould's sells pure maple syrup as well as its own dill and bread and butter pickles. During the limited season, the restaurant serves breakfast and lunch. Most diners order pancakes, waffles, or corn fritters with maple syrup, but you can also get a few sandwiches as well as homemade apple pie with cheddar cheese or ice cream. In 2009, the sugarhouse marked its fiftieth year. Open March to April and September to October.

Hamilton Orchards, 22 West St., New Salem, MA 01355; (978) 544-6867; www.hamiltonorchards.com. The season starts early with strawberries and continues all summer and fall with plums, cherries, peaches, raspberries, pears, apples, pumpkins, and gourds. The farm stand also has baked goods. Open weekends June through October; call for weekday availability.

Nourse Farms, 41 River Rd., Whately, MA 01373; (413) 665-2650 (24-hour berry information line); www.noursefarms.com. Best known to home gardeners around the Northeast as the premier source for berry plants, this nursery also operates a huge pick-your-own operation across the summer and into the fall. Because it raises plants for the berry industry, Nourse has the longest strawberry season in the state—from early June into August. You can also pick your own raspberries, blueberries, and rhubarb. Open daily June through September.

Best Ice Cream

Even sweets sometimes display a puritanical streak in the Connecticut Valley. Where else can you find cookies guaranteed to be all-natural— and vegan to boot? It's rumored that some children in the post-hippie hill towns have never seen white sugar. But fear not—like the rest of Massachusetts (where ice-cream consumption is the nation's highest), the Connecticut Valley has an inordinate fixation on super-premium frozen concoctions.

Bart's Homemade Ice Cream tops the list for most valley folk, who line up at Bart's Homemade Café in Amherst, where the brass ice-cream-cone knob on the door has been polished smooth by the fingers of the hungry hordes. Scoops, sundaes, shakes, malts, ice-cream sodas, and floats are all available in an exhausting list of familiar (and not-so-familiar) flavors. Our favorite is Mass Mocha: coffee ice cream with espresso-filled chocolate chunks, semisweet chocolate chunks, and a fudge swirl. Those with giant appetites can order the Bart's Blast sundae, which includes ten scoops of ice cream, five sauces, and five toppings.

Pine Hill Orchard and Bear Meadow Farm, 248 Greenfield Rd., Colrain, MA 01340; (413) 624-3325. How many ways can you use an apple? This inviting little complex by a small pond might be just the place to find out. Head to the Pine Hill Orchard farm stand for some of its own applesauce. (They also sell peach sauce, local honey, maple syrup, and cheeses.) Products with the Bear Meadow Farm label are made in the old sugarhouse on the property and

The alternative is **Herrell's** in Northampton, established in 1980 as the second venture of super-premium ice-cream pioneer Steve Herrell, originator of Steve's Ice Cream. He is generally credited in ice-cream circles for inventing the "smoosh-in"—the practice of mashing broken cookies or candy bars into already incredibly rich ice cream. That essentially infantile approach to ice cream is balanced, however, by some of his sophisticated flavors, such as Hearts and Flowers (with rosewater and lavender extracts), Burnt Sugar and Butter, and Mexican Chocolate. Confirmed chocoholics should probably zero in on the Quadruple Chocolate Sundae. This large sundae is constructed with Chocolate Pudding ice cream, hot fudge, real chocolate whipped cream, and M&Ms or any other chocolate smoosh-in your heart desires.

Bart's Homemade Ice Cream	Herrell's
103 North Pleasant St.	8 Old South St. (Thornes Marketplace)
Amherst, MA 01002	Northampton, MA 01060
(413) 253-9371	(413) 586-9700

include cinnamon cider jelly, apple blueberry preserves, and apple butter. (Bear Meadow also produces a number of private-label items, including those served at the Mount Washington Hotel.) While you're making your selections, sample "The Drink," a tasty concoction of apple cider, cider vinegar, grape juice, and honey. And don't forget that on weekends from Labor Day to Columbus Day, you can pick your own apples. Any day, you can grab a bag of Red Delicious,

Honeycrisp, Spencer, Macoun, Mutzu, or Empire apples at the farm stand. Select a perfect apple and take a big bite—the most simple of apple pleasures. Farm store open year-round.

Round Hill Orchard, 1 Douglas Rd. (Route 10), Southampton, MA 01073; (413) 562-4985. Round Hill has blueberries and raspberries when it opens in July, followed quickly by pears and apples. The farm stand also sells the orchard's own honey, and children can feed the horses and sheep. Open daily mid-July to mid-October.

Simple Gifts Farm, 1090 North Pleasant St., Amherst, MA 01002; (413) 323-9608; www.simplegiftsfarmcsa.com. An organic farm that's part of the nonprofit North Amherst Community Farm, Simple Gifts sells all of its meat, eggs, and dairy through CSA shares, but the extra produce makes its way to farmers' markets around the state and is available at the Amherst farm stand. The veggies run the gamut from arugula to zucchini, and include a wide range of heirloom tomatoes and some of the best garlic we've ever tasted.

Smiarowski Farm Stand & Creamy, 320 River Rd., Sunderland, MA 01375; (413) 665-3830. This vegetable-oriented farm stand invariably has a wide selection of red, white, and yellow potatoes, as well as several varieties of winter squashes, including buttercup, blue Hubbard, and acorn. Look also for native onions, carrots, lettuce, broccoli, beets, cucumbers, parsnips, and peppers. The adjoining food stand offers Polish specialties, including cabbage pierogi, golumpki (ground beef and rice wrapped in cabbage leaves

Roasted Garlic

Some of the region's finest garlic comes from the farms on the west side of the Quabbin Reservoir, in Belchertown, New Salem, and Pelham. Hard-stemmed garlic, in particular, can be extremely firm and difficult to peel—until it's roasted and mellowed. This approach comes from Jeremy Barker-Plotkin of Simple Gifts Farm in North Amherst.

1 head garlic
½ teaspoon olive oil

1. Cut off the top of the head of garlic so that the cloves are exposed.
2. Place head on aluminum foil and drizzle with olive oil. Wrap in foil and bake at 325°F for 1 hour.
3. Remove foil. Squeeze garlic cloves out of skins and use as a spread on French bread, as a rub for meats, or as a seasoning in salsa, salad dressing, or any savory dish.

Simple Gifts Farm

1090 North Pleasant St.
Amherst, MA 01002
(413) 323-9608
www.simplegiftsfarmcsa.com

and fried), and a popular kielbasa sandwich on rye bread. The kielbasa can be dressed with sautéed onions and peppers or sauerkraut, or just slathered with horseradish. The "creamy" also sells soft-serve ice cream, but you might prefer to hold out for homemade blueberry crisp with whipped cream. Open daily May through October.

Early May: **World's Largest Pancake Breakfast,** Main St. from State to Bridge St., Springfield, MA; (413) 733-3800. This pancake breakfast with live entertainment and family activities was named a "Local Legacy" by the Library of Congress.

Late June: **Lavender Festival,** Johnson Hill Farm, 51 Hog Hollow Rd., Buckland, MA 01370; (413) 625-6439; www.lavenderland.com. The hill towns around Greenfield have blossomed into one of North America's premier lavender-growing regions over the last few years. This annual event features local vendors selling wool, lotions, and other local products. You can also participate in culinary and craft herbal workshops, wind your way through a lavender-lined stone labyrinth, and purchase lavender plants.

Late August to early September: **Three-County Fair,** Fair St., Northampton, MA 01060; (413) 584-2237; www.3CountyFair .com. This annual agricultural fair has been a mainstay in the Northampton calendar since 1818, making it one of the oldest continuous fairs in the country. The Polish festival at the fair invariably blends oompah and dance music with the Polish-American cuisine of the Connecticut Valley's farmers. Other highlights include the New England championship horse-pulling competition and thoroughbred racing.

Mid- to late September:
Eastern States Exposition,
1305 Memorial Ave., West
Springfield, MA 01089; (413)
737-2443; www.thebige.com.
New England's counterpart to the
giant state fairs of the Midwest, the Big E features multiple stages
of famous-name performers, a big-top circus, a rodeo, and what
seems like miles of food vendors serving almost anything that can
be eaten off a stick, in a bun, or dipped in ketchup. In fact, the
hoopla is so overwhelming that you could forget to visit the extensive agricultural exhibits (marvel at the pickles, salivate over the
fruit pies) and the 4-H livestock judging. The fair's signature food,
the Big E Cream Puff, is sold inside the New England Center.

Late September: North Quabbin Garlic and Arts Festival,
60 Chestnut Hill Rd. (may vary year to year), Orange, MA 01364;
www.garlicandarts.org. This homegrown country fair and arts show
celebrates garlic in every form. About two dozen farms and vendors
participate, offering everything from fresh garlic to seed garlic to
barbecue sauce. The festival includes an art show and games. The
highlight is the garlic-eating contest.

Early November: Cider Days in Franklin County, various
locations; www.ciderday.org. The rural apple growers in the hill
towns west of Greenfield welcome the public for self-guided tours
of Franklin County orchards, tastings of sweet and hard ciders and

local cheeses, demonstrations of cider pressing, and workshops. Many activities center on the small village of Colrain, where apple growers in some of the most remote areas bring their often unusual varieties for display and sale. Area restaurants feature apples and cider on their menus.

Mid-November: Chocolate Dessert Buffet and Silent Auction, Clarion Hotel Conference Center, One Atwood Dr., Northampton, MA 01060; sponsored by AIDSCARE/Hampshire County; (413) 586-8288, extension 5. Pioneer Valley bakeries and restaurants donate more than seventy chocolate cakes, desserts, and cookie plates for sampling during the event, which benefits support programs for county residents living with HIV/AIDS.

Landmark Eateries

Amherst Chinese Food, 62 Main St., Amherst, MA 01002; (413) 253-7835; $$. When Tso-Cheng Chang opened Amherst Chinese in 1973, he also opened people's eyes to the differences between Chinese-American food and this cooking from his home region of Shandong, China. One of the keys to authenticity is that son Sidney runs the family farm in Whately, where he grows Chinese specialty produce used at the restaurant—hot peppers, baby bok choy, green eggplants, Chinese leeks, jade gourds, and the like. Be sure to try the bitter melon, traditionally cooked with black beans and pork.

The farm produce is also available at the Amherst Farmers' Market. Open daily for lunch and dinner.

Chef Wayne's Big Mamou, 63 Liberty St., Springfield, MA 01103; (413) 732-1011; $$. Wayne Hooker cooks with serious spice at Big Mamou, a Louisiana-style restaurant featuring both Cajun and Creole cooking. Among the most popular choices at this busy little place are crawfish, blackened shrimp, and catfish, although alligator and sausage jambalaya is available for adventurous eaters. The signature Big Mamou dish is a tangy combo of crawfish tails, shrimp, red peppers, yellow squash, broccoli, and scallions in a lobster and brandy cream sauce, served on puff pastry. Save room for some sweet potato pie or New Orleans bread pudding with whiskey sauce. Hooker was born in Hartford, Connecticut, but he honed his Cajun-Creole cooking through many trips to Louisiana. He says he'll talk to anyone he meets, "and I'm famous for getting myself invited home to dinner." Open Monday through Saturday for lunch and dinner. BYOB.

Davenport Maple Farm, 111 Tower Rd., Shelburne, MA 01370; (413) 625-2866; $. Dairy farmer and maple producer Norman Davenport and his wife, Lisa, operate a springtime sugarhouse restaurant, serving pancake and waffle breakfasts. They produce maple syrup, spread, candy, and granulated sugar, as well as maple-coated peanuts, cranberries, and soybeans. All the items are available by mail order and in local grocery and gourmet stores. Restaurant open

Saturday and Sunday for six weekends starting the first weekend in March.

Mike and Tony's Pizzeria at the Green Emporium, Town Common, Route 112, Colrain, MA 01340; (413) 624-5122; www .greenemporium.com; $$. This former village Methodist meeting-house was transformed to a fine-dining destination in 1992 and added a pizza oven in 2008 as part of a shift toward affordable gourmet dining. Chef Michael Collins emphasizes simple American bistro fare using a range of local products, from grass-fed organic beef to local cheeses, pickles, and even pies. The pizzas serve as a platform for imaginative toppings and combinations, such as cheddar cheese, apples, and herbes de Provence, or lavender and goat cheese. The lovely herb and flower gardens enhance the magical country experience. The restaurant serves lunch and dinner Thursday through Sunday.

Miss Florence Diner, 99 Main St., Florence, MA 01062; (413) 584-3137; $. The 1930s Worcester Dining Car Co. diner, about 3 miles west of downtown Northampton, opened in 1941. Except for an addition, little seems to have changed since, making the diner a favorite hangout of NoHo pop-culture vultures. Aim for a seat in the original section so you can watch the action at the grill. Miss Flo opens at 6:00 a.m. and serves breakfast all day. The diner fare is ultratraditional, but don't miss the cream pies—banana, chocolate, and coconut—made fresh on the premises daily.

Apple Pizza

Chef Michael Collins of Mike and Tony's Pizzeria at the Green Emporium in Colrain has long supported local agriculture in the upper Connecticut Valley and surrounding hill towns. For this apple pizza, he likes to use heirloom Northern Spy apples. He says baking the apples gives them a flavor unattainable any other way. For the sharp cheddar he sprinkles on top, he opts for Cabot. The company may be in Vermont, but it buys milk from most of the Colrain dairy farmers.

5 Northern Spy apples
½ pound ricotta cheese
1 pound pizza dough
3 whole star anise, ground and sifted to remove grit
½ teaspoon freshly ground black pepper

½ teaspoon dried herbes de Provence
¼ teaspoon finely chopped fresh rosemary
¼ pound sharp cheddar cheese, grated
2 teaspoons olive oil

1. Preheat oven to 350°F. Core 3 apples and bake for 45 to 60 minutes until soft. When cool, remove skins and mix baked apple puree with ricotta.
2. Increase oven temperature to 450°F. Roll out pizza dough into a 16-inch circle. Top with ricotta mixture, leaving an untopped rim of dough all around the edge.
3. Combine ground star anise, black pepper, and herbes de Provence. Sprinkle evenly on pizza. Sprinkle chopped rosemary over pizza.
4. Peel and core remaining 2 apples and cut into thin slices. Arrange on pizza. Sprinkle cheddar cheese over pizza and drizzle olive oil around the edges.
5. Slide pizza onto stone in oven and bake until bubbly and crisp (about 20 minutes). Serve with local hard cider.

Makes 1 16-inch pizza

Mike and Tony's Pizzeria at the Green Emporium
Town Common, Route 112
Colrain, MA 01340
(413) 624-5122
www.greenemporium.com

Paul & Elizabeth's, Thornes Marketplace, 150 Main St., Northampton, MA 01060; (413) 584-4832; www .paulandelizabeths.com; $$$. Vegetarians (and quasi-vegetarians) rejoice! While the Connecticut Valley is full of little places serving indifferent meatless food, Paul & Elizabeth's has elevated the preparation of natural foods to an art. Some seafood is served, but most dishes are vegetarian and many are vegan. The menu tilts toward noodles and rice (on the carb side) and beans and tofu (on the protein end), but a taste of the deep-fried tofu and mushrooms in ginger sauce could make you think twice about relegating soybeans to mere fodder. Salads are a culinary adventure, especially during the summer, when local farms produce all manner of raw delights. Even the pies, custards, and puddings offered are sweetened with honey or maple syrup instead of white sugar. Open daily for lunch and dinner, Sunday also for brunch.

Pulaski Club (Polish American Citizens Club), 13 Norman St., Chicopee, MA 01013; (413) 534-7388; $. The food service at this local community hall is one of the valley's best-kept secrets, known by locals of Polish descent and by impoverished students looking for a solid meal at a great price. The traditional Polish and Polish-American foods are all made from scratch, including golumpki (stuffed cabbage rolls, breaded and fried), pierogi (huge dumpling pies, big enough to cut), and kielbasa. Open Wednesday through Saturday, 11:00 a.m. to 5:00 p.m.; take-out available.

Red Rose Restaurant Pizzeria, 1060 Main St., Springfield, MA 01103; (413) 739-8510. Back in 1963, Edda Caputo took over an ice-cream store and started selling pizza for three tables and takeout. The rest, as they say, is history. "My mom didn't believe in day care, so my two sisters and I grew up under the pizza bench," says Tony Caputo, who joined the business in 1986. Several expansions later, the restaurant seats about four hundred, and it's often full at lunchtime.

Despite the crystal chandeliers, marble statues, and Bay of Naples murals, pizza is still a mainstay. Italian-Americans from all over western Massachusetts come for a big Sunday afternoon meal, and during the week, diners rise from their tables with substantial doggie bags of shrimp scampi, arancini (rice balls), chicken Marsala, or the locally famed eggplant rollatini (rolled eggplant filled with ricotta and baked in tomato sauce). The family buys local eggplant in season and slices and freezes it to be able to serve this signature dish all year long. Open Tuesday through Saturday for lunch and dinner, closed Monday.

Sienna, 6 Elm St., South Deerfield, MA 01373; (413) 665-0215; www.siennarestaurant.com; $$$. Chef-owner Karl Braverman operates this fine-dining outpost in low-rent South Deerfield, just off I-91. The steadily dependable white-linen restaurant places a strong emphasis on local products, and it interprets contemporary American cuisine with just the faintest of French accents. Braverman's crab cakes, for example, arrive on a tasty salad of shaved fennel, mesclun greens, and orange segments with a dollop of crème fraîche. Pan-seared venison plays off snappy parsnips and a sherry vinegar demi-glace. Not only does Sienna serve nicely decadent desserts, it also offers an ever-changing cheese plate. Open Monday and Wednesday through Saturday for dinner.

South Face Sugarhouse, 755 Watson–Spruce Corner Rd., Ashfield, MA 01330; (413) 628-3268; www.southfacefarm.com; $. A succession of owners have made maple syrup commercially on this farm for more than a century and a half, and some of the massive, gnarled trees might well be the original stock. Grade A and B maple syrup, maple cream, and maple-coated walnuts are available by mail order or through the Web site. For six weekends, beginning the first weekend of March, the sugarhouse and restaurant are open for classic maple breakfast fare, which incorporates ingredients from other local farms (Heath blueberries, Millers Falls eggs) and locally baked bread (for French toast).

Student Prince/The Fort, 8 Fort St., Springfield, MA 01103; (413) 734-7475; $$$. If you want to see the movers and shakers of Springfield, make a reservation at the long-reigning king of the city's fine dining. Established in 1935 as the Student Prince Café, the complex of rooms also includes the Fort Dining Room. All the rooms are dark and gemütlich, and the menu remains resolutely Teutonic, with a few touches of circa-1955 American steakhouse. Best bets include spicy sauerbraten, delicate Wiener schnitzel, *zwiebelfleisch,* Hungarian goulash, and the peppery braised rabbit (*hasenpfeffer*). Open daily for lunch and dinner.

Amherst Brewing Company, 24 North Pleasant St., Amherst, MA 01002; (413) 253-4400; www.amherstbrewing.com. This ten-barrel brewpub is strategically located just about halfway between the Amherst College and University of Massachusetts campuses, and upperclasspersons (as they're called in Amherst) constitute a substantial segment of the clientele. Head brewer John Korpita makes a broad range of ales in German, English, and Pacific Northwest styles as well as a few lagers. The light Honey Pilsner (a slightly malty lager with hints of honey and crisp German hops) remains ABC's most popular. Open daily.

Berkshire Brewing Company, 12 Railroad St., South Deerfield, MA 01373; (413) 665-6600; www.berkshirebrewingcompany.com. Berkshire Brewing's signature 22-ounce bottles are available in gourmet and wine shops, and many western Massachusetts pubs have its products on tap. This tiny brewery goes to the trouble of brewing both an American-style and a British-style pale ale (Steel Rail Extra Pale and Berkshire Ale Traditional, respectively). Many small breweries make cautious beers—never very malty, never very sharp with hops, usually light rather than heavy. BBC, on the other hand, is willing to go to extremes, punctuating its wheat beer with strongly spicy hops, for example, or emphasizing the sweet malt of its seasonal porters or Oktoberfest beers.

Craft Brew Basics

We grew up on American beer, which meant that it came in three varieties: the brown bottle, the green bottle, and the can. Everything else was just marketing. But the emergence of craft brewing (brewpubs and 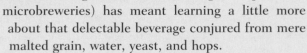 microbreweries) has meant learning a little more about that delectable beverage conjured from mere malted grain, water, yeast, and hops.

Practically speaking, Massachusetts brewers make only two types of beer. Lager beers are fermented with a yeast that resides on the bottom of the vessel. They are usually fermented at temperatures below 50°F and are often aged up to a few months before serving. Ales employ top-fermenting yeasts and warmer temperatures (60–70°F). Lagers tend to be smooth and thin; ales are often thick, cloudy, and full of fruity flavors. We've heard beer aficionados compare the two styles to white and red wines, respectively.

Go to any brewpub, though, and you'll encounter a bewildering number of beers (usually ales) with all sorts of names. Here's a glossary to help sort them out.

Bitter ale: This is another name for pale ale, but a bitter ale usually has a higher hop content and more alcohol than an India Pale Ale (IPA). Extra Special Bitter (ESB) is usually hoppier and even more alcoholic, and it often has a little more body and a redder color. It is generally the beer by which you can judge the skill and style of a brewmaster.

Bock: This dark lager tends to have more than 6 percent alcohol and is often brewed seasonally, around Christmas or the vernal equinox. Dopplebock (a Belgian term) refers to a stronger version.

Brown ale: Popular in England and Scotland, brown ales are less common among Massachusetts craft brewers. They tend to be sweeter and more full-bodied than IPA, ESB, or amber ale. Some have a nutty quality, like toasted hazelnuts.

Oktoberfest lager: At its best, this is a rich, copper-colored, malty beer with a sharp bite of hops—worth celebrating with a fall party.

Pale ale: This is a light-bodied ale fairly low in alcohol—generally the most popular ale among Americans brought up drinking "light" beer. IPA is a variation with more hops in the brew, which gives it a sharper taste. IPAs were created to make ale stable enough to ship on sailing vessels from England to the troops in India, hence the name.

Pilsner lager: Most American commercial beers emulate the Pilsner style, which originated in the town of Pilsen in the Czech Republic. (The original thirteenth-century brewery still makes Pilsner Urquell.) Pilsner is light and delicately hopped with a gentle, lingering, bitter aftertaste from the use of Czech hops.

Porter: An ale sometimes confused with stout, porter derives a similar dark color from the use of dark malts, not from roasted grain. Porters found in Massachusetts brewpubs tend to be fairly alcoholic and thin-bodied compared to stout. They often have an appealing burnt sugar aftertaste.

Stout: This black ale gets its color from roasted barley added to the brew, which also gives it a creamy body and a certain sharpness. Alcohol content can be quite low, as in the classic Guinness stout, but maltiness makes the drink seem heavier.

Wheat: Wheat beer is brewed by substituting a portion of malted wheat for malted barley. Most Massachusetts wheat beers are light and unfiltered, a style called Hefeweizen. Dark wheat beer is called Dunkelweizen.

Northampton Brewery, 11 Brewster Court, Northampton, MA 01060; (413) 584-9903; www.northamptonbrewery.com. The pioneer in the Pioneer Valley (as the Springfield-Greenfield piece of the Connecticut River Valley is sometimes called), this brewpub has been creating classic ales in a former carriage house behind Northampton's downtown parking garage since 1987. The food menu is a bit more ambitious than that of some brewpubs, with several light pastas and roasted meat dishes, but, as with most breweries, eating is a secondary consideration. Many of the ales created here adhere to the philosophy of the Real Ale movement—delicate, perishable, artistic, yet still unpretentious. The best bet is usually the cask-conditioned special (often a bitter), sipped on a warm evening on the rooftop. Open daily.

Paper City Brewing, 108 Cabot St., Holyoke, MA 01040; (413) 535-1588; www.papercity.com. Owner Jay Hebert, an ardent homebrewer, launched Paper City in 1995, on the fifth floor of an old warehouse building overlooking one of Holyoke's industrial canals. Fittingly enough, the 1996 initial offering from head brewer Rick Quackenbush was named Holyoke Dam Ale. Now with Ben Anhalt heading up the brewing, the company counts its Ireland Parish Golden Ale as the flagship and brews a hop-laden Indian Ale (named in honor of the Indian motorcycles Hebert collects) as well as several seasonal brews. Rollie's Premium Style Root Beer is also made on the premises. Though you can buy the products in most area package and liquor stores, you might want to take a tour (available weekdays from 9:00 a.m. to 5:00 p.m. and by appointment). In addition to sampling the offerings, you'll get a chance to admire memorabilia from vanished breweries of the Connecticut Valley, especially Hampden Brewery, as well as Hebert's vintage motorcycles.

People's Pint, 24 Federal St., Greenfield, MA 01301; (413) 773-0333; www.thepeoplespint.com. Aptly named, this friendly brewpub captures the spirit of a British or Irish local. The bar food is very much of the place—that is, more than half vegetarian and terribly socially conscious. (All the brewpub waste is recycled; all the food is locally grown if possible.) The pub is uncluttered by showy brewing equipment—that whole operation has been moved to a brewery on Hope Street. Owners Dan Young and Alden Booth are at their best with substantial, English-style brews. Their ESB (Extra Special Bitter) is aromatic and fruity with a nice herbal hop snap. On Wednesday, Friday, and Saturday nights, you can sip your suds to live music. Open daily.

Wine Trail

Chester Hill Winery, 47 Lyon Hill Rd., Chester, MA 01011; (413) 354-2340; www.blueberrywine.com. *Vinifera* wine grapes can't take the winters at an elevation of more than 1,300 feet in the Berkshires, but blueberries abound, and they have a similar profile of fruit acids and tannins. Chester Hill picks and crushes its own berries and makes three blueberry wines—a "nou-

Pork Tenderloin with Maple Glaze

Tangy cider vinegar, sweet maple syrup, and the herbal scent of sage make this version of roast pork provided by the North Hadley Sugar Shack an especially local treat.

2 12- to 14-ounce pork
   tenderloins
2 teaspoons dried sage leaves
Salt and pepper to taste
1 tablespoon butter

6 tablespoons pure maple syrup
6 tablespoons apple cider
   vinegar
2 teaspoons Dijon mustard

1. Rub pork with sage and sprinkle with salt and pepper.
2. Melt butter in a large sauté pan and brown pork over medium-high heat, turning occasionally until brown on all sides, about 6 minutes.
3. Reduce heat to medium-low, cover, and cook pork, turning occasionally, about 15 minutes more, or until a meat thermometer shows an internal temperature of 150°F. Remove pork to platter.
4. Whisk 5 tablespoons maple syrup, 4 tablespoons cider vinegar, and 2 teaspoons mustard in bowl.
5. Put the remaining 2 tablespoons of vinegar in the sauté pan, bring to a boil, and scrape up browned bits.
6. Return pork to pan, add syrup-vinegar-mustard mixture, and glaze pork for 2 minutes. Lower heat and cook for 2 more minutes.
7. Remove pork from pan and slice. Add the remaining tablespoon of maple syrup to the glaze remaining in pan. Stir and warm, then spoon glaze over the pork slices.

Serves 8

**Boisvert Farm and North
Hadley Sugar Shack**

**181 River Dr. (Route 47)
Hadley, MA 01035
(413) 585-8820
www.northhadleysugarshack.com**

veau" style ready by Thanksgiving of the harvest year ("New Blue"); a dry oak-aged red that pairs well with pungent cheeses, red meat, or chocolate ("Best Blue"); and a port-style sweet wine ("Bay Blue") that's aged in oak and fortified with brandy. The winery also produces some serviceable whites from Seyval Blanc grapes grown in New York's Finger Lakes region. The wines are available at many western Massachusetts package and liquor stores or at the winery itself. Open June to December, Saturday and Sunday from 1:00 to 5:00 p.m.

West County Winery, 106 Bardswell Ferry Rd., Shelburne, MA 01370; (413) 624-3481; www.west countycider.com. Only the quirks of Massachusetts law make West County a winery, for its real products are a range of small-batch hard ciders crafted from both single varietals and custom blends. The cider-making style continues to evolve at West County, ranging from simple American ciders to fruitier English versions to more refined, elegant styles reminiscent of Normandy and Brittany. Alcohol content tends to range from 6 to 7 percent, and most varieties are naturally sparkling. On Cider Days (see Food Happenings), West County opens for tastings.

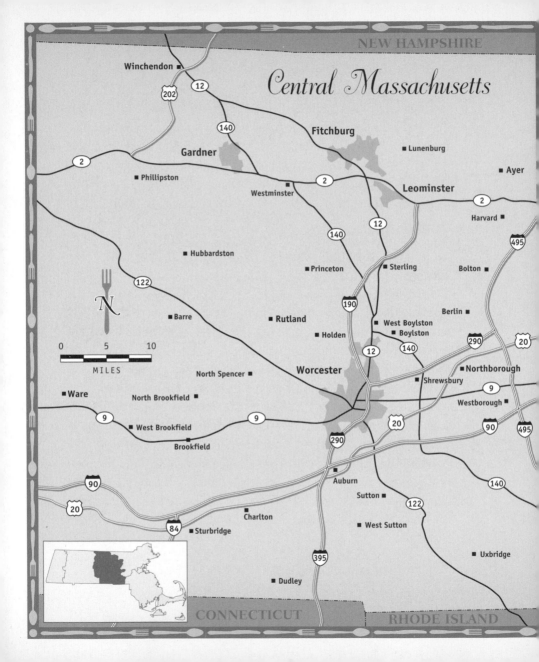

Central Massachusetts

Highway builders of the twentieth century took a dim view of central Massachusetts, assuming that travelers would like to get through it as quickly as possible. As a result, the flavor of the region remains mostly intangible until you get off the main roads and onto the byways. Turn off and drive just out of earshot of the highway, however, and you will encounter another world. Even New England's vaunted fall foliage can barely compare with apple blossom time along the Nashoba and Nashua River valleys, when a sudden breeze can create a snowstorm of pink and white petals. A seminal figure in the settling of the West, John Chapman was born in this orchard country, in Leominster, in 1774. In 1797 he started moving west with his Bible preaching and his apple seedlings, always one step ahead of the waves of settlement. Johnny Appleseed, as they called him, left, but the apples persist. Not all of the region is so bucolic. A string of industrial cities lines

Route 2 west of the orchards, and Worcester itself introduces a gentle, low-rise, urban sprawl into the center of central Massachusetts. These locales harbor food lovers' destinations every bit as endangered as the family farm: the classic roadside diners of the 1930s and 1940s. In an age of corporate fast food, the diners seem almost surreal—havens of home-slung hash, eggs over easy, and "wouldja like a warm-up on that, hon?"

West of the city, the landscape opens up into the rolling high country of the Worcester Hills. Many of the state's dairy cattle roam these upland meadows, and you will even find tracts grazed by buffalo and nibbled by dairy goats. Some of these backcountry farms can be tricky to find, but once you've navigated the back roads, you'll be rewarded with treats such as truly fresh milk, farmstead cheese, and homemade dairy ice cream. Turn southward from Worcester and the microclimate changes to produce moist, warm summers that support some of the state's most productive vegetable and berry farmers. We have highlighted some of the larger operations, but from the first asparagus of May to the last gourds and pumpkins of November you can drive through the agricultural countryside and find dozens of makeshift farm stands—often a card table and an honor-system coffee can for payment. Look, too, for the "Buy Local" sticker or sign at stores or even plastered on intersection telephone poles and marked with an arrow. They'll lead you to the best and freshest produce, meat, poultry, and dairy products.

Alta Vista Farm, 80 Hillside Rd., Rutland, MA 01543; (508) 886-4365; www.altavistabison.com. We can't guarantee cloudless skies or an absence of discouraging words, but Alta Vista is definitely the home where the buffalo roam—and have been since the Mann family bought their first heifer calves from South Dakota in 1968. In 1993 the farm sold off its last remaining beef cattle to focus entirely on bison. Now a herd of American bison grazes lazily in the hilltop fields surrounded by trees. The iconic ruminants, outlined against the New England sky, make a striking tableau. The farm specializes in selling hides and bison meat. "People have been reading about the health benefits and they want to try it," says Nancy Mann. Because bison meat does not marble, a bison roast is actually lower in calories, fat, and cholesterol than a same-size serving of roast chicken. You can purchase frozen ground bison, bison patties, shank, stew meat, rib steak, strip steak, sirloin steak, and roasts. Open Friday through Sunday all year.

Specialty Stores & Markets

Country Gourmet, 547 Summer St., Barre, MA 01005; (978) 355-6999 or (888) 355-6999; www.thecountrygourmet.net. Owner Sally Harrington (sometimes confused with her coffee-grinding trademark mouse, Java Belle) believes that every cook deserves the best. Her small shop virtually overflows with such sought-after tools as Chicago Metallic professional baking tins, Henckels knives, and Scanpan Titanium pots and pans. Harrington stocks more than a hundred bulk herbs and spices, which are available with a minimum 25-cent purchase, and has 750 members in her coffee club, which provides a free pound of coffee after a purchase of twelve pounds. Country Gourmet also has an extensive line of kitchen and table linens. "You have to have a great-looking table to show off good food," says Harrington.

Eaton Farm Confectioners, 30 Burbank Rd., Sutton, MA 01590; (508) 865-5235; www.eatonfarmcandies.com. Some of Lynwood Eaton's candy recipes date back to the nineteenth century, but this small shop on a backcountry farmstead (Burbank Rd. is off of Sibley Rd.) is best known for its thoroughly modern "ultimate candy sensation." In the mid-1990s, one of Eaton's employees invented the Peanut Butter Lust Bar, a concoction of peanut butter, crisped rice, marshmallows, cashews, and chocolate chips surrounded with milk chocolate. The San Diego Zoo can't keep them on the shelves, but you can stock up through mail order or by visiting the shop. (If you visit, you will probably be offered a sample.)

Ed Hyder's Mediterranean Marketplace, 408 Pleasant St., Worcester, MA 01609; (508) 755-0258. There's good reason that Ed Hyder's own name is part of his shop's title. He's the kind of hands-on proprietor who's enthusiastic about his products and always pleased to help his customers. The wide-ranging selection of imported cheeses and to-die-for Greek olives is reason enough to visit, and you'll probably exit laden with specialty meats, exotic nuts and oils, premium tea, and some of the obscure Middle Eastern spices (zaatar, anyone?) that you must have but can't find at Stop & Shop. (Hyder estimates that he carries more than 2,000 items.) Best of all, the prices are set for everyday, not special occasion, shoppers.

Hebert Candies, the Candy Mansion, 575 Hartford Turnpike, Shrewsbury, MA 01545; (508) 845-8051; www.hebertcandies.com. One of the giants among regional candymakers, Hebert makes 130,000 bars of chocolate a day, along with all sorts of filled and dipped candies, including cognac, apricot brandy, peach brandy, Irish cream, and rum cordials. The company was launched in 1917 when Frederick Hebert paid eleven dollars for a copper kettle, knife, thermometer, table, marble slab, and stove. For thirty years he developed and made candies that were sold throughout central Massachusetts in small neighborhood stores. In 1946 he bought a Tudor-style stone mansion in Shrewsbury and launched what the company calls America's first roadside candy store. Frederick Hebert is credited with perfecting white chocolate in the United States after having tasted it in Europe. The company claims the Geneva as its signature sweet. You can watch through a glass window as workers make the bite-size pieces of white, mocha, and dark chocolate, each with or without a toasted almond. You can also find the Hebert family candies at **E.J. Candies,** One River Rd., Sturbridge, MA 01566 (508-347-3051) and at **Colonial Candies,** 47 Sugar Rd. (exit 27 off I-495), Bolton, MA 01740 (978-779-6586).

Priscilla Hand Made Candies, 4 Main St., Gardner, MA 01440; (978) 632-7148. Second location at 10 Walden St., Concord, MA 01970; (978) 371-0585. Located in the heart of Gardner, Priscilla was founded in 1936. Virginia Trudel explains that although the shop makes all sorts of milk and dark chocolates with nuts, chewy centers, and soft centers, it is best known for its French Roll. "It was my father's recipe. We are the only ones who make it," she says. "If you weren't from Gardner, you wouldn't know what it was." For the record, the French Roll has a chocolate center that has been flattened, dipped in milk chocolate, and rolled in crushed cashews. This location is both the candy-making facility and a retail store.

Publick House Bake Shoppe, 277 Main St. (Route 131), Sturbridge, MA 01566; (508) 347-3313; www.publickhouse.com. As the quaint spellings suggest, the Bake Shoppe at this eighteenth-century inn is a logical place to find such recherché treats as molasses-ginger hermit cookies and a Joe Frogger, a large molasses cookie that holds its freshness so well that fishermen used to take them to sea. The shop also sells some of the inn's own brand of Indian pudding, various relishes, strawberry jam, apple butter, and a whole range of mustards and ice cream toppings.

Smith's Country Cheese, 20 Otter River Rd., Winchendon, MA 01475; (978) 939- 5738; www.smithscountrycheese.com. Dave and Carol Smith milk a herd of about 150  Holsteins at Otter River Farm and use much of the milk to produce their farmstead cheddar, Havarti-style, and Gouda-style cheeses in sizes that range from small wheels to massive blocks. They also pack spreadable cheese in five-pound and eight-ounce tubs. You can buy whole cheeses or shrink-wrapped wedges at many shops around Massachusetts or directly at the farm store.

St. Joseph's Abbey, 167 North Spencer Rd. (Route 31), North Spencer, MA 01562; (508) 885-8720; www.spencerabbey.org. The monks of the Cistercian Order of the Strict Observance, founded by reformist Benedictine monks in 1098, follow an austere life of prayer, contemplation, and manual labor. Hospitality has always been a special work of monks, who have a long tradition of preserving foods to offer their guests. The twenty-eight selections of fruit and wine jellies, jams, and marmalades made by the Spencer monks since the 1960s are part of that tradition. The monks produce more than two million jars a year and sell them at supermarkets and stores in New England. But experiencing the silent beauty

Pasta with Tomato Sauce, Broccoli, and Goat Cheese

This easy variant of a classic summer pasta with vegetables comes from Westfield Farm. Cooking the broccoli with the pasta saves a preparation step, and the goat cheese creates a creamy sauce without masking the summery flavors of the fresh vegetables and basil.

1 tablespoon olive oil
2–3 large cloves garlic, minced or pressed
2 pounds fresh tomatoes, peeled, seeded, and diced,
    or 1 28-ounce can tomatoes, seeded and diced
¼ teaspoon sugar
Salt to taste
1 tablespoon slivered fresh basil
Freshly ground pepper to taste
12 ounces fusilli, penne, or other pasta
1 pound broccoli, broken into florets, stems peeled and chopped
3 ounces (about ⅓ cup) goat cheese, crumbled

1. Bring a large pot of water to boil while you make the tomato sauce.

of the monastery gives each jar a little more meaning. A gift shop located at the foot of the abbey's driveway is open daily; afternoon only on Sunday. Look for some of the more unusual items, such as Ginger Preserve, Kadota Fig Preserve, and Sherry Wine Jelly.

2. Heat the olive oil in a large, heavy-bottomed nonstick skillet over medium-low heat, then add the garlic. Cook, stirring, just until it begins to color, 30 seconds to 1 minute, then add the tomatoes, sugar, and salt.

3. Raise the heat to medium, bring to a simmer, and cook, stirring often, 15 to 20 minutes, or until the tomatoes have cooked down, smell fragrant, and are beginning to stick to the pan. Remove from the heat and stir in the basil and pepper. Adjust the salt.

4. When the water reaches a rolling boil, add 2 to 3 teaspoons salt and the pasta. Stir until the water comes back to a boil. Cook the pasta for 6 minutes, then add the broccoli. Continue cooking another 4 minutes, stirring occasionally, until the pasta is done but still firm to the bite (al dente).

5. Drain the noodles and broccoli together when the pasta is al dente, and toss with the tomato sauce and the goat cheese. Divide at once among four warm plates.

Serves 4

Westfield Farm

28 Worcester Rd.
Hubbardston, MA 01452
(978) 928-5110
www.chevre.com

Westfield Farm, 28 Worcester Rd., Hubbardston, MA 01452; (978) 928-5110; www.chevre.com. When Bob and Debbie Stetson decided to branch out from their award-winning goat cheeses to make a few exceptional cow's-milk cheeses, they settled on milk from Otter

River Farm (see Smith's Country Cheese) for their Hubbardston Blue Cow and Capri Camembert Cow. They also make goat-milk versions of the blue, including a blue log with a strikingly blue edible rind formed by Roquefort mold during the aging process. Westfield Farm produces about 900 pounds of soft, unaged goat cheese per week, including a Plain Capri (simple chèvre) and flavored logs of Herb, Herb Garlic, Pepper, Chive, and Smoked. When you drive up, don't be surprised—the operation seems shockingly small to be producing cheeses with such sophistication and big flavors. The shop also sells Smith's Country Cheeses.

Farmers' Markets

Auburn Farmers' Market, Auburn Library parking lot, Route 12, Auburn. Saturday from 9:30 a.m. to 2:00 p.m., mid-May to late October.

Barre Farmers' Market, Barre Common, Barre. Saturday from 9:00 a.m. to 12:30 p.m., mid-May to October.

Fitchburg Farmers' Market, Wallace Civic Center parking lot, John Fitch Highway, Fitchburg. Friday from 8:45 a.m. to noon, July to mid-October.

Gardner Farmers' Market, Monument Square (Park Street side), Gardner. Thursday from 9:00 a.m. to noon, May to October.

Holden Farmers' Market, Damon House parking lot, Holden center. Tuesday from 3:00 to 7:00 p.m., May through October.

Sturbridge Farmers' Market, Basketville parking lot, Route 20, west of entrance to Old Sturbridge Village, Sturbridge. Thursday from 11:00 a.m. to 3:30 p.m., mid-June to October.

Worcester Farmers' Market, Beaver Brook Park parking lot, west side of 306 Chandler St., Worcester. Monday, Wednesday, and Friday from 9:30 a.m. to 2:00 p.m., mid-June through October.

Farm Stands

Berberian's Farm, 68 Otis St., Northborough, MA 01532; (508) 393-8079. You'll drive past fields and fields of vegetables when you turn off Route 20 toward the farm—a spread that gives credence to Berberian's claim to have the greatest variety of homegrown produce in New England. Should it be late summer, you'll smell the onions before you even open the car door. At the height of the season, boxes and flats are full of the farm's own scallions, arugula, dandelion greens, mint, dill, rhubarb, parsley, cilantro, basil, celery, Romano beans, yellow beans, green beans, carrots, beets, Chinese cabbage, lettuces (iceberg, salad bowl, red leaf, Simpson, buttercrunch, Boston, romaine), escarole, squash (acorn, blue Hubbard, buttercup, butternut, Cousa, summer, zucchini), cabbage, cauliflower, potatoes (red, white, Yukon gold), peppers (red, green,

sweet Italian, sweet Hungarian, sweet banana, hot Hungarian, jalapeño, hot cherry, Thai dragon, hot finger), Butter and Sugar corn, cucumbers, tomatoes (plum, beefsteak, cherry, grape), cucumbers, pickling cukes, Armenian cucumbers, and eggplant. As if its own production were not enough, Berberian also sells locally grown nectarines, peaches, blueberries, and raspberries, as well as locally packed turkey and chicken potpies. Open year-round; call for hours.

Berlin Orchards, 200 Central St., Berlin, MA 01503; (978) 838-2400; www.berlinorchards.com. The orchard occupies the former Chedco Farm, where the foundation herd of America's Guernsey cattle was raised in the early twentieth century. An indoor farmers' market is located in the antique former barn, and Berlin Orchards serves as a combination farm stand and pick-your-own orchard, with more than 200 acres growing more than twenty varieties of apples, as well as pears, peaches, pumpkins, squash, and berries. During the fall you can watch through windows as cider is pressed at the back of the barn. There is also a bee observation window. Berlin has its own maple sugarhouse and offers pancake breakfasts year-round. From May to October, ice cream is made on the premises. You can pick your own apples in season. Open daily year-round.

Bolton Orchards, 125 Still River Rd., Bolton, MA 01740; (978) 779-2733; www.boltonorchards.com. One of the very large suppliers of apples to the Boston market, Bolton Orchards has 250 acres in active production, growing twenty-five different apple varieties, fifteen types of peaches, and five types each of nectarines and plums. Long fields also grow tomatoes, squash, and pumpkins. Bolton presses a blended cider through the fall season and, from mid-October until almost Christmas, also produces a sweet, light yellow cider pressed from Golden Russet apples. Far from being a mere farm stand, the store can serve as one-stop shopping: it carries a full line of dry goods; a wide variety of canned goods, jellies, jams, and preserves; and all manner of pickled items in canning jars, including hot asparagus bullets, pickled beets, dilled pickles, pickled garlic, and spicy dilled beans. This is also a fabulous spot to stop for baked goods and snacks while touring the area's orchards, as Bolton has its own bakery (top item: apple pies) and sells a variety of breads, cookies, and cakes from other small bakers in the region. Open daily.

Brookfield Orchards, 12 Lincoln Rd., North Brookfield, MA 01535; (508) 867-6858; www.brookfieldorchardsonline.com. Open all year, the country store at Brookfield Orchards is famous (at least locally) for its hot apple dumplings and ice cream served in the snack bar. The bakers also make apple pies and coffee cakes and a range of homey cookies. In September and October, when the pick-your-own portion of the apple harvest season is in full swing, the snack bar also offers hot dogs, hamburgers, chili, and macaroni and cheese. The country store sells the farm's apples and cider and the whole gamut of country store fare, including penny candy, jams, honey, collectibles, and crafts. Open daily 9:00 a.m. to 5:00 p.m.

Carlson Orchards, 115 Oak Hill Rd., Harvard, MA 01451; (978) 456-3916; www.carlsonorchards.com. Possibly the largest cider producer in the state (the Whole Foods Market, Roche Bros., Donelan's, and Market Basket chains carry their cider), Carlson is a no-nonsense working farm and orchard—no petting zoo, no hay rides, just fruit and vegetables. Pick-your-own blueberries are available around mid-July; peaches and nectarines from early August into September. Carlson grows fifteen varieties of apples to pick in September and October. These include Gingergold, Royal Gala, Empire, Cameo, Macoun, Cortland, Red Delicious, and McIntosh. Business manager David Weiher says the hottest new apple is Honeycrisp, a golden eating apple, but he is most proud of Carlson's success with peaches (seven varieties) and nectarines (four varieties). "Most people don't believe it's possible to grow peaches in New England," he says. Not everything is pick-your-own: All the fruits are available by the pound in the rudimentary shop, which also sells the orchard's applesauce, apple juice, apple cider vinegar, mulling spices, jams, jellies, and preserves. Open when harvesting; call for hours.

Carter & Stevens Farm Store, 500 West St. (Route 22), Barre, MA 01005; (978) 355-4940; www.carterandstevensfarm. com. Leaving the kids home when you visit this farm store is a form of cruel and unusual punishment. Principally a dairy farm that packages its own milk in glass bottles, Carter & Stevens also has a free farm animal petting zoo, makes and sells ice cream from its milk, and operates an outdoor open-fire barbecue restaurant in the summer. The store carries some of the farm's own vegetables and produce from other central Massachusetts farms, as well as Carter & Stevens's grass-fed ground beef and steaks. The farm also produces honey and maple syrup, both for sale at the store. Open late May through October; call for hours.

Clearview Farm, 4 Kendall Hill Rd., Sterling, MA 01564; (978) 422-0442; www.clearviewfarmstand.com. This venerable hilltop farm was first planted more than two centuries ago and has been in Diane Melone's family since 1906—a "long line of Yankees," she jokes. In fact, if encouraged, she'll admit to being a descendant of Mary E. Sawyer, the author (so people in Sterling claim) of the nursery rhyme "Mary Had a Little Lamb." Diane and her husband, Rick, grow a wide variety of vegetables ("Rick mulls over the seed catalogs over the winter looking for new things to try," Diane says), including chile peppers. Their orchards have five varieties of freestone peaches, which they sell at the farm stand for a few weeks before opening up the orchards to people who want to pick. Clearview also has pick-your-own pumpkins and fall raspberries. The farm stand is open daily from mid-August through Thanksgiving, and the farm offers hayrides to the orchards on weekends from mid-September through Columbus Day. Along with their beautiful produce, the Melones also sell honey from their own hives, their own cider, and several types of locally produced cheeses.

Apple Pie with Dried Apricots and Pineapple

Eileen Maher Kronauer is the apple pie lady of Harvard, Massachusetts. The book she co-wrote with her husband, Charles, called Apple of Your Pie, *is one of the best histories of apples and pie making in New England—and an incredible source for great variations on that most American of desserts, apple pie. This pie is one of Eileen's personal favorites, created in a moment of inspiration with ingredients she had on hand. She suggests refrigerating the pie for at least ten minutes before baking (unless you are using a light ceramic plate that could crack). She advises that ceramic, stoneware, or glass pie plates are better than metal because they allow the bottom crust to brown more evenly and the resulting pie is less likely to be soggy.*

Brandy Pastry

3 large egg yolks, slightly beaten
6–7 tablespoons brandy
2 cups all-purpose flour
2 tablespoons sugar
½ teaspoon salt
1¾ sticks (14 tablespoons) cold, unsalted butter, cut into ½-inch pieces

1. In a small bowl, stir together egg yolks and brandy until smooth.
2. Combine flour, sugar, and salt in a large bowl. Using a pastry blender or two knives, cut in butter until mixture resembles coarse meal, with large pea-size bits. Chill mixture in refrigerator for 10 minutes.
3. Sprinkle 3 tablespoons of egg-brandy mixture over the dry ingredients. Stir with a wooden spoon and continue adding egg-brandy mixture 1 tablespoon at a time until dough begins to clump together. Reserve at least 3 tablespoons egg-brandy mixture.
4. Form dough into two balls, flatten each into a 4-inch disk, wrap in waxed paper or plastic wrap, and refrigerate for at least 30 minutes. Prepare the filling (see below) while the dough is chilling.

5. Roll out one disk, for the bottom pastry, on a lightly floured surface. Roll evenly until circle of crust is about 4 inches wider than diameter of pie plate. Keep the other disk refrigerated.
6. Transfer the pastry to a pie plate, then trim the edge and moisten with some of the remaining egg-brandy mixture. Cover and refrigerate the pie shell while rolling out the top pastry.
7. Preheat oven to 425°F.
8. Roll out the second disk for the top pastry. Spoon the prepared filling into the pie shell and place the second pastry on top.
9. Trim the edge of the top pastry, then fold the top and bottom pastry edges under and crimp decoratively. Cut several small slits in the pastry top or prick with a fork to allow steam to escape. To give the top crust a golden color and crisp texture, brush the top and sides of the pastry with the remaining egg-brandy mixture and sprinkle with sugar before baking.
10. Bake the pie at 425°F for 20 minutes, then reduce the heat to 400°F and bake for another 30 minutes, or until the crust is golden brown. Cool for 20 minutes before serving.

Fruit Filling

3 tablespoons apricot preserves
¼ **cup sugar**
⅓ **cup brandy**
½ **cup chopped dried pineapple and apricots**

7 Golden Russet apples, peeled, cored, and cut into chunks
2 tablespoons all-purpose flour
¼ **teaspoon ground nutmeg**

1. While the dough is chilling, heat apricot preserves, sugar, and brandy in a saucepan, stirring until smooth. Add dried fruit. Stir together.
2. Place apples in a large bowl. Stir in apricot mixture. Sprinkle flour and nutmeg over fruit and toss well. Use mixture to fill pie shell.

Serves 8

Apple of Your Pie
(978) 456-6965
www.appleofyourpie.com

Crystal Brook Farm, 192 Tuttle Rd., Sterling, MA 01564; (978) 422-6646. Cheesemaker Ann Starbard milks a herd of fifty Saanen and Alpine goats to produce both a feta-style cheese and a range of plain and flavored soft chèvres. (Flavors include garlic and basil, chive, dill, cracked black pepper, and sun-dried tomato and basil.) She also sells goat cheese marinated in olive oil. Open daily March through December.

Dick's Market Garden, 647 Northfield Rd., Lunenburg, MA 01462; (978) 582-4896; www.dicksmarketgarden.com. Probably best known to Boston and Cambridge shoppers as "that farm with the incredible vegetables" at many of the farmers' markets, Dick's also has a stand at the farm open from Mother's Day weekend through Halloween (call for hours). Greenhouses on the property (Dick's also sells garden and landscape plants in the spring) let the Violette family extend the season in the fall with such spring-like delicacies as tender lettuce and pea tendrils.

Hyland Orchard, 199 Arnold Rd., Sturbridge, MA 01566; (508) 347-7500; www.hylandorchard.com. Offering wagon rides and hayrides and music festivals, Hyland Orchard also has pick-your-own apples and pumpkins in September and October and peaches in August (call for hours). In March, the farm runs pancake breakfasts every weekend. The tap room for Pioneer Brewing (see below) is also on the property, and the farm shop has cider and maple syrup made on the premises, ice cream, and jellies, jams, honey, and baked goods.

Keown Orchards, 9 McClellan Rd., Sutton, MA 01590; (508) 865-6706; www.keownorchards.com. Although most people visit during the height of the apple harvest, when Keown has more than sixty varieties available for picking, there's something endearing about stopping in late in the season when the wood-burning stove is fired up hot with apple-wood prunings and the aromas of mulled cider and apple pies in the oven fill the air. The farm is open for events from apple blossom tours in mid-May to Sutton pre-Christmas celebrations in December, but the farm stand doesn't get going until mid-July, when the vegetable harvest begins to roll in. Among the apple varieties are at least twenty heirlooms, including a few varieties of crab apple (the only apple native to North America), Rhode Island Greening, Hubbardston, Westfield, and the one-time king of these hills, Red Astrachan. Keown also has pick-your-own peaches, nectarines, and sweet cherries. Open daily from mid-May through December.

Misty Brook Farm, 830 Springhill Rd., Barre, MA 01005; (413) 477-8234. Located in the gentle microclimate east of the Quabbin Reservoir, Misty Brook raises organic grass-fed beef and dairy cattle, as well as free-range pigs and poultry, and grows a variety of organic fruit and vegetable crops that range from watermelons to potatoes. Eggs, pork, veal, and raw cow's milk are available all year, while beef is available in the fall. The stand also sells Babcia's Farm pasture-fed organic chicken stock, beef stock, lard, and baked goods. Call for hours.

Red Apple Farm, 455 Highland Ave., Phillipston, MA 01331; (978) 249-6763; www.redapplefarm.com. In addition to a farm stand crammed with goodies—cider doughnuts, fudge, maple candy and sugar—Red Apple operates one of the most extensive pick-your-own operations in the middle of the state. The season begins with both wild and cultivated blueberries (hint: the wild are more expensive and more work to pick—and worth every bit of extra effort) in mid-July. It's the only spot we know that has dig-your-own potatoes—in six varieties, no less! Peaches, pears, and raspberries round out the fruits. The farm stand, open daily from mid-July through December, also carries a lot of jams, jellies, relishes, pickles, and salsas. The best-seller of the bunch, though, is the Vidalia onion salad dressing.

Sholan Farms, Upper Pleasant St., Leominster, MA 01453; (978) 840-FARM; www.sholanfarms.com. The last apple orchard in Leominster, birthplace of John Chapman (aka Johnny Appleseed), Sholan Farms was purchased by the city in 1999 to prevent conversion of the farmland into a subdivision of 150 single-family homes. Conservation-minded volunteers have been reclaiming and restoring the orchard and working to renovate the barn. Ten varieties are available for picking—Vista Bella, Jersey Mac, Gingergold, Paula Red, McIntosh, Cortland, Empire, Golden Delicious, Macoun, and Red Delicious—from very late July into early November, Thursday through Sunday.

January through March: **Dinner in a Country Village,** Old Sturbridge Village, Route 20, Sturbridge, MA 01566; (508) 347-3362; www.osv.org. When winter hits, Old Sturbridge Village emphasizes indoor activities. At these special dinners you learn how early New Englanders prepared a delicious meal over the hearth. Costumed interpreters direct the proceedings, but the guests do the chopping, mixing, and basting, using early-nineteenth-century tools and techniques.

Mid-May: **Quaboag Valley Asparagus & Flower Festival,** Town Common, Route 9, West Brookfield, MA 01585; (508) 867-1421. Diederik Leertouwer came to the United States in 1784 to promote trade between his native Netherlands and New England. With his wife and daughter, he later settled in West Brookfield, where he lived from 1794 to 1798. Local legend has it that Leertouwer imported asparagus from his homeland and was the first to plant it in this country. Wild asparagus continues to grow in the area and a few farms also cultivate it. This annual spring festival features homegrown and homemade agricultural products and a generally festive atmosphere, including Maypole dancing for children and lots of homemade foods.

Late August: **Ware Grange Fair,** Belchertown Rd., Ware, MA 01082; www.massgrange.org. If you're particularly good at pickling or growing champion green beans or basil, this is your chance to vie for recognition. Any resident of Massachusetts is eligible to enter the fair competition and need not be a Grange member. Categories include vegetables, fruit, herbs, eggs, canned goods, poultry, and farm crops. An old-fashioned ham and bean supper caps the festivities.

Late September: **Agricultural Exhibition,** Old Sturbridge Village, Route 20, Sturbridge, MA 01566; (508) 347-3362; www.osv .org. This early-nineteenth-century forerunner of today's community agricultural fairs features exhibitions of livestock and produce. Home gardeners show off their heirloom vegetables, flowers, and herbs—antique varieties only.

Mid-October: **Brookfield Apple Country Fair,** Brookfield Common, Brookfield, MA 01535; (508) 867-9553; www.apple countryfair.com. This fund-raiser to send the local sixth grade class to environmental summer camp has two major draws: a raffle for a community-made quilt and a massive bake sale of apple pies. There's also a pie-judging contest, live music, and more than seventy local craftspeople and vendors selling their wares.

Late October: **Annual Applefest,** Wachusett Mountain Ski Area, 499 Mountain Rd., Princeton, MA 01541; (978) 464-2300; www .wachusett.com. The entire Wachusett area is major apple country, and this fall festival is a cross between an agricultural fair and an Oktoberfest. Look for apple pies and cider as well as sausages, German music, craft exhibitions, a farmers' market, and pie-baking and pie-eating contests.

Coney Island Lunch, 158 Southbridge St., Worcester, MA 01608; (508) 753-4362; www.coneyislandlunch.com; $. No visitor to Worcester should be allowed to leave the city without making a pilgrimage to this neon-bedecked palace where the lowly dog is elevated to an icon of pop culture. The place still serves the best hot dog in town for less than two bucks. Grab a tray and get in line—it shuffles through quickly. The house classic Coney Island is a hot dog with mustard, onions, and chili sauce.

El Basha, 424 Belmont St., Worcester, MA 01604; (508) 797-0884; $$. El Basha West, 256 Park Ave., Worcester, MA 01609; (508) 795-0222; El Basha, 2 Connector Rd., Westborough, MA 01581; (508) 366-2455; $$. The original El Basha has become a fixture in Worcester—a popular Lebanese family restaurant that adheres to halal dietary laws. Stuffed grape leaves are the signature dish. If you have a hankering for smoky eggplant, tabouli, and a pervasive taste of green olives, this is the spot for you in central Massachusetts. The newer El Basha West and the Westborough outpost offer the same menu. Diners unfamiliar with real Middle Eastern cooking are invariably surprised by the subtlety of the seasoning and preparation. Fans of the beloved but defunct El Morocco say El Basha West deserves to be its successor.

Harrington Farm, 178 Westminster Rd., Princeton, MA 01541; (978) 464-5600; www.harringtonfarm.com/restaurant.html; $$$.

Classic Diners

Over the half century between 1907 and 1957, the Worcester Lunch Car and Carriage Manufacturing Company helped create one of the most enduring icons of the American roadside—the diner. Known affectionately as Worcester Lunch, the company transformed the humble horse-drawn lunch wagons invented in Providence, Rhode Island, into compact metal diners with galley kitchens, long counters lined with stools, and a wall of small booths.

Over the years, the company built 651 diners, and many of them are still found along the streets and highways of central Massachusetts. Worcester Lunch was slow to adopt the streamlined, chromed look that the other two major diner builders employed after World War II. As a result, Worcester diners have a distinctive look of period graphics on porcelain-enamel exteriors. Many have real wood trim and wooden booths inside.

Three lovingly maintained Worcester diners still operate in their home city, serving such diner classics as meat loaf, burgers, grilled cheese sandwiches, and eggs any style at all hours. The **Miss Worcester Diner** (300 Southbridge St., Worcester, MA 01608; 508-753-5600) is yellow with blue trim and classic lettering. The **Boulevard Diner** (155 Shrewsbury St., Worcester, MA 01604; 508-791-4535), built in 1936, is registered as a National Historic Landmark. With its bold illuminated clock and extensive neon, it is guarded around the clock by surveillance cameras. Essentially across the street, the **Parkway Diner** (148 Shrewsbury St., Worcester, MA 01604; 508-753-9968) is covered with pebbled cement that obscures its 1934 exterior. Inside, however, it retains the original features, including a second counter and row of stools in lieu of the usual booths. The Parkway is also known locally for its red-sauce Italian specials. All three serve breakfast and lunch daily and are sometimes open around the clock (or nearly) on the weekends.

This country inn (just three rooms) and restaurant is the baby of John Bomba, an acclaimed chef and graduate of the Culinary Institute of America. On summer evenings the dining room extends to tables set on the "farmer's porch" that overlooks the front lawn and pond. Bomba does his best to give an American interpretation to the French country inn, with a menu that usually includes hearty fare such as venison loin served on a base of creamy polenta flecked with white truffles. The New American menu changes seasonally. Open for dinner Friday and Saturday.

J's at Nashoba Valley Winery, 100 Wattaquadoc Hill Rd., Bolton, MA 01740; (978) 779-9816; www.nashobawinery.com; $$$. Executive chef Steve Sprague displays real finesse and panache in this restaurant associated with the pioneering fruit winery. The New American menu, which changes seasonally and showcases the fruits, vegetables, herbs, and flowers grown on the grounds, is frankly much more sophisticated than the relatively straightforward fruit wines made next door. Start with caramelized sea scallops, for example, and move on to a large piece of halibut grilled with lovage and thyme from the kitchen garden. Luncheon fare is less daunting but equally tasty—a pizza margherita, for example, or one of several entree salads that can also be packed up as picnic fare. Open for lunch and dinner Wednesday through Saturday and brunch on Sunday.

Salem Cross Inn, Route 9, West Brookfield, MA 01585; (508) 867-8337; www.salemcrossinn.com; $$$$. A family restaurant since 1961, the Salem Cross occupies a restored 1705 home, filled with an extensive collection of colonial- and federal-period antiques. The restaurant always has a fairly traditional American-Continental menu, but the "fireplace feasts" offered select nights November through April are even more fun. These eighteenth-century-style meals are prepared on the open hearth of the fieldstone fireplace, with prime rib turned over the cherry-log fire on a circa-1700 roasting jack and apple pie baked in the 1699 beehive oven. Fireplace feasts are on Saturday and Sunday in late November and all of April, and Friday through Sunday from December through March. Reservations essential.

Ted's Montana Grill, Union St., Westborough, MA 01581; (508) 366-5050; www.tedsmontanagrill.com; $$. We're always reluctant to recommend chain restaurants, but if you have a hankering to try bison meat before you head to Alta Vista Farm (see above) to buy some, this is the place. Who better to introduce bison to Massachusetts than a man who has a big bison spread himself, Ted Turner? The meat is lower in fat and cholesterol than beef and is offered in several forms (burger, steak, short ribs, chili).

Twigs Cafe, Tower Hill Botanic Garden, 11 French Dr., Boylston, MA 01505; (508) 869-6111; $. The home of the Worcester County Horticultural Society occupies a hilltop with sweeping views down to the Wachusett Reservoir and acres of beautiful flower and vegetable

Blueberry Bread Pudding

Cecile Collier, chef of Twigs Cafe at Tower Hill Botanic Garden, says that this dessert is popular even during the warmest, stickiest days of the summer because visitors to Tower Hill are invariably people who appreciate the fresh flavors of in-season fruits and vegetables.

4 eggs
2 cups half-and-half
¼ cup whole milk
¾ cup plus 2 tablespoons sugar
1 tablespoon vanilla extract

7–8 slices stale bread, crusts removed
1 cup blueberries
Nutmeg to taste

1. Preheat oven to 350°F. Combine and blend eggs, half-and-half, milk, ¾ cup sugar, and vanilla.
2. Tear up bread and mix with blueberries. Place in a 9 x 5-inch loaf pan. Pour egg mixture over bread and berries in pan. Sprinkle with nutmeg and 2 tablespoons sugar.
3. Place loaf pan into a larger baking pan that has been filled halfway with hot water. Bake for 45 minutes to 1 hour.
4. Serve pudding warm, pairing each dish with a small sidecar of vanilla ice cream.

Serves 4

Twigs Cafe
Tower Hill Botanic Garden
11 French Dr.
Boylston, MA 01505
(508) 869-6111

gardens. But the hungry traveler has two other good reasons to visit: the small demonstration orchard of more than thirty heirloom apple trees (scions are sometimes sold to home orchardists in the spring) and Twigs, where chef CeCe Collier thinks nothing of incorporating snippets from the gardens into her light, fresh midday dishes. Have a salad with heaps of edible flowers or a plate of scones with herbal tea. Open Tuesday through Sunday for lunch.

Brewpubs & Microbreweries

Pioneer Brewing Company, 195 Arnold Rd., Fiskdale (Sturbridge), MA 01566; (508) 347-7500; www.pioneerbrewingcompany.com. Based on the old song, and a rate of 7.5 bottles of beer per minute, Pioneer estimates that it is located 450 bottles of beer on the wall from Boston, 1,350 bottles of beer on the wall from New York, and 338 bottles of beer on the wall from Hartford, Connecticut. Who said brewers took themselves seriously? The brewery occupies a 12,000-square-foot former barn at Hyland Orchard (see above). Its flagship beer is the Pioneer Pale Ale, a medium-bodied brew with a rich copper color. The Pioneer Industrial Pale Ale carries a sharper hops flavor and more alcohol. Look for an additional ale, which changes from season to season. It could be a Bock aged in bourbon barrels, a Bavarian-style wheat beer, or a hearty dark English-style ale. Open Tuesday through Thursday from 3:00 to 8:00 p.m., Friday through Sunday from noon to 8:00 p.m.

Brew It Yourself

There's a Scrub-a-Dub across Route 9 from their location, but the only suds that interest the folks at **Deja Brew** in Shrewsbury come from pouring a bottle of home brew into a beer mug. The first brew-on-premises operation in Massachusetts, Deja Brew lets aspiring home-brewers (and home winemakers) practice their craft in a retail environment. They provide the recipes, ingredients, brewing kettles, storage areas, and bottling equipment. Even better, they clean up the mess. This means your cellar or garage need not smell like a brewery—unless the bottles explode after you get them home because you ignored the brewer's advice and added too much sugar before capping them. Deja Brew has prepackaged more than sixty beer recipes and more than a dozen wine recipes for use on the premises. Each beer batch makes six dozen 22-ounce bottles. Wine runs are five gallons.

If you get hooked, you'll find that homebrewers tend to be an enthusiastic bunch, and brewer/vintner Bruce Lucier is no exception. He runs **West Boylston Homebrew Emporium,** a store that provides everything for making beer at home—including all sorts of grains, spices, gadgets, and brewing chemicals you didn't think you needed but absolutely cannot live without. Novices will appreciate the canned and boxed kits, while experienced (or, as they prefer to style themselves, "visionary") homebrewers can mix and match yeasts, dry malts, crystal malts, malt extracts, and different styles of hops and hop extracts. The shop also carries winemaking supplies, including a wide range of concentrated grape juices for no-hassle vinting. If you want to introduce your kids to classic soda flavors, you can purchase the ingredients for sarsaparilla, spruce beer, and birch root beer, as well as orange soda, ginger ale, and cream soda.

Deja Brew
510B Boston Turnpike Rd. (Route 9)
Shrewsbury, MA 01545
(508) 842-8991
www.deja-brew.com

West Boylston Homebrew Emporium
Causeway Crossing Mall
45 Sterling St. (Route 12)
West Boylston, MA 01583
(508) 835-3374
www.wbhomebrew.com

Wachusett Brewing Company, 175 State Rd. East (Route 2A), Westminster, MA 01473; (978) 874-9965; http://wachusettbrew .com. Three friends who confess to developing a significant "appreciation" for beer as students at Worcester Polytechnic Institute opened Wachusett in 1994. With an annual production of fewer than 8,000 barrels, WBC is a true microbrewery and its beers are available solely within state lines. They're easiest to find closest to the source—i.e., in almost every central Massachusetts package store. Year-round products include a pale ale (Country Ale), a wheat ale with blueberries, Nut Brown Ale, an IPA, and Black Shack Porter. The company also brews a summer wheat ale with a hint of lemon, Winter Ale (a Scotch-style amber), and Quinn's Irish (an Irish-style pale ale available around St. Patrick's Day). Condensed tours are offered Wednesday through Friday from 1:00 to 4:00 p.m. and full tours are available on Saturday from 1:00 to 4:00 p.m. Families are welcome, but children are not allowed to taste.

Wine Trail

Nashoba Valley Winery, 100 Wattaquadoc Hill Rd., Bolton, MA 01740; (978) 779-5521; www.nashobawinery.com. Nashoba Valley Winery is as much a destination as a winery. Acres and acres of fruit trees surround the property, and the grounds are deliberately set up to encourage picnicking. Or picking, for that matter—pick-your-own is available for raspberries, peaches, blackberries, plums, and apples. If you don't pick them, they'll likely end up in the wines. NVW was a regional pioneer in developing fine fruit wines and has the blue ribbons to prove it. Apple wines (from a sparkling brut and several dry varietals to the semisweet Maiden's Blush) remain the core of the offerings. Other wines incorporate blueberries, cherries, plums, and peaches. In recent years, the winery has also begun making a few grape wines as well: Chardonnay, Vidal Blanc, Riesling, and Gewürztraminer. Open daily year-round for tastings and sales. Tours Saturday and Sunday 11:00 a.m. to 4:00 p.m.

Obadiah McIntyre Farm Winery, at Charlton Orchards, 44 Old Worcester Rd. (Route 20), Charlton, MA 01507; (508) 248-7820; www.charltonorchard.com. Owner Nate Benjamin Jr.'s Charlton Orchards produces wonderful apples, peaches, pears, strawberries, and blueberries, and the farm store, open daily from June to January and weekends the rest of the year, has quite a local following for its apple pies and ciders. But Benjamin began planting *vinifera* and French-American hybrid wine grapes in the 1990s, and in 2002 opened Obadiah McIntyre Farm Winery, named for the man who received the farm as a land grant in 1733. Benjamin makes fruit wines from apples, strawberries, blueberries, raspberries, peaches, blackberries, and pears. One of the apple wines is aged up to a year in oak to impart complexity. He's also vinting wines from Riesling, Chardonnay, Zinfandel, Chambourcin, and Cabernet Sauvignon grapes.

Cranberry Apple Chutney

J's restaurant at Nashoba Valley Winery tries to use local products and the winery's fruit wines whenever possible. The balance of sweet and tart in this chutney depends on the variety of apple used. We suggest heirloom Golden Russet or Roxbury Russet apples for a piquant version that pairs well with roast pork, duck, or wild game. This recipe makes about 12 pints of chutney for canning.

2 tablespoons vegetable oil

3 cups diced Bermuda onions

12 cups diced apples

2 tablespoons chopped fresh sage

4 cups dried cranberries

3 cups cranberry apple wine (several regional winemakers produce a cranberry apple wine)

1 teaspoon cinnamon

½ teaspoon ground thyme

Pinch of ground cloves

2 teaspoons ground cardamom

½ teaspoon ground fennel seed

½ teaspoon ground nutmeg

2 teaspoons salt or to taste

½ cup sugar

¾ cup orchard honey

¾ cup pure maple syrup

3 teaspoons fresh-squeezed lemon juice

2 splashes grenadine syrup

1 cup Baldwin apple wine (or substitute any other dry apple wine or hard cider)

2 tablespoons cornstarch

1. In a large stockpot over medium heat, combine the vegetable oil, the onions, and a third of the apples. Sauté until the apples begin to sweat, then add the sage, cranberries, another third of the apples. Deglaze the pot with cranberry apple wine.

2. Bring to a boil, then boil for 2 minutes, stirring frequently. Then reduce heat and add the cinnamon, thyme, cloves, cardamom, fennel, nutmeg, salt, sugar, honey, maple syrup, and lemon juice.

3. Simmer until the apples have softened, the cranberries have hydrated, and the wine has reduced. Lower the heat and add the remaining apples, the grenadine syrup, and the apple wine.

4. Cook at a low simmer for 10 minutes, continuing to stir.

5. Pour the chutney into a large mixing bowl and let it cool for a few minutes.

6. Meanwhile mix the cornstarch with approximately 1 cup cold water to make a slurry (it should have a smooth consistency like heavy cream). Add the slurry to the chutney while it's still hot, stirring to combine well. This will lighten the color.

7. Serve the chutney warm, chill it for up to 2 hours, or jar it while still hot (180°F or more).

Fills a dozen 12-ounce canning jars

Nashoba Valley Winery
100 Wattaquadoc Hill Rd.
Bolton, MA 01740
(978) 779-5521
www.nashobawinery.com

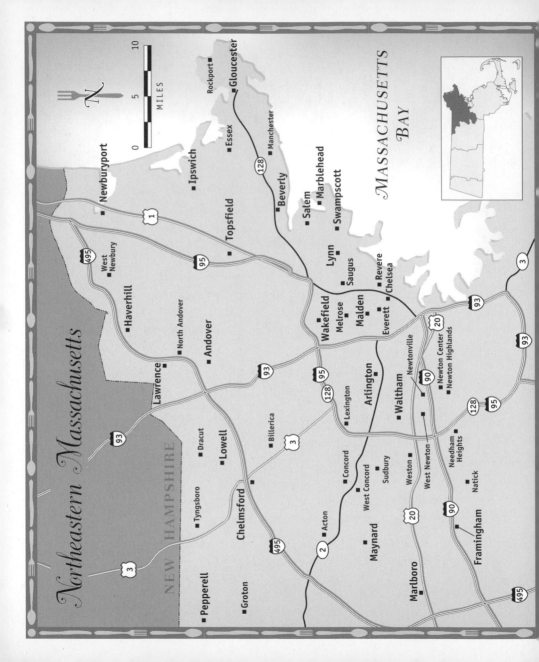

Northeastern Massachusetts

The Gloucester fisherman is as iconic a figure in American myth as the lumberjacks of Minnesota and the cowboys of the Southwest. He is forever fixed in his yellow raingear, gritting his teeth in the face of a storm and hauling his lines to feed a hungry nation. With declining fish stocks and other economic opportunities available, the number of Gloucester fishermen has dwindled, but representatives of this venerable breed still stride the docks of Cape Ann, and the shore towns north of Boston retain a fishing identity.

"North Shore fish" used to mean cod, but these days it's more likely to refer to clams or lobsters. The sandy flats and marshy inlets north of rocky Cape Ann remain some of the world's most pristine and productive shellfishing beds, and the restaurants of northeastern Massachusetts revel in the bounty of the nearby sea and the orchards and fields of the Merrimack Valley. Even in this age of agricultural conglomeration, family farms persist in the rural areas north and west of Boston. Pushed out of their own local markets by nationwide distributors, they thrive by supplying restaurants and selling directly to consumers at farm stands and, increasingly, at weekly farmers' markets. When driving back roads in the summer, keep your eyes peeled for small roadside stands operated by dairy farmers who make their own ice cream.

As you get closer to metropolitan Boston, where old fishing and farming towns have matured into commuter suburbs, you'll also find a proliferation of fine bakeries, gourmet shops, and restaurants. And in communities like Chelsea, Everett, and Malden, you'll find substantial immigrant populations that have brought their own cuisines intact from the old country.

Made or Grown Here

The Candy Shoppe, 135 American Legion Highway, Revere, MA 02151; (781) 485-4500. Next Halloween, surprise the kids in your neighborhood with retro treats from this factory outlet store of the New England Confectionery Company: Necco Wafers, Mary Janes, Sky Bars, or Clark Bars. Or, for Valentine's Day, stock up on those pastel-colored, chalky conversation hearts, first manufactured in Cambridge in 1902. Open weekdays 8:30 a.m. to 5:00 p.m.

Carolyn's Homemade, P.O. Box 1221, Concord, MA 01742; (978) 369-2940; www.40parklane.com. Carolyn Harby Schaefer started making spiced pecans and walnuts in her Concord kitchen and met with such success selling them locally that she moved into a commercial kitchen in 1991. She changed the company name from Carolyn's Kitchen to 40 Park Lane in 2008, while changing the product line to Carolyn's Homemade. The kosher products include three flavors of spiced pecans and walnuts (sweet and salty, orange, and coconut ginger), spiced peanuts, and spiced pecans covered in milk and dark chocolate, as well vinegars, mustards, and herbal rubs. Available at select stores nationwide, by mail order, and through the Web site.

George Howell Coffee Company, 312 School St., Acton, MA 01720; (978) 635-9033; http://terroircoffee.com. George Howell might just be the most fanatical coffee aficionado on the planet, and his tiny Terroir coffee exists to promote the idea of single-source fine coffees as the gastronomic pinnacle of the coffee world—rather like single-vineyard wines. Howell's approach is even more radical in that he makes the growers part of the process of developing spectacular coffees and pays them accordingly. The results are on the pricey side, but they represent arguably the best and most sophisticated choice of fine coffees in the world. Terroir sells via its Web site and through a few high-end specialty shops and fine restaurants.

Harbor Sweets, 85 Leavitt St., Salem, MA 01970; (978) 745-7648; www.harborsweets.com. In 1973 Ben Strochecker decided he wanted to create the best piece of candy in the world. What he ended up

with was the Sweet Sloop, a sailboat-shaped piece of almond buttercrunch covered in white chocolate and dipped in dark chocolate
and crushed pecans. Although Harbor Sweets now produces a broad
line of premium chocolates, the sailboats still lead the company's
regatta. Strochecker now spends his time on the tennis court while
former part-time candy dipper Phyllis LeBlanc has risen through
the ranks to become CEO and owner. Harbor Sweets chocolates are
found in hundreds of gourmet and gift shops across the country,
and you can visit the factory shop (call for hours), where you'll see
the chocolates being made and wrapped. Also available by mail
order and through the Web site.

Nashoba Brook Bakery, 152 Commonwealth Ave., West Concord,
MA 01742; (978) 318-0006; www.slowrise.com. Breadmakers have
a penchant for philosophy, and Nashoba Brook is no exception.
Principally a wholesale bread bakery, Nashoba Brook bakes about a
half dozen varieties daily, none of which contains oil, milk, sugar,
or eggs. The bakery's own sourdough starter (begun a decade ago
with wild yeast harvested from Concord grapes) is a marvel, producing an intense Old World flavor, yet giving the breads a true loft.
The company also makes authentic French breads with unbleached
flour. Available at many eastern Massachusetts specialty groceries
and at the bakery cafe, which does a booming business in healthy
sandwiches, soups, and salads.

Owens Poultry Farm, 585 Central Ave., Needham Heights, MA
02494; (781) 444-1861. Looking at the one-story brick building

in the middle of suburbia, you'd never guess there was a full-scale turkey and chicken farm out back. The Owen family has been selling poultry here since 1935, and besides fresh chicken, ducks, and other birds (as well as eggs), the farm shop also has frozen chicken and turkey meat, potpies, and casserole dishes. In fact, you can get a Thanksgiving dinner any time of year. Not only does the store have fresh roasted turkey breast, it also carries turkey gravy, cooked trays of squash, stuffing, mashed potatoes, and green bean casserole.

Shaw Farm Dairy, 195 New Boston Rd., Dracut, MA 01826; (978) 957-3011; www.shawfarm.com. Founded in 1908, Shaw Farm is the last independent farm dairy in the greater Lowell area. It bottles fresh milk in glass quarts as well as plastic pints and makes its own ice cream; its products are widely available in northeastern Massachusetts at farm stands and some grocery stores. During warm weather, the dairy operates its own ice-cream stand, where most of the fifty-plus flavors are available. The staff is always coming up with new taste sensations. "We get bored," says Janet McGann, "so we say, 'Let's come up with something new' and start tossing ideas around." Those ideas have included vanilla brownie, Kahlúa brownie, and coffee Oreo. Vanilla's the top-selling flavor, but orange pineapple also does well. The farm store is open daily, and you can walk up to the barns and visit the seventy-five or so Holsteins that provide the milk. Down at the store, peek through a window in back and you'll see the bottling machine splash milk into gleaming glass bottles, then plop and crimp a cap on top. In 2008, Shaw Farm inaugurated a certified organic product line under the New England Organic Creamery label. If you e-mail ahead for a reservation (see the Web site), you can join one of the Monday night barn tours.

Valley View Farm, 278 High St., Topsfield, MA 01983; www .valleyviewcheese.com. Peter and Elizabeth Mulholland milk a small herd of Anglo-Nubian goats to produce fresh Valley View Chevre (plain and seasoned versions), soft-ripened white-rind Topsfield Round, pyramidal soft-ripened Highlander cheese, and a crumbly but creamy feta. They also buy Jersey cow's milk from Appleton Farms in Ipswich (a heritage farm) to make a soft-ripened cheese like an unusually creamy Camembert. Several eastern Massachusetts restaurants serve the Mulhollands' cheeses, which are also available at regional cheesemongers and specialty gourmet shops.

Zorro Chocolates; (800) 936-2218; www.zorrochocolates.com. Ed Fox launched Zorro (Spanish for "fox") when he was laid up painfully awaiting back surgery and realized, despite everything, how much pleasure he took from 70 percent cacao dark chocolate. Fox infuses the flavors into the chocolate for an intense, consistent taste in every bite. He also tempers the bars very carefully, for the most pleasurable mouthfeel. Two of Zorro's best-selling flavors are dark chocolate with Chimayo chiles and fleur de sel and dark chocolate with star anise. Zorro Chocolates are only sold by phone or Web order, since Fox feels normal distribution means customers get the candy past its peak.

Big Sky Bread Company, 105 Union St., Piccadilly Square, Newton Center, MA 02159; (617) 332-4242. In our book, there are two strains of great breadmaking in Massachusetts—the crusty European-style loaves and the squared-off, richly flavored, high-rising soft loaves that owe their resurgence to the rediscovery of breadmaking by the sixties counterculture. Big Sky falls into the sophisticated neo-hippie camp, with outstanding honey whole wheat; light, dark, and marble rye breads; and egg-rich loaves such as raisin challah and Swedish tea ring. Big Sky's most unusual breads are those with fruit, such as strawberry bread or peach and vanilla bread.

Bread & Chocolate Bakery Cafe, 108 Madison Ave., Newtonville, MA 02460; (617) 243-0500; www.breadnchocolate.com. Trained as an artist, then as a chef, Eunice Feller has a knack for making pastries as beautiful as they are tasty. She also manages just the right balance between fussy French pastry (little chocolate mousse cakes, for example) and down-home American baked goods (like her oaty peanut butter cookie laced with chocolate chips). For people who can't decide on their breakfast pastry, Feller makes a donut muffin. Lunch is a treat, with sandwiches, soups, salads, and comfort food entrees such as baked mac and cheese, chicken potpie, and the quiche of the day.

Lemon Blackberry Pound Cake

Chef-owner Eunice Feller at Bread & Chocolate Bakery Cafe puts a summer seasonal twist on this classic pound cake.

1 cup (2 sticks) unsalted butter, at room temperature

3 cups sugar

3 cups cake flour

½ teaspoon baking soda

½ teaspoon salt

6 large eggs, at room temperature

1 tablespoon lemon zest

3 tablespoons lemon juice

8 ounces sour cream

3 pints fresh blackberries, slightly crushed

Powdered sugar

1. Preheat oven to 325°F. Butter and flour a large Bundt pan.
2. Using an electric mixer, beat butter and sugar at high speed in a large bowl for 5 minutes.
3. Sift together flour, baking soda, and salt. Set aside.
4. When butter and sugar is light and fluffy, add eggs one at a time, beating well after each addition. Then beat in lemon zest and lemon juice.
5. Reduce mixer speed to low. Add flour mixture and beat until just mixed. Scrape down bowl and beat in sour cream until just mixed. Gently fold in crushed blackberries by hand.
6. Spoon batter into prepared pan and bake 50 to 60 minutes, or until a toothpick inserted near center of the cake comes out clean.
7. Cool cake in pan on a rack for 15 minutes, then invert rack over cake and reinvert cake onto rack. Let cool, then dust with powdered sugar.

Makes 12–16 slices

Bread & Chocolate Bakery Cafe

108 Madison Ave.
Newtonville, MA 02460
(617) 243-0500
www.breadnchocolate.com

Cafe Zabaglione, 1 Market St., Ipswich, MA 01938; (978) 356- 6484. The casual bar-cafe annex to a more formal restaurant, Cafe Zabaglione combines the best of a fine bakery with a European cafe atmosphere—which is to say, it has a seasonal liquor license and pours cordials, champagne, and other drinks with the sweets from late spring through December. You can get sandwiches, muffins, biscotti, and cookies to eat here or take away, but the best offerings are those in the pastry case, where you'll find such European classics as a tall white chocolate cake studded with raspberries, blueberry flan, tiramisu, Opera cake (dark chocolate cake, mocha filling, chocolate ganache icing), and chocolate mousse served in a crisp wafer cone topped with whipped cream.

China Fair, 70 Needham St., Newton Highlands, MA 02461; (617) 332-1250; www.chinafairinc.com. If you're equipping a kitchen from scratch, you could do worse than to start at China Fair, which carries an extensive generic line of pots and pans, kitchen utensils, and specialty items such as cookie cutters in unusual shapes (dinosaur, coffeepot, house, saw, hammer, cowboy boots, sailboat, palm tree . . .), quesadilla presses, pressure cookers, pizelle makers, waffle makers, and sandwich presses. You'll also find shelf after shelf of casserole dishes, gratin plates, and pie plates. Once you've outfitted the kitchen, you can move on to the dining room, as China Fair sells a great deal of casual dinnerware. In fact, many local restaurants come here for their table settings. The paper goods annex has anything you'd ever need for a big party, from invitations to banners and noisemakers to paper cups and plates.

Chocolate Café, 6 School St., Manchester-by-the-Sea, MA 01944; (978) 526-0040; www.nantucketchocolatier.com/ChocolateCafe. cfm. This elegant little shop in tony Manchester-by-the-Sea carries a full line of exquisitely crafted truffles and fine dipped chocolates. Order a coffee or hot chocolate and some of the chocolate-dipped ginger cookies for a sophisticated break at one of the handful of tables.

Dante Confections, 199 Boston Rd., Billerica, MA 01821; (800) 933-2683; www.danteconfections.com. Piano maker turned chocolatier Santi Falcone is such a perfectionist that it takes months of experimentation before he introduces a new truffle flavor. Fortunately, he's been at it awhile, so he has twenty-six flavors for you to enjoy as you wait for the next great inspiration. Falcone hasn't forgotten his Sicilian origins: He makes a tiramisu truffle and another flavored with limoncello.

Gigi's Mozzarella House, 355 Broadway, Everett, MA 02149; (617) 387-6810. Located in a clapboard building at the edge of a parking lot behind a funeral home, Gigi's isn't the easiest place to find. But it's worth the search to buy the soft young cheeses— mozzarella, bocconcini, ricotta, and "fresh cheese" similar to farmer cheese—as well as the firmer scarmoza, aged for three to four months. Gigi's is a small operation, with big cheese vats in the back and an informal counter just inside the door where the cheesemaker will dry her hands and ring up your purchase. Most of the cheese goes to restaurants and grocery stores, but you get it cheapest and freshest from the source.

Il Pastificio, 328 Broadway, Everett, MA 02149; (617) 387-3630. Spend time with shop owner Antonio Dello Iacono and you'll earn a degree in the do's and don'ts of southern Italian cooking. His small shop has more varieties of fresh pasta than we've ever seen before, all made with "time and patience," he says. Select a pasta and he'll advise on which homemade sauce makes the best match. A fine capellini, for example, requires a light marinara sauce that keeps the pasta loose and easy to turn. (Dello Iacono never uses a spoon.) In his quest for the perfect pairing of pasta and sauce, he continues to experiment and churn out new shapes. His bombolotti, a chunky tube with a star-shaped interior, can hold up to hearty Bolognese sauces (with or without mushrooms). His Sicilian-style twisted cannolicchio has enough grooves to hold rich sauces such as pesto or Alfredo. Once you've got the pasta and sauce, you can round out the meal with homemade spumoni ice cream and a selection of Italian cookies for dessert.

Katz Bagel Bakery, 139 Park St., Chelsea, MA 02150; (617) 884-9738. The Katz (pronounced "kates") family has been making and selling bagels from this location since 1940, when Chelsea was a city of Jewish immigrants and supported a dozen synagogues. Although now more than half Hispanic, Chelsea still has pockets of European Jewish immigrants, and Richard Katz carries on his

Russian immigrant father's line of work for an increasingly diverse clientele. His old-fashioned New York–style bagels are smaller than the homogenized and Americanized versions prepared by the fast-food giants, and far tastier. They're crunchy on the outside, soft on the inside, and they come in garlic, raisin, plain, egg, pumpernickel, sissle, and onion. The bakery also sells "teething bagels"—a dozen small bagels on a string to help babies through the pain of teething.

La Chapincita Market, 424 Moody St., Waltham, MA 02453; (781) 894-9552. Many New England Latino markets cater to Dominicans and Puerto Ricans, but La Chapincita focuses mostly on the foods of Mexico, Guatemala, El Salvador, Costa Rica, Honduras, and Peru. In practice, this means a great selection of dried chile peppers, a lot of canned goods from Mexico, fresh Mexican tortillas and Salvadoran arepas, and dried corn husks in case you're making your own Mexican tamales. On Saturdays, the shop also has fresh homemade Guatemalan-style pork tamales wrapped in banana leaves. You can wash down your spicy repast with Mexican sodas in such classic fruit flavors as mango, tamarind, pineapple, and limón.

Lakota Bakery, 1375 Massachusetts Ave., Arlington, MA 02476; (781) 646-0121; www.lakotabakery.com. If you're a cookie freak, you've probably encountered Lakota's splendid cookies at select gourmet shops, coffee emporia, and delis. They run the gamut from orange chocolate chip and "old-school peanut butter" (glazed with chocolate and chopped peanuts) to traditional ginger and less-traditional chocolate ginger cookies. Linzer cookies come in raspberry as well as strawberry and apricot. But Lakota's biggest hits are sandwich cookies that catapult the Oreo into another dimension. They include lemon, mint, vanilla, and mocha buttercream between the cookie layers. Lakota sometimes bakes a pie or two, but the shop is really a cookie specialist.

Mrs. Nelson's Candy House, 292 Chelmsford St., Chelmsford, MA 01824; (978) 256-4061. An entire display case facing the entrance at this old-fashioned candy shop at the edge of a strip mall is filled with milk, dark, and white chocolate barks variously combined with pecans, cashews, almonds, nut crunch, and thin slabs of peanut butter or mocha candy. Barks are a specialty of Mrs. Nelson's, though this venerable candymaker also handcrafts fine dipped chocolates and slabs of rich fudge. With advance notice, you can have boxes of chocolates customized with your initials. Mrs. Nelson may have retired in the 1980s, but the classic candies continue.

Penzeys, 1293 Massachusetts Ave., Arlington, MA 02476; (781) 646-7707; www.penzeys.com. Many cooks have encountered Penzeys Spices as a Wisconsin mail-order outfit. But if you want to see and sniff more than 250 herbs and spices, you have to visit a store. This Arlington shop is the sole Massachusetts outpost at this writing, and it's a great place to pick up zaatar, Ceylonese cinnamon, and different strains of oregano suited to different cuisines.

Prides Crossing Confections, 590 Hale St., Prides Crossing (Beverly), MA 01965; (978) 927-2185; www.pridescrossing confections.com. The green miniature chalet-style building at the commuter rail stop might look like a train station, but it's the home of Christopher Flynn's candy-making operation. While Flynn makes outstanding clusters, bark, and soft-center choco-lates, he's best known for his creamy caramels, either coated with chocolate or as the body of his nut-studded, chocolate-coated turtles.

Priscilla Candies, 428 Essex St., Lawrence, MA 01840; (978) 682-2893; www.priscillacandies.com. An old-line candy store (since 1928), Priscilla Candies creates the usual array of mouthwatering dipped chocolates, barks, and chocolate-enrobed nuts. But it's also one of the last places where nice big candy canes—up to three feet long!—are made by hand. The twisting process is very similar to that used in making glass, but glass doesn't have the concentrated peppermint oil that gives Priscilla's canes their delectable flavor.

Shubie's Liquor & Marketplace, 16 Atlantic Ave., Marblehead, MA 01945; (781) 631-0149. Shubie's modestly advertises itself as carrying the "best in specialty foods, cheeses, wines, and spirits," and it's the truth. What's even better is that they believe in letting customers taste  before they buy, and there's usually an array of cheeses, salsas, crackers, and dips to whet your appetite. The selection of wines from California, Australia, New Zealand, and Europe emphasizes small producers who supply quality for the dollar. The cheese case, while relatively small, includes a number of fine chèvres, some outstanding Dutch cheeses, and just a few select French options. The range of culinary oils is broad, embracing several single-olive oils from parts of Spain, Italy, France, and Morocco, and the vinegars include long-aged balsamics and perky Jerez vinegars as well as some made from late-harvest Riesling grapes and d'Anjou pears. Shubie's excels at prepared foods to reheat at home: maple–Dijon mustard grilled chicken, roasted vegetables, four-cheese lasagna, and rosemary beef stew. Sweets include their own scone-sized cookies as well as the full line of Dancing Deer cookies and cakes.

Tito's Bakery, 333 Broadway, Chelsea, MA 02150; (617) 884-3313. The Hispanic markets of eastern Massachusetts get many of their pastries from Tito's, but the sweets are sweetest at the source. Turnovers (empanadas) are filled with a range of luscious concoctions, from pineapple, guava, and apple to cheese and raspberry.

Read All About It

The largest cookbook store in the country, Jessica's Biscuit, started in the early 1980s with a classified ad in *Gourmet* magazine offering a single cookbook. It garnered all of seven orders, but founders David Strymish and Mark Landau pressed forward and were able to expand from David's living room into two small back rooms in his father's bookstore, New England Mobile Book Fair. Today the company has a staff of twenty-two and stocks more than 8,000 titles, including many that are out of print, at discounts of up to 75 percent. The company performs a great service to home cooks, finding and reprinting classic cookbooks that have lapsed from print, including one of our favorites, *Charles Virion's French Country Cookbook*. The easiest way to order is through the Web site, but a large portion of the stock is also available at New England Mobile Book Fair.

Jessica's Biscuit
(800) 878-4264
www.ecookbooks.com

New England Mobile Book Fair
82–84 Needham St.
Newton Highlands, MA 02461
(617) 964-7440
www.nebookfair.com

The caramel-filled turnover—nuked for ten seconds—is a hot taste of heaven. In addition to coffee and chocolate, you can get cool and creamy milkshakes with papaya, pineapple, or guanabana. Tito's style is more Argentine than Mexican, so there's also a thick flan and a scrumptious bread pudding.

Tuck's Candies, 15 Main St., Rockport, MA 01966; (800) 569-2767; www.tuckscandy.com. Walter F. Tuck began making candies in Rockport in 1929 and established such a high standard that he became a Massachusetts confectionery hero—one of the true pioneers. Bob and Dan Tuck (second and third generation, respectively) continue the tradition. The chocolate-covered buttercrunch was Tuck's calling card for many years, but Tuck's has kept up with changing tastes: Some of the most popular candies now are the chocolate-covered pretzels, caramel nut patties, and fudge.

Turtle Alley Chocolates, 91A Washington St., Gloucester, MA 01930; (978) 281-4000; www.turtlealley.com. Also Museum Place Mall, Suite 110, Salem, MA 01970; (978) 740-0660. The aroma of chocolate smacks you in the face as you walk in the door of the tiny Washington Street shop where the staff mixes fudge and hand-dips chocolates behind the counter. When owner Hallie Baker was growing up in Gloucester, she had a pet turtle—now she makes a whole menagerie of the sweet critters in milk, dark, and white chocolate with pecans, macadamias, almonds, and (her favorite) cashews. (She says the cashews look most like flippers.) The shop also produces truffles, brittles, and barks. Try the tulip—a Brazil

The Saintly Sandwich

THE BREAD MAKES THE SANDWICH, proclaims the sign in the front window of Virgilio's Italian Bakery & Groceria, established in 1939 by Joseph Virgilio Sr. Fittingly, the bread in question is the St. Joseph roll, a pillowy white bread with a slight crunch to the crust, originally made on the saint's feast day. Now the rolls are baked daily in the shop's original round shape or as the submarine roll that is filled with Italian cold cuts, provolone cheese, lettuce, tomato, pickles, oil, and oregano to create Virgilio's signature St. Joseph Roll Sandwich. "My father invented the sandwich for the fishermen who would hang around the shop," recalls Rosemary Virgilio. She and her brothers continue the tradition, which is a good thing—aficionados say the sandwich can't be duplicated.

Virgilio's Italian Bakery & Groceria
29 Main St.
Gloucester, MA 01930
(978) 283-5295

nut wrapped in caramel, sprinkled with chocolate shots, and dipped in milk or dark chocolate. All products are also available by mail order or on the Web site.

Ye Olde Pepper Candy Company, 122 Derby St., Salem, MA 01970; (978) 745-2744 or (866) 393-6533; www.yeoldepeppercandy. com. Also 137 Main St., North Andover, MA 01845; (978) 689-3636. In business since 1806, this is possibly the oldest candy company in the country. The house specialty is the Gibraltar, available in lemon or peppermint. The candy, which consists of sugar and oil, is hard when first made but mellows to the texture of an after-dinner mint and supposedly never spoils (a jar of Gibraltars on the counter dates from 1830). The company claims the Gibraltar is the first candy made commercially in the United States. Ye Olde Pepper also pioneered the Blackjack molasses stick candy, another American first. But they've kept up with the times, and you'll find a full assortment of hard candies and chocolates at this landmark store.

Farmers' Markets

Arlington Farmers' Market, Russell Common parking lot, Arlington center. Wednesday from 1:00 to 6:30 p.m., mid-June to late October.

Chelsea Farmers' Market, Chelsea Square, Chelsea. Saturday from 9:00 a.m. to 1:00 p.m., late July to October.

Framingham Farmers' Market I, St. Tarcisius Church parking lot, Waverly St., Framingham. Wednesday from 3:00 to 6:00 p.m. and Saturday from 9:00 a.m. to noon, mid-July to October.

Framingham Farmers' Market II, Village Green, Edgel Rd., Framingham. Thursday from 12:30 to 5:30 p.m., mid-June through October.

Haverhill Farmers' Market, GAR Park, Main St. (Route 125), Haverhill. Saturday from 8:00 a.m. to 1:00 p.m., mid-June through October.

Ipswich Farmers' Market, Ebsco parking lot, Estie's St., Ipswich. Saturday from 9:00 a.m. to 1:00 p.m., July through October.

Lawrence Farmers' Market, Appleton Way, Lawrence. Wednesday from 8:30 a.m. to 4:00 p.m., late June to late October.

Lowell Farmers' Market, City Hall Plaza, Arcand Dr., Lowell. Friday from 3:00 to 7:00 p.m., mid-July to mid-October.

Lynn Farmers' Market, Olympia Square, intersection of Washington and Exchange Streets, Lynn. Thursday from 11:00 a.m. to 3:00 p.m., July through October.

Marblehead Farmers' Market, Middle School, Vine St., Marblehead. Saturday from 9:00 a.m. to noon, mid-June to mid-October.

Maynard Farmers' Market, Clock Tower Place, Mill Pond parking lot, Maynard. Saturday from 9:00 a.m. to 1:00 p.m., late June to early October.

Melrose Farmers' Market, City Hall parking lot off Main St., Melrose. Thursday from 10:00 a.m. to 3:00 p.m., June to mid-October.

Natick Farmers' Market, Natick Common, downtown Natick. Saturday from 9:00 a.m. to 1:00 p.m., June to October.

Newton Farmers' Market, Cold Spring Park, 1200 Beacon St., Newton Highlands. Tuesday from 1:30 to 6:00 p.m., early July to late October.

Topsfield Farmers' Market, Topsfield Fair Grounds, Route 1, Topsfield. Saturday from 7:00 a.m. to noon, early July to late September.

Waltham Farmers' Market, Sovereign Bank parking lot, Main and Moody Streets, Waltham. Saturday from 9:30 a.m. to 2:30 p.m., mid-June to late October.

 *Farm Stands*

Northeastern Massachusetts farms are not as well organized as those in the rest of the state when it comes to promoting themselves as a group to consumers, but the BuyFresh Web site contains some very good information on farms, farm stands, and farmers' markets in the region. Visit www.buyfresh.org.

Autumn Hills Orchard, 495 Chicopee Row, Groton, MA 01450; (978) 448-8388; www.autumn hillsorchard.com. The vistas at Autumn Hills are some of the most jaw-dropping of any of the orchards in this region. Spanning more than seventy acres with more than 8,000 trees, the fruited ridges look out to panoramic views of mountains in both Massachusetts and New Hampshire. The orchard grows more than twenty apple varieties (including the heirloom Cox's Orange Pippin), as well as Italian prune plums, peaches, some pears, and fall-bearing raspberries. All fruits are available pre-picked or as pick-your-own. Call for hours, beginning in late July.

Belkin Family Lookout Farm, 89 Pleasant St. South, Natick, MA 01760; (508) 653-0653; www.lookoutfarm.com. The land of Lookout Farm has been tilled since 1651, making it one of the oldest working farms in North America. With more than 180 acres of grape arbors, orchards, berry patches, and vegetables, Lookout has a vast array of produce throughout the growing season, including you-pick strawberries, peaches, plums, nectarines, several varieties of apples, and fall pumpkins. Open late April through October.

Hutchins Farm, 754 Monument St., Concord, MA 01742; (978) 369-5041; www.hutchinsfarm.com. A pioneer of conscientious organic farming (since 1973), Hutchins not only has a wide array of produce for sale from June through October but also sells organic vegetable and herb plants in the spring. Many of the varieties are unavailable in garden centers or even from other farms, largely because they come from expensive seeds or from cuttings taken from the farm's own plants. Hutchins also sells organic growing supplies, including bagged compost and row covers. Check the Web site for a terrific chart indicating availability of various crops.

Kimball Fruit Farm, 184 Hollis St., Pepperell, MA 01463; (978) 433-9751; www.kimballfruitfarm.com. From the time the Cambridge farmers' market opens in May until the middle of July, we wait with barely restrained anticipation for the first tiny but explosively delicious peaches from Kimball. They mark the beginning of an eight- or nine-week season of peach after peach, as we glut ourselves on stone fruit the way some people devour corn and tomatoes. Of course, Kimball also has great corn, great tomatoes, bushy fresh herbs, and some of the best, most vigorous leaf lettuces we've ever seen. And when peach season is done, there are still the apples (including hard-to-get Russets), which we keep buying until they're gone. Kimball sells extensively at farmers' markets around eastern Massachusetts, but it's worth a drive to the farm itself, located west of Lowell on the New Hampshire border. The farm stand is open daily June through Thanksgiving and sporadically the rest of the year. Pick-your-own strawberries, raspberries, apples, and pumpkins.

Land's Sake, Inc., Newton and Wellesley Streets, Weston, MA 02193; (781) 893-1162; www.landssake.org. Once an outlier of the Arnold Arboretum in Boston, this preserve of suburban forest and

Verrill Farm Corn and Tomato Tart

This recipe is a perennial favorite at Verrill Farm's Corn & Tomato Festival. Jennifer Verrill Faddoul recommends using Sweet 100 cherry tomatoes, which are a small variety best left whole. Other cherry tomato varieties can be substituted, she says. We've found that larger tomatoes tend to make a watery tart. (If using standard tomatoes, peel, chop, and drain well before using.) For variations on the tart, add chopped bacon or chopped jalapeño peppers.

Tart Crust

This recipe makes three single pie shells. Use a 9- to 10-inch ceramic pie plate or a tart pan.

2½ cups flour	**1 teaspoon salt**
8 ounces (2 sticks) butter	**¼ cup water**

1. Preheat oven to 375°F.
2. Pulse flour, butter, and salt in food processor until mixture resembles corn kernels.
3. Add water and pulse until mixture forms a ball.
4. Divide dough into three parts, roll out, and place in three pie pans. Freeze two for future use.
5. Cover edges of pastry with aluminum foil to prevent burning. Bake in 375°F oven for 10 to 15 minutes. Remove from oven when the crust is very lightly browned and the surface of the dough is set.
6. Remove foil, let crust cool, and add filling.

Tart Filling

½ cup chopped onion
1 clove garlic, chopped
3 tablespoons olive oil
5 ears corn, uncooked, kernels off
Salt and pepper to taste
¼ cup shredded smoked cheddar

½ pint Sweet 100 cherry tomatoes
3 scallions (green and white parts), chopped
2 eggs
½ cup milk
½ cup cream

1. Preheat oven to 375°F.
2. Sauté onion and garlic in olive oil until translucent. Add corn and cook 5 to 10 minutes. Add salt and pepper to taste and remove pan from heat.
3. Put half of corn mixture in cooked pie shell. Layer shredded cheese on top. Add remaining corn mixture. Place cherry tomatoes and scallions on top.
4. Whisk eggs, milk, and cream with a pinch of salt and pour over tart.
5. Bake at 375°F for 30 minutes or until filling is set.

Serves 6

Verrill Farm
11 Wheeler Rd.
Concord, MA 01742
(978) 369-4494
www.verrillfarm.com

farmland is a public experiment in land management combined with environmental education. Pick up a tree map and go for a walk, and take advantage of the certified organic farm, which offers pick-your-own blueberries, raspberries, strawberries, vegetables, and herbs. Open daily mid-June through October.

Russell Orchards, 143 Argilla Rd., Ipswich, MA 01938; (978) 356-5366; www.russellorchardsma.com. Located on the road to Crane Reservation (and the famous bird-watching strand of Crane Beach), Russell Orchards is as much an agritourism destination as a farm, offering hayrides, barn tours, and group picnics. About 120 acres are under cultivation, and Russell has pick-your-own strawberries, vegetables, blueberries, and apples. The gift shop even sports its own bakery. The busy farm winery produces an extensive line of hard ciders and perries (7–8 percent alcohol) as well as a long list of fruit wines (11–12 percent alcohol) from the farm's own fruit (except for the blueberry varietals). We know no other commercial winery in New England that makes dandelion wine—an old-fashioned favorite that turns a summer yard blight into a winter delight. Open daily May through November.

Verrill Farm, 11 Wheeler Rd., Concord, MA 01742; (978) 369-4494; www.verrillfarm.com. Verrill Farm has more than three centuries of continuous history as productive farmland, dating back to a colonial-era grant, and, in conjunction with a state program to maintain sustainable agriculture, the Verrill family has placed the property under an Agricultural Preservation Restriction that will keep it as farmland in perpetuity. Fans of heirloom produce especially love Verrill for its range of strawberries and tomatoes, but the farm grows almost all the vegetable crops feasible in Zone 6. Several top Boston and Cambridge restaurants (including Hamersley's Bistro and Rialto) buy directly from Verrill. Pick-your-own strawberries, raspberries, and pumpkins. The on-site bakery and deli turns out delicious breads, muffins, fine pastries, soups, sandwiches, and ready-to-heat entrees. Open daily year-round.

Wilson Farms, 10 Pleasant St., Lexington, MA 02173; (781) 862-3900. The immense post-and-beam farm stand at Wilson Farms so dwarfs everything around it that you could make the mistake of thinking that this is a supermarket with a farm attached. Actually, Wilson Farms sells crops from its thirty-three-acre spread in Lexington as well as from additional acreage in New Hampshire. But to keep the market stocked all year, the store also carries a full range of domestic and imported produce, more than 200 cheeses, its own bakery goods as well as those from surrounding artisanal bakeries, and the farm's own eggs and poultry. Its flower section is one of the best in the state. Much of the Lexington acreage is devoted to strawberries, including some day-neutral varieties, which help ensure a long harvest, from mid-June until mid-August. Open Wednesday through Monday year-round.

Fisherman's Fleet, 689 Salem St., Malden, MA 02108; (781) 322-5200; www.freshfish.net. This retail fish market is just the tip of the iceberg for this fourth-generation family-owned company that packs and ships top seafood around the country. Walk in the door and you're hit with the fresh, clean smell of the sea and confronted with tanks of swimming lobsters segregated by size. The Graffeos started shipping fish to friends in Florida in 1996, and the direct-sale business has exploded since, with good-value clambakes and lobster bakes that include everything but the pot. The shop is often ice-cold—all the better to keep the fish fresh. We particularly like being able to point to a slab of tuna or a side of swordfish and explain just how thick we'd like the steaks cut.

Ipswich Shellfish Fish Market, 8 Hayward St., Ipswich, MA 01938; (978) 356-6941; www.ipswichfishmarket.com. Ipswich Shellfish is a giant wholesale distributor of fresh fish and shellfish, and this modern market adjacent to the warehouses and shipping terminal puts owner Chrissi Pappas's personal stamp on the operation. In addition to a full line of the freshest catch (and all the shellfish you can imagine), the shop also offers prepared seafood entrees such as lobster pie, chowders, and stuffed fish. The shelves, refrigerator cases, and freezers are filled with imported cheeses, smoked fish, oils, vinegars, mustards, breads,

Rice, Lobster, and Cucumber Salad

Chrissi Pappas, proprietor of Ipswich Shellfish, hails from Thessaloniki in Greece. This refreshing salad blends the flavors of her native cuisine with sweet North Shore lobster.

1 cup white basmati rice
¾ cup chopped fresh dill
¾ cup thinly sliced scallions
½ cup lemon juice
¼ cup olive oil
Salt and pepper to taste

1½ pounds lobster meat, chopped, tail meat reserved
1 head romaine or Bibb lettuce
1 large English cucumber, peeled and chopped in ½-inch dice

1. Heat 1½ cups lightly salted water in a saucepan with a tight-fitting lid. When water begins to simmer, stir in rice. Continue stirring until water comes back to a simmer. Place lid on pan and reduce heat. Cook rice for 16 minutes, then remove from heat. Let stand 5 minutes before removing lid. Remove rice to a bowl to cool before proceeding.
2. In a large bowl, whisk together dill, scallions, lemon juice, olive oil, and salt and pepper.
3. Stir in cooked rice until well coated with dressing.
4. Reserving tails, add lobster meat to rice and gently toss to coat.
5. Line a serving dish with lettuce leaves and mound rice on top. Garnish with reserved lobster tails and chopped cucumber.

Serves 4

Ipswich Shellfish Fish Market
8 Hayward St.
Ipswich, MA 01938
(978) 356-6941
www.ipswichfishmarket.com

pastas, sauces, and condiments. Frozen ravioli are filled with shrimp, lobster, or duck and Brie. You can also arrange to have lobster and Ipswich clams shipped anywhere in the country.

Roy Moore Lobster Company, 39 Bearskin Neck, Rockport, MA 01966; (978) 546-6696. You can buy live clams, crab, and lobsters here, but most people come to eat them on the premises, preferably out back on the deck, looking across to Motif No. 1. This may be the most authentic bit of old Bearskin Neck left in a district where tourism has otherwise overwhelmed the original reasons to visit. BYOB. Open late March through October.

Food Happenings

May: **Taste of Essex,** Essex Room, Woodman's, 121 Main St. (Route 133), Essex, MA 01929; (978) 768-7335. A gala food and wine reception features specialties from Essex restaurants as a benefit for local scholarships.

June: **New Fish Festival,** Gloucester House Restaurant, 63 Rogers St., Gloucester, MA 01930; (978) 283-1601. Chefs from restaurants all over Cape Ann participate in a cooking contest to highlight the appeal of underutilized species. Events like this introduced Americans to monkfish a few decades ago, and made it a new star of the fish menu.

Mid-June: **Strawberry Festival,** Russell Orchards, 143 Argilla Rd., Ipswich, MA 01938; (978) 356-5366; www.russellorchardsma .com. Admission to this annual celebration of the first sweet crop of summer is free. Homemade strawberry shortcake is the star of this event, along with other food samples and wine tastings, live folk music, and hayrides. Pick-your-own strawberries in season.

Mid-August: **Gloucester Waterfront Festival,** Western Ave. and Stacey Blvd., Gloucester, MA 01930; (978) 283-1601. A pancake breakfast on Saturday and a gala lobster bake Sunday afternoon anchor this celebration of Gloucester. Musicians play the whole time and artists and artisans display their wares.

Labor Day Weekend: **Mahrajan Lebanese Festival,** St. Anthony's Church parking lot, 145 Lawrence St., Lawrence, MA 01841; (978) 685-7233. Tables of such Lebanese delicacies as falafel, kebabs, kibbe, spinach pies, and hummus are the highlight of this cultural festival, which includes live Lebanese and American music and belly dancing performances.

September: **Fall Festival,** various locations, Marblehead, MA 01945; (781) 631-2868. Hayrides and a crafts fair supplement the main event: tastings of chili and chowders from local restaurants.

***Late September:* Essex Clamfest,** Memorial Park, Essex, MA 01929; (978) 283-1601. Essex has been famous for its clams for more than three centuries, and a chowder-tasting competition is at the heart of this annual celebration, which also includes arts and crafts, games, and live entertainment.

***Early to mid-October:* Topsfield Fair,** 207 Boston St. (Route 1 North), Topsfield, MA 01983; (978) 887-5000; www.topsfield fair.org. Established in 1818, the Topsfield Fair proclaims itself America's oldest continuously operating country fair. It's notable for several cooking contests, a beer-making competition, and its beekeeping and honey exhibit. The New England Giant Pumpkin Contest, held on opening day, is the World Series and Superbowl rolled into one for the horticultural subculture of giant pumpkin growers. Cash prizes range up to $3,500. Minimum entry size begins at 350 pounds, and truly mammoth vegetables are featured. The 2007 winner, for example, tipped the scales at 1,673 pounds.

Learn to Cook

Create-a-Cook, 53 Winchester St., Newton, MA 02461; (617) 795-2223; www.createacook.com. Create-a-Cook offers four-session cooking courses and Monday night advanced workshops for adults, but the real lure is the classes for children, with five seven-week terms each school year. The classes are broken into six age groups, for kids three to fifteen. The staff are all professional chefs, and they also offer a special program of three-hour adult cooking parties that include a chef, recipes, food, the professional kitchen, and all the cleanup.

Newton Community Education, 140 Brandeis Rd., Newton Center, MA 02459; (617) 559-6999; www.newtoncommunityed .org. Newton is a cook's town, and this education program offers a host of classes from basic wine appreciation to creamy desserts to detailed courses in such ethnic cuisines as Persian, Moroccan, Caribbean, East African, and Indian.

Landmark Eateries

Duckworth's Bistrot, 197 East Main St., Gloucester, MA 01930; (978) 282-4426; www.duckworthsbistrot .com; $$$. A young Ken Duckworth was the final chef at the famed Maison Robert in Boston, and when that temple of French haute cuisine closed in 2004, the people of Gloucester were the beneficiaries. His bistro serves casual but authentically French food, making great use of North Shore shellfish and the Gloucester catch, as well as produce from Merrimack Valley farms. We also love Duckworth's approach to moderation: Almost every dish (including a killer seafood stew any other restaurant would call bouillabaisse) is available in half or full portions, and the eclectic wine list includes many choices by the glass and by the half bottle. Open Tuesday through Saturday for dinner in winter, Tuesday through Sunday in summer.

Il Capriccio, 888 Main St., Waltham, MA 02453; (781) 894-2234; www.ilcapricciowaltham.com; $$$. From the nondescript exterior you'd never guess that Il Capriccio is an elegant northern Italian restaurant with intimate tables and a dynamite wine list. We like the true Italian style of the menu—pastas as half courses between appetizers and entrees, salads as a tangy palate cleanser

between entree and dessert. The kitchen is bold, roasting halibut with olives, capers, lemon, and tomato, for example, or stuffing pork loin with sumptuous chanterelle mushrooms. Open for dinner Monday through Saturday.

Ithaki, 25 Hammatt St., Ipswich, MA 01938; (978) 356-0099; www .ithakicuisine.com; $$$. The first hint at Ithaki's cuisine is provided by the exterior: four Corinthian columns supporting an angled pediment in imitation of the Parthenon. The Greek and Mediterranean cooking is far more up to date, and the stylish interior is purely contemporary. Ithaki is famous for its delectable version of moussaka: layers of potato and eggplant covered in béchamel and topped with shaved Romano cheese. Open for lunch Tuesday through Saturday, dinner Tuesday through Sunday.

Kelly's Roast Beef, 410 Revere Beach Blvd., Revere, MA 02151; (781) 284-9129; $. This year-round kiosk has been a Revere Beach fixture since the days when only sailors and tough guys sported tattoos. The ostensible specialty is the sliced roast beef sandwich, but the perfectly fried seafood is an even better choice. Order fish-and-chips or a fried shrimp basket, wander across the road to the beach to sit on the seawall, and munch away as the waves roll in and the jetliners swoop down to land at nearby Logan Airport. Open daily for lunch and dinner.

Lobster Pool, 329 Granite St. (Route 127), Rockport, MA 01966; (978) 546-7808; $. This unpretentious beachside seafood shack (delicious chowders, big portions of grilled fish, sweet steamed clams) also has one of the best locations on Cape Ann. Time your visit to sit out on the back deck and watch the sun set over Folly Cove. Open April through November (call for hours).

Longfellow's Wayside Inn, 72 Wayside Inn Rd., Sudbury, MA 01776; (978) 443-1776 or (800) 339-1776; www.wayside.org; $$. This country inn has been taking in and feeding travelers since 1716, though it finally became famous when Henry Wadsworth Longfellow used it as a setting for his 1863 book, *Tales from a Wayside Inn.* The setting couldn't be more colonial, although the cozy Tap Room with its wood-burning fireplace is actually a 1929 addition, built by Henry Ford back when he was thinking of making the place a base for his

Steak and Clam Road Feasts

Northeastern Massachusetts has some of the state's strangest restaurant architecture and signage. The strangest of all must be the **Hilltop Steak House** in Saugus, founded by Frank Giuffrida, a butcher from Lawrence, in 1961. The 68-foot-tall neon cactus sign is visible from miles away, and the herd of fiberglass steers out front leaves no question that this place is about meat, plain and simple. Hilltop is as legendary for its long waits (reservations for parties of eight or more only) as for the 18-ounce bone-in sirloin. The restaurant also has an on-premises butcher shop, should you still be hungry. It is open daily for lunch and dinner.

Somewhat more subtle, **Clam Box of Ipswich** was built in 1938 by Dick Greenleaf to resemble the open-flapped pasteboard box in which fried clams are served. Some aficionados of North Shore bivalves rank the Clam Box above Woodman's, citing superior breading (pastry flour followed by cornmeal) and the unique blend of meat and vegetable fats in which they're fried. Enjoy the dining room or the outdoor picnic tables. Open daily June through September; call for off-season hours. No credit cards.

Hilltop Steak House

855 Broadway (Route 1)
Saugus, MA 01906
(781) 233-7700
www.hilltopsteakhouse.com

Clam Box of Ipswich

246 High St. (Route 1A)
Ipswich, MA 01938
(978) 356-9707
www.ipswichma.com/clambox

American history village. Several dishes are Wayside Inn traditions, including the crumb-topped lobster pie with béchamel sauce. The pastry cook works wonders with flour and meal ground at the mill along a stream on the property, producing airy breads and corn muffins, delicate pie crust, and silky Indian pudding. The flour and meal are also available in the gift shop.

Lumière, 1293 Washington St., West Newton, MA 02465; (617) 244-9199; www.lumiereres taurant.com; $$$. Set in a former ice-cream parlor, Lumière glows with spare, contemporary style—both in the decor of the small room and chef-owner Michael Leviton's French dishes. The food is lusty (pork terrine with cornichons and coarse mustard) as well as silky and subtle (big disks of seared sea scallops against dark and earthy wild mushrooms and creamy potato mousse). Desserts feature the full flavors of bistro fare with a more polished execution. Don't miss the dried apricot tarte tatin dabbed with crème fraîche and surrounded by Muscat sauce. Open for dinner daily.

Red Rock Bistro, 141 Humphrey St., Swampscott, MA 01907; (781) 595-1414; www.redrockbistro.com; $$$. Almost every table at Red Rock has a water view, and in warm weather, there's the option of dining on the two outdoor patios with waves crashing below. In any season, try to time dinner for a great sunset view of the Boston skyline. The menu is primarily seafood (with steak, coq au vin, and pork ribs for non–fish eaters), with simple dishes such as grilled swordfish with mashed chickpeas and a salad of roasted red peppers with feta cheese. During the summer, simple fish shack fare (fried clams, lobster rolls) is also available at a take-out window on the sidewalk. Open for lunch Monday through Saturday, brunch Sunday, and dinner nightly.

Stonehedge Inn, 160 Pawtucket Blvd., Tyngsboro, MA 01879; (978) 649-4400; www.stonehedgeinn.com; $$$$. The heart of the Stonehedge Inn's country getaway is the gourmet experience of Left Bank restaurant and the world-class 100,000-plus-bottle Stonehedge cellars. Proprietor Levent Bozkurt has been buying case upon case of great wines for many years, laying them aside until they're ready to drink. This is one of the rare places in New England where you can taste verticals of famous Bordeaux and Burgundies. Stonehedge also does a monthly wine dinner, pairing the courses with the wines of one company. The winemaker or estate owner is usually on hand to discuss the wines. Left Bank serves a seasonal cuisine driven largely by what's available from nearby fishermen and farmers. For a lighter repast, book a table for afternoon tea with a full complement of dainty sandwiches, sweet scones, tea cookies, and other pastries. Open daily for tea, nightly for dinner. (Also daily for breakfast for inn guests.)

Woodman's of Essex, 121 Main St. (Route 133), Essex, MA 01929; (978) 768-6057; www .woodmans.com; $. "'Twas a brave man who first did eat an oyster," quipped author Jonathan Swift, but that pioneer couldn't hold a candle to Lawrence "Chubby" Woodman, who seems to have been the first to bread and fry a clam. He did so in 1914, and his once-tiny seafood shack has prospered and grown into the iconic Woodman's of Essex, where the family continues the tradition. The "in-the-rough" seafood restaurant is less rough than others, offering spacious and sunny dining rooms as well as picnic tables and a large parking lot (an important feature in parking-starved Essex, one of the great historic shipbuilding towns of the North Shore). Woodman's also ships live lobsters and clams. Open daily year-round for lunch and dinner.

Brewpubs & Microbreweries

Mercury Brewing Company, 2 Soffron Lane, Ipswich, MA 01938; (978) 356-3329; www.mercurybrewing.com. This small brewery, which recently relocated downtown, built its reputation on Ipswich Ale, a finely crafted English-style ale that serves as the flagship of a more extended line that includes an IPA, a stout, a porter, and a bitter.

Stonehedge's Maple Syrup Crème Brûlée

Executive chef David Bressler of Stonehedge Inn & Spa makes this New England version of a classic French dessert using pure Vermont maple syrup. Excellent Massachusetts syrup will also work.

2 cups heavy cream
½ fresh vanilla bean or 2
   teaspoons vanilla extract
1 egg, plus 4 egg yolks
7 tablespoons pure maple syrup

4 tablespoons raw sugar, for
   topping
6 4-ounce brûlée molds (about
   1 inch deep and oval
   shaped)

1. Preheat the oven to 325°F. Pour cream into a nonreactive saucepan over medium heat. Slice the vanilla bean, if using, in half lengthwise with a sharp paring knife. Separate seeds from skin by scraping the bean with the knife. Place seeds or vanilla extract in the cream. Scald the cream by heating it until bubbles start to form at the edge of the pan. Remove from the heat.

2. In a large mixing bowl, whisk together the whole egg, egg yolks, and maple syrup until well blended. Continue to whisk while slowly pouring the hot cream into the egg mixture and whisk until the mixture is smooth and homogenous in color. Strain the mixture through a fine-mesh sieve, to remove vanilla bean pieces and any overcooked eggs, into a large measuring cup with a spout.

3. Place the molds on a baking sheet with sides at least 1 inch high. Fill the molds half full with the custard and set the sheet in the oven (it's easier to transfer the sheet with the molds only half full). Finish filling the molds to the top. Using hot water from the tap, pour enough water into the baking sheet to reach halfway up the sides of the molds.

4. Bake for approximately 45 minutes. The custard should tremble slightly when gently shaken. If you detect any liquid under the skin, the custards are underbaked. Return them to the oven and check them every 5 minutes or so.

5. Remove the molds from the water bath and place on a cooling rack for 30 minutes. Refrigerate for at least 2 hours or up to 3 days before serving; the custard will finish setting in the refrigerator.

6. When ready to serve, preheat your oven broiler. If condensation has occurred during chilling, carefully blot custards with a paper towel. Place the molds on a clean baking sheet. Sprinkle 2 teaspoons of sugar over the top of the custards. Make sure to spread the sugar evenly. Place the sheet about 4 inches under the broiler and broil until the sugar is caramelized. Keep a close eye on the brûlées; they are finished when they are lightly browned. Serve immediately.

Serves 6

Left Bank at Stonehedge Inn
160 Pawtucket Blvd.
Tyngsboro, MA 01879
(978) 649-4400
www.stonehedgeinn.com

Mercury has branched out into a line of Stone Cat beers and ales that more closely resemble traditional North American beers. At the same time, it has introduced colorful soft drinks under the Mercury Soda label. Ipswich Ale is available at most serious taverns and all package stores in eastern Massachusetts. Stone Cat and Mercury Soda have more limited distribution, mostly on the North Shore and Cape Ann. Tours are available; call for information. The new facility also has a pub for tasting both beer lines along with some grub. Call for hours.

Salem Beer Works, 278 Derby St., Salem, MA 01970; (978) 745-2337; www.beerworks.net; $$. One of the state's pioneer brewpubs, Salem Beer Works sits on the waterfront like a pirate at the mouth of a harbor, beguiling passersby with the wafting aromas of freshly brewed ales and hot charcuterie. Big TV screens highlight sporting events, and soaring ceilings give the room a warehouselike feel, so it doesn't seem crowded, even when every seat is taken. Best food bets are the barbecue plates; best beers, the simple ales. Open daily.

Watch City Brewing Company, 256 Moody St., Waltham, MA 02453; (781) 647-4000; www.watchcitybrew.com; $$. A brewpub that matches its beers nicely with the food, Watch City has built its reputation on copper-colored, fruity American ale with a bit more hops bite than most, now being made as Mongrel Red IPA. We're fonder, however, of Moody Street Stout, with its overtones of coffee, chocolate, and nuts and its creamy richness. Compared to the sweetness of, say, Guinness, Moody Street is dry stout, which gives a greater clarity to its overtones. While Watch City has the usual bar-food suspects (buffalo wings, popcorn shrimp), it also serves grilled steak tips, skillet-roasted marinated salmon, and pan-seared tuna with orange-ginger sauce. Open daily.

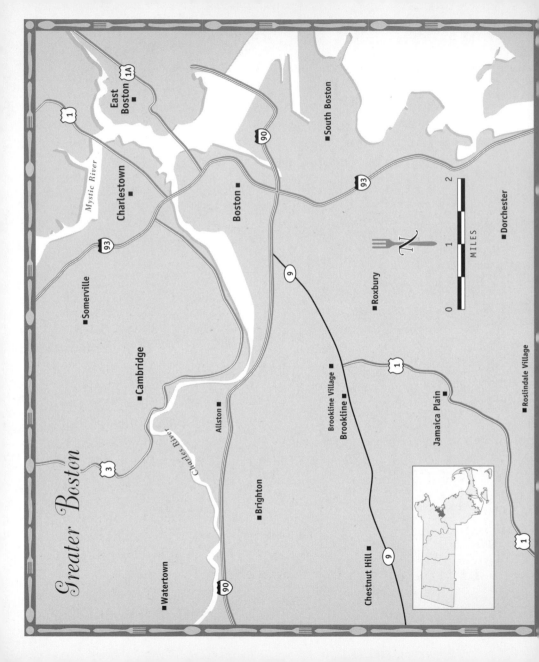

Greater Boston

From our home in mid-Cambridge, we can walk ten minutes or less and find ourselves in the midst of a Portuguese neighborhood in one direction, a Caribbean neighborhood in another. Our halal butcher and grocer is around the corner from our Portuguese wine merchant, who's across the street from a fine-dining restaurant that draws on the traditions of the American South. Our Korean grocer is a hundred yards from our Brazilian sausage store, which is next to an Irish pub across the street from a Mexican taqueria, a few blocks from the restaurant where we go for Indian roadhouse chow. The families of the kids who walk past our window on the way to the high school speak more than forty languages as their native tongues.

Home to new immigrants and old established families, Greater Boston has an exciting mix of cuisines and culture, where the venerable American myth of the melting pot yields to the modern paradigm of the multi-ethnic stew. Everyone brings a different spice to the table—and we all feast together.

Boston also has a distinct restaurant culture. The dining scene—who's cooking where, what's the hot new dish, who has the best bartender—is constant grist for local press, Internet enthusiast sites, and casual conversation. It is no fluke that most of the Massachusetts restaurants with national or international reputations are found in Greater Boston. The city has thousands of places to eat—and several hundred where you can dine. What you'll find here are a few historic restaurants, the home kitchens of some of Boston's leading chefs, and a handful of special places that reflect their neighborhoods and hint at the city's cultural diversity.

While Greater Boston doesn't raise much of its own food (apart from those of us with community gardens), it's an amazing place to shop—whether you're dickering over flats of fresh fruit with Haymarket vendors at the end of the day or wandering wide-eyed down the aisles of the Hong Kong Supermarket in Allston, struck dumb by the unending choices. Fresh produce flows into the farmers' markets, fresh fish into the fishmongers. With the finest foods coming to Boston from all over the state—indeed, from all corners of the earth—the taste of the city is truly world class.

Made or Grown Here

Dancing Deer Baking Company, 77 Shirley St., Boston, MA 02119; (888) 699-DEER (3337); www.dancingdeer.com. Noting the growing popularity of gourmet coffee, Dancing Deer was founded in

1994 to create high-quality sweets to go with that refined cup of joe. Using all-natural ingredients, the company bakes cookies (chocolate tangerine, sugarcane lime, molasses clove . . .) and cakes (chocolate espresso, maple pumpkin cranberry, blueberry pecan streusel . . .) that are so good that tea and milk drinkers snatch them up as well.

The products are sold in grocery and gourmet stores (and some enlightened coffee shops) throughout Massachusetts and around the country in Whole Foods and Wild Harvest grocery stores. They can also be ordered online. All orders are baked from scratch.

Iggy's Bread of the World, 130 Fawcett St., Cambridge, MA 02138; (617) 924-0949; www.iggysbread.com. Iggy's chewy-crusted European-style artisan breads pop up in the bread baskets of many of the best restaurants in eastern Massachusetts. Four of their basic breads—country sourdough, whole wheat sourdough, pillowy Francese, and seedless white rye—are priced low to make them accessible to everyone. Some of the others (including a divine olive loaf) bring rather higher prices, both at this bakery and at natural food stores and gourmet grocers.

Taza Chocolate, 561 Windsor St., B206, Somerville, MA 02143; (617) 623-0804; www.tazachocolate.com. Launched in 2006, Taza is the region's sole chocolate maker that takes the process from the bean to the bar. Founders Alex Whitmore and Larry Skolnick travel to cacao-growing regions (mostly the Dominican Republic and Costa

Cubano, the Sandwich with Attitude

"The thing about Cuban food," an older Cuban immigrant friend laments, "is that you have to be a Cubano of a certain age to recognize the real thing. After 1960 there were all kinds of things we didn't have—like meat."

Be that as it may, the Cubano sandwich—consisting of a long pressed bun filled with ham, roast pork, cheese, and pickle—has become a staple in Boston. Aficionados argue about what makes an authentic Cubano, and whenever the subject comes up, someone laments how no one makes a Cubano like Uncle Octavio in Miami.

Maybe not, but the Dominican owners of El Miami in Jamaica Plain make a Cubano so good that Cuban players from all the visiting baseball teams head to this casual sandwich shop for dinner. Perhaps less authentic, the Cubano at Chez Henri, an upscale French-Cuban restaurant in Cambridge, is the popular choice of hipsters who order them at the bar.

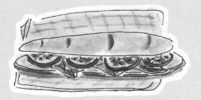

Chez Henri

1 Shepard St.
Cambridge, MA 02138
(617) 354-8980

El Miami

381 Centre St.
Jamaica Plain, MA 02130
(617) 522-4644

Rica) to buy the top of the crop directly from certified organic growers—a process known as Direct Trade, which is much more stringent than Fair Trade about quality and economic justice. "It was very hard at first to find organic cacao that was also excellent," Whitmore admits. "Some farmers took the attitude that they would get a premium price for organic and didn't really have to take care with the beans." Taza light-roasts 150-pound sacks of cacao right at the factory. The light roast, as with coffee, preserves "fruity, natural flavors," says Whitmore. Then Taza grinds the nibs and blends them with organic sugar, vanilla, almonds, or cinnamon, depending on the variety. "All the ingredients are from the tropics," Whitmore points out. In all cases, the chocolate qualifies as minimally processed. The company makes smooth dark chocolate bars of 60, 70, and 80 percent cacao, as well as grittier Mexican-style tablets. All the products are available at farmers' markets in Greater Boston, at about four hundred stores nationwide, and by ordering from the Web site. Check the Web site for occasional open houses and free factory tours.

Specialty Stores & Markets

A. Bova & Sons Modern Bakery, 134 Salem St., Boston, MA 02109; (617) 523-5601. Part of the charm of Bova is that, name aside, there's little "modern" about it. In fact, this is one of the most old-fashioned of the North End's bakeries, and the best-selling items are the various forms of puffy white Italian bread. "Of course, the cannoli go pretty good, too," say the staff. With a delicate crust that crumbles as you bite down and a fresh ricotta filling (with or without chocolate chips), they should. Bova even has a window on Salem Street for takeaway pizza slices. Breads are only part of the story, however. The bakery makes fine anise cookies, sugar cookies in a variety of shapes, cakes, pies, and several types of cheesecake. Best of all, Bova is open around the clock, in case you need to pick up some cannoli after the bars close.

Baltic European Deli, 632 Dorchester Ave., South Boston, MA 02127; (617) 268-2435. Half the people, young and old, wandering into this bright little shop in Andrew Square speak Polish as a first language, and you could have a hard time identifying some of the imported groceries unless you, too, have a smattering of the tongue. But food is universal, and the pictures give you a good idea—jars of preserved raspberries and cherries, instant borscht mix, Wawel chocolates from Kraków. Polish, German, and Russian baked goods at the front of the store vary from sweet coffee cakes to hearty rye breads that will stave off the chill of winter. The cold cuts, meats, and kielbasa come from smokehouses around New England, but they're done in classic Baltic style. The freezer case is full of such delights as pierogi, stuffed cabbage rolls, and imported Polish butter. For an idea of how these are all supposed to taste, have lunch or dinner across the street at **Café Polonia** (611 Dorchester Ave., South Boston, MA 02127; 617-269-0110), which is also owned by the Barcikowski family.

Berezka, 1215 Commonwealth Ave., Allston, MA 02134; (617) 787-2837. Berezka specializes in Russian and eastern European foods, from canned borscht to tins of caviar and frozen dumplings (potato, cheese, veal, and even cherry). Most of the signage is in the Cyrillic alphabet. Berezka offers frozen fillets of flounder, turbot, whiting, sea perch, sturgeon, sea bass, golden carp, catfish, and red carp, as well as delectable tiny Arctic shrimp. The dried and smoked fish include salmon, sevruga, Nova lox, rainbow trout, herring, and shad. A fresh pastry case is loaded with supersized desserts—chocolate balls, pastries laden with fruit—and another case holds several dozen cakes, tortes, and mousses. In the cold cuts case are more than twenty varieties of salami (PLEASE ASK FOR A TASTE, a hand-lettered sign implores).

BMS Paper Co., 3390 Washington St., Jamaica Plain, MA 02130; (617) 522-1122; bmspaper.com. Don't let the name fool you—BMS furnishes restaurants and caterers rather than supplying party goods (though you will find balloons and paper plates). Many of the no-frills aisles in this cavernous warehouse are lined with restaurant-size jars and cans of everything from peaches in syrup to baked beans to mayonnaise. But home cooks aspiring to a professional kitchen will also find whisks, tongs, and cake pans in every imaginable size, industrial aluminum pots and pans (up to fifty-gallon stockpots), and enough white crockery and salt and pepper shakers to stock the average roadside diner a hundred times over. If you need cardboard cake boxes or large disposable aluminum lasagna pans (foil or plastic lids), this is your place.

The Butcherie, 428 Harvard St., Brookline, MA 02146; (617) 731-9888. If it's kosher, it's probably available here. Every variety of New York and Israeli kosher canned and dry goods are stacked high on the shelves, but what really packs in the customers is the deli area with fresh kosher meats, sausages, fish, latkes, and blended grain and vegetable salads. Knishes are available in turkey, vegetarian, sweet potato, and potato. The Butcherie also sells several varieties and grades of caviar, sliced smoked salmon, and a tremendous variety of frozen kosher hors d'oeuvres. Closed Saturday.

Cardullo's Gourmet Shoppe, 6 Brattle St., Cambridge, MA 02138; (617) 491-8888; www.cardullos.com. Opened in 1950, when Vienna sausages still passed as gourmet food, this pioneering Harvard Square shop has introduced generations of Bostonians to the likes of such French specialties as foie gras, confit of duck, and escargot (all packed in tins), as well as cider vinegar from Normandy and sea salt gathered early in the morning by a "master salt maker." The Cardullos recognize, however, that great food need not be haute. Along with the chocolates, coffees, teas, oils, vinegars, maple syrups, and lobster pâtés, they also stock what they claim is the largest selection of hot sauces in New England. Check it all out in the shop or online. Printed catalog available on request.

The Cheese Shop, 20 Fleet St., Boston, MA 02109; (617) 570-0007. This cheesemonger opened in 2009 as the primary distributor of the ricotta and mozzarella made fresh daily in Quincy by Purity Cheese Company. The shop also carries dozens of imported Italian cheeses and meats, such as several types of Parmigiano-Reggiano—ranging in age up to four years—and four different prosciuttos, all from Parma. The real master of the cheese wheels is Tom Burns, who has an uncanny ability to shave a huge block of extremely firm cheese within a few hundredths of the weight you request. "The only thing better than the products," says Burns, "is the help." He's got that right.

Chocolee Chocolates, 83 Pembroke St., Boston, MA 02117; (617) 236-0606; www.chocoleechocolates.com. A self-taught pastry chef, Lee Napoli was almost singlehandedly responsible for revolutionizing dessert in several Boston fine restaurants. One of the founders of the Professional Pastry Guild of New England, her latest venture in the South End is devoted to the sweet art of chocolates. You can always count on five exquisite truffles (hazelnut, espresso, white chocolate pistachio, Moroccan mint, and spicy poblano pepper), along with her signature bark of toasted almonds and semisweet chocolate. What else is on hand depends on how the spirit has moved her, but it always represents the pinnacle of the chocolatier's art.

Christina's Spice and Specialty Foods, 1255 Cambridge St., Cambridge, MA 02139; (617) 492-7021. **Christina's Homemade Ice Cream** next door is known for its delicious flavors, which employ exotic spices (and a lot of mango pulp). This adjunct shop simply extends that palate for the pantry, with a tremendous range of bulk spices (four kinds of cinnamon, for example), cans of mango pulp, and a broad selection of dried chile peppers. If you're looking for inspiration to repaint your kitchen, look no farther than Christina's colorful bags of ground spices.

Dave's Fresh Pasta, 81 Holland St., Somerville, MA 02144; (617) 623-0867; www.davesfreshpasta.com. Dave Jick not only crafts fresh pasta sauces and raviolis (lobster, porcini mushroom, shrimp and roasted garlic, artichoke fontina, and crab and sweet red pepper, among others), he also teaches occasional classes on making fresh pasta and sauces. Moreover, the shop sells sandwiches made to order, gelato, a large line of mostly European cheeses, and a nice selection of small-vineyard wines.

Flour Bakery, 12 Farnsworth St., Boston, MA 02210; (617) 338-4333 and 1595 Washington St., Boston, MA 02118; (617) 267-4300; www .flourbakery.com. From morning muffins to lunchtime sandwiches

Jordan Marsh Blueberry Muffins

In the decades following World War II, the center of retail Boston was the inter-section of Winter, Summer, and Washington Streets, still known as Downtown Crossing. Two local department stores, Filene's and Jordan Marsh, anchored the district. Both companies have since been absorbed by other retail chains, and the Jordan Marsh name has vanished. But old-timers still bask in the memory of the store bakery's blueberry muffins. The recipe was supposedly secret, but this ver-sion, by legend passed hand to hand from an employee to friends, tastes like the real McCoy.

½ cup (1 stick) unsalted butter	**½ teaspoon salt**
1 cup sugar	**A scant ¾ cup milk**
2 eggs	**1 teaspoon vanilla**
2 cups flour	**2½ cups blueberries**
2 teaspoons baking powder	**2 teaspoons sugar, for topping**

1. Preheat oven to 375°F. Using a mixer on low speed, cream butter and sugar until fluffy. Add eggs, one at a time, and mix until blended.
2. Sift dry ingredients and add alternately with milk and vanilla.
3. Mash ½ cup berries and stir in by hand. Add the rest of the berries whole and stir in by hand.
4. Grease muffin tins well with butter and grease top surface of pans as well. (Muffins will spill over.) Pile batter high in each muffin tin. Sprinkle sugar over tops.
5. Bake for 30 minutes or until cake tester comes out clean. Cool in tins for at least 30 minutes.

Makes a dozen muffins

(like roasted lamb with tomato chutney and goat cheese) to bread for the dinner table and an "ooey-gooey caramel tart" for dessert, Flour simply revels in the joy of baked goods and the fun of sharing them. Founder Joanne Chang has been featured in most of the United States' major food magazines.

Formaggio Kitchen, 244 Huron Ave., Cambridge, MA 02138; (617) 354-4750. **South End Formaggio,** 268 Shawmut Ave., Boston, MA 02118; (617) 350-6996; www.formaggiokitchen.com. Ihsan Gurdal has devoted his life to the pursuit of exotic cheeses, and these two shops are widely considered among the great cheese-mongers of the world. (Even West Coast gourmet restaurants order cheese from Gurdal.) The Cambridge location has an aging cellar, allowing Gurdal to purchase cheeses when they are available but sell them only when they are ready. At any given time, the shops will have maybe fifty cheeses in the cases, ranging from unpretentious Canadian and New England cheddars to such rarities as a Bleu de Termingnon made by hand by an elderly lady in the French Alps. Both shops also have fresh breads, pasta, desserts, spices, and a small number of sausages and cold cuts of the same quality as the cheeses.

Greenhills Traditional Irish Bakery, 780 Adams St., Dorchester, MA 02124; (617) 825-8187; www.greenhillsbakery.com. The big sellers at this truly traditional bakery, operated by Dermot and Cindy Quinn since 1991, are Irish soda bread and brown bread (the oat-based Celtic version, not the steamed Boston style). The

bakery also makes a sturdy whole wheat bread
and a white yeast bread and offers sandwiches
at lunchtime. Desserts include Boston cream pie,
sherry trifle, Irish sponge cake with jam and cream,
and apple squares with sliced apples and a biscuitlike crust. For real
Irish traditionalists, the Quinns import Cadbury chocolates, Bird's
Trifle Mix, golden syrup, black treacle, Erin dried soups, Chivers
jams and marmalades, and the peculiar breakfast cereal known as
Flahavan's Progress Oatlets.

Hong Kong Supermarket, 1 Brighton Ave., Allston, MA 02134;
(617) 787-2288. This Boston branch of the New York area's Asian
food empire offers one-stop shopping for more than twenty varieties of fresh fish, hundreds of varieties of noodles, more than
twenty variants of soy sauce, and a meat case where you can buy
various organ meats and animal parts rarely seen in American markets. One stop at Hong Kong is like cruising all the little markets of
Chinatown—from wriggling eels to fresh longan and durian fruits.
Tea lovers and adherents of Chinese medicine will be heartened by
such drinks as Healthy Eyesight Tea, Healthy Kidney and Back Tea,
Healthy Spleen Tea, Internal Cooling & Cleansing Tea, Cholesterol
Normalizer Tea, and those all-time favorites, Dieter's Green Tea,
Beauty-Slim Tea, Thé Super-Slim, and Extra Strength Dieters' II True-
Slim Tea. The store's adjoining food court (the Food Connection)
abounds with quality Asian street food, from Vietnamese salads to
Indian curries.

Japonaise Bakery, 1020 Beacon St., Brookline, MA 02146; (617) 566-7730; also Porter Exchange Building, 1815 Massachusetts Ave., Cambridge, MA 02140; (617) 547-5531; www.japonaise bakery.com. This small shop blends Japanese flavors with European pastry traditions. The signature pastry is the Japonaise—layers of green-tea sponge cake filled with green-tea mousse. But the most popular cake is a similar concoction that owner Hiroko Sakan modestly calls strawberry shortcake—strawberries and sponge cake with vanilla Bavarian cream. One of the more exotic treats is the Azuki cream, a croissant with red beans incorporated into the dough filled with light whipped cream and dusted with powdered sugar—the ethereal Japanese version of a cream donut.

Kupel's Bakery, 421 Harvard St., Brookline, MA 02146; (617) 566-9528. Kupel's is best known in this predominantly Jewish neighborhood for its stupendous bagels—light rye, pumpernickel, sissle, marble rye, and corn. You can also pick up the bakery's own bagel spreads, ranging from flavored cream cheeses to salmon mousse. In addition to bagels, Kupel's also makes sourdough, sissle, pumpernickel, cinnamon raisin, spinach, and oat bran breads, as well as flaky, bite-size rugalach. Closed Saturday.

L.A. Burdick Chocolates, 52D Brattle St., Cambridge, MA 02138; (617) 491-4340; www.burdickchocolate.com. Many Cantabridgians blame L.A. Burdick for those few extra inches around their waists. This shop and cafe sells the company's extravagantly rich chocolates—made in Walpole, New Hampshire, with high-cocoa-butter dark chocolate imported from France, Switzerland, and Venezuela.

Fillings are made from scratch with local milk, cream, and honey; cooked fruits; fresh-brewed coffees and teas; and nuts and dried fruits from California and Turkey. The cafe's hot chocolate (in dark, milk, or white) is so popular that it is served iced in the summer. The goodies are also available on the Web site, but order early for the holidays. Since the company uses no preservatives, it is unable to produce enough chocolates to meet the demand.

Las Ventas, 700 Harrison Ave., Boston, MA 02118; (617) 266-0905; www.lasventasspain.com. If you have an uncontrollable hankering for *membrillo* (quince paste), *pimentón la vera* (toasted Spanish paprika), or thin, incredibly luxurious slices of *jamón ibérico* (prosciutto-like ham from acorn-fed black-footed pigs), you can satisfy it at this Spanish epicurean grocer. Manager Luis de Haro also carries close to a hundred cheeses from all over Spain, including many artisanal cheeses made only at a single farm.

Lionette's Market, 577 Tremont St., Boston, MA 02118; (617) 778-0360; www.goeboston.com. If you want to buy local, buy at Lionette's. The beef is grass-fed from Vermont and Massachusetts farms; the poultry free-range from New England, New York, and Quebec; and the cheeses from some of the best tiny dairies around New England (including Maine's fabulous Seal Cove chèvre). The market buys a pig every week and makes its own charcuterie, offering house-made sausages, bacon, ham, and pâtés. Sustainable agriculture never tasted so good.

Modern Homebrew Emporium, 2304 Massachusetts Ave., Cambridge, MA 02140; (617) 498-0400; www.wbhomebrew.com. Part of the same group of hobby shops as the West Boylston Homebrew Emporium (see Central Massachusetts), Modern has everything you'd ever need to make your own beer or wine, including imported varietal grape juice from all over the world and the rhizomes to get you started growing your own hops.

Mix Bakery, 36 Beach St., Boston, MA 02111; (617) 357-4050. The crowds line up at midday for the tasty Vietnamese sandwiches, but the real specialties at Mix are the Hong Kong–style pastries, including a sponge cake layered with sliced fruit and whipped cream. Baked "pies" that are more like turnovers range from savory (filled with shredded pork or black beans) to sweet (lotus seeds, for example). You can also get chocolate mousse cake, cream horns, lemon cream rolls, and elegantly decorated napoleons, as well as owner Grace Kwong's favorite, lotus-seed cake with a salty whole egg yolk on top.

Petsi Pies, 285 Beacon St., Somerville, MA 02143; (617) 661-7437; also 31 Putnam Ave., Cambridge, MA 02139; (617) 499-0801; www.petsipies.com. There's a lot to be said for doing one thing so well that the world beats a path to your door. Renee McLeod (whose childhood nickname, pronounced "peet-see," gives the bakery its name) is a pie genius. At either location, expect half a dozen sweet

Taste of the Streets

Boston's Little Italy and Chinatown are some of the tastiest (and most ethnic) parts of the city. One whiff of the garlic and olive oil wafting from restaurant doors in the North End tells you that the district is among the best-established Italian communities in the country. To find out where the locals buy their goods, sign up for the North End Market Tour, a half day of walking and tasting with Italian food expert Michele Topor. She's on a first-name basis with all the shop owners, who will almost certainly offer you samples of prosciutto and salami, mozzarella and ricotta, biscotti and amaretti, and bread hot from the oven. The tours last three and a half hours and happen on Wednesday, Friday, and Saturday. Reservations are essential. Mandarin-speaking superchef Jim Becker pulls back the curtains of the Asian community with his Boston Chinatown Market Tour, which concludes with a dim sum lunch, on Thursday and Saturday mornings.

L'Arte di Cucinare

6 Charter St.
Boston, MA 02113
(617) 523-6032
www.cucinare.com

pies in three sizes and a few savory pies (like chicken potpie) in two sizes. Of course, she also makes some mean cookies, brownies, and scones.

Rubin's, 500 Harvard St., Brookline, MA 02446; (617) 731-8787; www.rubinskosher.com. This landmark deli has been the kitchen away from home for generations of Eastern and Central European Jewish immigrants since it opened in 1927. The full-service deli sells superb brisket, pastrami, beet salad, chopped beef liver, chopped chicken liver, knockwurst, pickled herring, latkes in uncountable variations, potato kugel, sweet potato kugel, and good old plain tuna salad. You can order sandwiches or have some of the other dishes warmed to eat at the tables—or stock up and take them home for a feast. Closed Saturday.

Salem Street True Value Hardware Store, 89 Salem St., Boston, MA 02113; (617) 523-4759. North End residents come here for paint and nails, sure, but they also come for stovetop espresso and cappuccino makers, ravioli forms, pasta machines, hand-cranked cavatelli makers, pizelle bakers, meat grinders and sausage stuffers, cannoli forms, and canning and bottling supplies (for putting up your homemade tomato sauce and wine). This being Boston, they also come for the selection of beanpots.

Salumeria Italiana, 151 Richmond St., Boston, MA 02109; (617) 523-8743; www.salumeriaitaliana.com. When you step in the door, there's no question about the cuisine, but you might wonder if you've stepped through warp space and wound up in Italy. Italian opera plays over the sound system, a stack of dried cod meets you just inside the door, and at the holiday season, huge stacks of panettone (a sweet bread studded with dried fruit) practically obscure the rest of the interior. Once you tear yourself away from the shelves laden with green and black olive paste, various tapenades, artisanal olive oils, and half a dozen types of balsamic vinegar, head to the refrigerated cases in the back for dozens of dried sausages, whole Parma hams, prosciutto shanks, and—during the fall and early winter—fresh white truffles. "They're $2,000 a pound," apologizes Tony, "but they're just as expensive in Italy. Would you like a sniff?" he asks, holding the jar. Given an affirmative, he jokes, "That's $20," and offers the open jar.

Savenor's, 160 Charles St., Boston, MA 02114; (617) 723-6328; also 92 Kirkland St., Cambridge, MA 02139; (617) 576-6328; www.savenors market.com. Julia Child catapulted this butcher shop into the limelight as the place to go for prime rib, rack of lamb, venison, buffalo, wild boar, goose, pheasant, or poussin. Those less at home in the kitchen than the French Chef might opt for the pork loin already stuffed with prosciutto, provolone, and spices, or the leg of lamb with goat cheese, herbes de Provence, garlic, and rosemary. Or pick up some duck foie gras, salmon pâté, Stilton cheese, and a crusty loaf of bread for a picnic on the banks of the Charles River.

Serenade Chocolatier, 5 Harvard Square, Brookline Village, MA 02445; (617) 739-0795; also 2 South Station, Boston, MA 02110; (617) 261-9941; www.serenade chocolatier.com. This small shop carries on the Viennese chocolate-making tradition, so it is no surprise that its signature sweet is the Viennese truffle, alternating layers of dark and milk chocolate blended with hazelnut butter. Serenade also creates more conventional truffles flavored with raspberry, champagne, Irish cream, and Kahlúa, as well as dipped fruits, nut clusters, caramel patties, buttercrunch, and a variety of creams. For an elegant Old World treat, nothing is better than Serenade's marzipan truffle or chocolate-covered marzipan.

Sevan's Bakery, 599 Mount Auburn St., Watertown, MA 02472; (617) 924-9843; www.sevanboston.com. "We start at 5:00 in the morning and make everything in the kitchen in the back," says the counter man as he points at display cases full of Armenian specialties. Look for stuffed grape leaves, peppers, or cabbage leaves; eggplant stuffed with meat or with onion, garlic, and tomato; turnovers filled with cheese and peppers, spinach, or spinach and cheese; or *bogacha,* a turnover-like savory made with a rich pastry dough and filled with cheese, spinach and cheese, or chicken. Baklava is made with walnuts or pistachios, or with a rich custard instead of nuts. You can complete your feast with fresh-baked breads, including *lahmejun* (sort of a thin-crust, cheeseless Armenian pizza), goat and sheep cheeses from the Carpathians and the Near East, and a variety of olives from the olive bar that gives the market a tangy aroma.

Shalimar India Food & Spices, 571 Massachusetts Ave., Cambridge, MA 02139; (617) 868-8311. While it seems that there is an Indian restaurant on every block in Cambridge's Central Square, we'd wager that all the chefs count on this well-stocked shop when they find themselves short on cardamom or star anise. If you want to create Indian food at home, check the freezer cases for frozen samosas (with lamb, cheese, or vegetable fillings), as well as naan, roti, paratha, and other Indian breads. Then look for the packaged gourmet spice blends with recipes on the back. We're particularly fond of the chicken vindaloo, a spicy, garlicky stew seasoned with the Vindaloo Masala blend. Round out your meal with garlic, mint, coconut, tamarind, or coriander chutney. Easier yet, pick up some lamb vindaloo to take home at the small fast-food counter at the rear of the market.

Sofra Bakery and Cafe, 1 Belmont St., Cambridge, MA 02138; (617) 661-3161; www.sofrabakery.com. Flavors of the eastern Mediterranean waft out the door of this tiny bakery-cafe practically on the Watertown–Cambridge line. *Sofra* is an old Arabic word denoting both a picnic and a kilim rug—a synonym for hospitality. Diners fill up the few low tables and munch on flatbread sandwiches and updated *mezze* dishes (lentils with caramelized onion, Moroccan carrot salad, smoky eggplant with pine nuts). You can also choose from a limited line of intense sweets, such as brown-butter bread pudding (weekends only) or chocolate-hazelnut baklava. Breakfast treats include Persian spiced doughnuts or eggs poached in tomato with curry and pita crumbs. Open Monday through Friday from 7:00 a.m. to 7:00 p.m., Saturday from 8:00 a.m. to 6:00 p.m., and Sunday from 8:00 a.m. to 3:00 p.m.

Syrian Grocery Importing Company, 270 Shawmut Ave., Boston, MA 02118; (617) 426-1458. From the end of the nineteenth century until World War II, the South End boasted a large population of immigrants from the Middle East (including Lebanese poet/philosopher Kahlil Gibran, who grew up here). The immigrants' families have largely dispersed over the last half century, but Syrian Grocery remains. Many supplies that aren't available elsewhere in the city can be found here, from the ground sumac that Near Eastern grandmothers must have to zaatar (latest spice darling of gourmet chefs) to the graduated sieves needed to roll your own couscous from semolina flour. (If you don't know how, they'll also sell you one of Paula Wolfert's books that explains the process.) Old-fashioned wooden bins and screw-top jars of exotic spices and herbs fill the shelves.

Tatte Pâtisserie and Café, 1003 Beacon St., Brookline, MA 02446; (617) 232-2200; www.tattecookies.com. Baker Tzurit Or and three assistants can barely keep up with the demand for Or's specialty "cookies," such as XXL fig biscotti ("so they won't end so fast") and her signature nut boxes. The boxes are made of buttery pastry and filled with a mix of caramel and pistachios, almonds, hazelnuts, or walnuts—or an assortment. Her chocolate halvah bomb is just that—chocolate layers enveloping a halvah center. Although Or sells a lot of her goodies wholesale to restaurants and specialty stores, the cafe is also open daily for retail customers.

Tealuxe, Zero Brattle St., Cambridge, MA 02138; (617) 441-0077; also 108 Newbury St., Boston, MA 02116; (617) 927-0400; www.tealuxe.com. Dying for a cuppa? In this java-jive world, tea lovers often get little respect, but not so at Tealuxe, a tea bar that stocks more than a hundred varieties of premium tea from around the world. You can purchase by the gram (figure two grams per cup) for brewing at home or order a pot for sipping in the shop (perhaps along with a crumpet, a scone, or a piece of shortbread). Tealuxe also sells stylish teapots and rakish cup and saucer sets, as well as countless tea accessories. The bulk teas come with instructions on brewing temperature (some teas, for example, are best brewed at 180°F rather than with boiling water), brewing time, and amount to use. Top sellers include Irish breakfast, masala chai, blood orange sencha, organic gunpowder, peachy white, dragon pearl jasmine, China oolong, vanilla, blue flower Earl Grey, and red groats (an herbal infusion high in vitamin C).

Tropical Foods, 2101 Washington St., Roxbury, MA 02119; (617) 442-7439. As the name suggests, this supermarket at the corner of Melnea Cass Blvd., just a block out of Dudley Square, carries the ingredients for Jamaican, Barbadian, and Haitian home cooking. But it caters equally to family tastes formed in the steamy antipodes of the American South. The meat case holds every edible part of the pig: chitterlings, ears, trotters, and snout, as well as the usual chops, roasts, fatback, and bacon. Caribbean foods, including Jamaican soft drinks, Parrot-brand coconut juice, and the Goya line of Hispanic groceries, abound. The market is divided into two large rooms, with meats and groceries in the first section and fresh vegetables, bulk beans (more than a dozen varieties), and rice in the second. Tropical tubers alone are staggering in their diversity, including white and yellow true yams, sweet potatoes, yucca, yautia, African yams, malanga coco, fresh batata, and several kinds of potatoes.

Farmers' Markets

Although **Haymarket** is considerably larger than the typical farmers' market, it's a throwback to the era of outdoor central markets. Vendors set up their tables along Blackstone Street in Boston, in front of the halal markets on the back side of Faneuil Hall Marketplace on Friday afternoons and all day on Saturday. They offer some amazing bargains that get more amazing as the end of the day approaches—especially if you're willing to take an entire case of broccoli, a flat of strawberries, or a basket of peaches. Because most of the food at Haymarket is highly perishable produce, the vendors want to move it at discount prices.

ABCD Mission Hill Farmers' Market, Brigham Cir., intersection of Huntington Ave. and Tremont St., Roxbury. Thursday from noon to 6:00 p.m., July to October.

Cambridge/Central Square Farmers' Market, parking lot No. 5, Bishop Allen Dr., Central Square, Cambridge. Monday from 11:30 a.m. to 6:00 p.m., late May to mid-November.

Cambridge/Charles Square Farmers' Market, Charles Hotel Courtyard, Harvard Square, Cambridge. Friday from noon to 6:00 p.m. and Sunday from 10:00 a.m. to 3:00 p.m., June to late November.

Cambridge/Harvard University Farmers' Market, corner of Oxford and Kirkland Streets, Cambridge. Tuesday from 12:30 to 6:00 p.m., mid-June to October.

Cambridge/Kendall Square Farmers' Market, 500 Kendall St., Cambridge. Thursday from 11:00 a.m. to 2:30 p.m., June to early November.

Cambridgeport Farmers' Market, Morse School parking lot, Magazine St. and Memorial Dr., Cambridge. Saturday from 10:00 a.m. to 2:00 p.m., June to late October.

Charlestown Farmers' Market, Thompson Square on Main and Austin Streets, Charlestown. Wednesday from 2:00 to 7:00 p.m., mid-July to late October.

City Hall Plaza Farmers' Market, Boston City Hall Plaza, Government Center, Boston. Monday and Wednesday from 11:00 a.m. to 6:00 p.m., late May to late November.

Copley Square Farmers' Market, Copley Square along St. James Ave., Boston. Tuesday and Friday from 11:00 a.m. to 6:00 p.m., late May to late November.

Dudley Farmers' Market, Town Common, Dudley St. and Blue Hill Ave., Roxbury. Tuesday and Thursday from 3:00 to 7:00 p.m., June to October.

Fields Corner Farmers' Market, Park Street shopping center parking lot, Park St., Dorchester. Saturday from 9:00 a.m. to noon, mid-July to October.

Franklin Park Farmers' Market, Franklin Park Rd. at main entrance to zoo, Dorchester. Sunday from 1:00 to 4:00 p.m., mid-August to late October.

Jamaica Plain Farmers' Market, Bank of America parking lot, Centre St., Jamaica Plain. Tuesday from noon to 5:00 p.m. and Saturday from noon to 3:00 p.m., July to October.

Roslindale Farmers' Market, Adams Park at Washington St. and Cummins Highway, Roslindale Village. Saturday from 9:00 a.m. to 1:00 p.m., late June to October.

Somerville/Davis Square Farmers' Market, Day and Herbert Streets parking lot, Davis Square, Somerville. Wednesday from noon to 6:00 p.m., late May to late November.

Somerville/Union Square Farmers' Market, Union Square Plaza, Somerville. Saturday from 9:00 a.m. to 1:00 p.m., June to late October.

South Boston Farmers' Market, parking lot on West Broadway by Mt. Washington Bank, South Boston. Monday from 10:00 a.m. to 6:00 p.m., mid-July to October.

South End Farmers' Market, South End Open Market, 540 Harrison Ave., Boston. Sunday from 10:00 a.m. to 5:00 p.m., May to October.

Farm Stands

A. Russo & Sons, 560 Pleasant St., Watertown, MA 02472; (617) 923-1500; www.russos.com. A pioneer in specialty produce, Russo is principally a wholesaler of fruits and vegetables to some of the Boston area's leading restaurants, including East Coast Grill, Rialto, and L'Espalier. But this large farm stand (or small market, depending on how you look at it) on the Waltham line in Watertown is chock-full of delights for the home cook, too. Russo carries more wild and exotic mushrooms (both fresh and dried) than any other supplier to the public in the region. If something is in season somewhere, it's available at Russo, making the store an essential stop if, say, you develop a sudden craving for blackberries in January. Boston area cooks also appreciate the broad selection, generous packaging, and low prices on fresh herbs.

Allandale Farm, 259 Allandale Rd., Brookline, MA 02467; (617) 524-1531; www.allandalefarm.com. Open April into November, Boston's last working farm devotes its primary efforts to CSA (community-supported agriculture), a program where consumers buy shares in the season and pick up harvests from June into October. The farm stand carries the surplus, as well as some products from other local farms and suppliers (like a Hingham coffee roaster).

Fishmongers

Court House Fish Market, 484 Cambridge St., Cambridge, MA 02141; (617) 876-6716. The residents of Portuguese East Cambridge love their fish, and Court House caters to them by including mackerel and large sardines among the choices on the big beds of ice. Of course, you can also find everything else that's come into Fish Pier in Boston, along with fresh clams and oysters trucked in from Cape Cod and the North Shore. Directly adjacent to the fish market,

Court House Seafood Restaurant (617-491-1213) is a casual lunch place with fried, steamed, and broiled fish and a few stir-fries. Pick a fillet at the fish market and they'll cook it for you at the restaurant while you wait.

J. Hook, 15 Northern Ave., Boston, MA 02210; (617) 423-5501; www.jameshooklobster.com. Bostonians were aghast when the iconic barn-red wooden warehouse on Fort Point Channel burned to the ground in May 2008—but thanks to fellow seaport fishmongers, J. Hook was open for business days later and has rebuilt on its prime site between the new and old bridges over Fort Point Channel. Principally known as a lobster broker and wholesaler, Hook also deals in crabs, clams, oysters, scallops, and varying types of finfish (depending on the recent catch). You can even pick up a hot bowl of chowder or a fish sandwich to tide you over until you get home to boil those lobsters.

Morse Fish Company, 1401 Washington St., Boston, MA 02118; (617) 262-9375. Located across Washington Street from Holy Cross Cathedral since the days when Roman Catholics routinely ate fish on Fridays, Morse continues to thrive on customers who eat fish because they like it, not because they have to. The harbor is deceptively close, and Morse carries the full line of the local fresh catch. The Formica and fluorescent interior isn't exactly high style, but you can sit at one of the tables to enjoy a plate of fried fish-and-chips from the short-order kitchen.

Wulf's Fish Market, 407 Harvard St., Brookline, MA 02146; (617) 277-2506. Wulf's brings the same kind of care and skill to cutting and selling fish that a master baker brings to bread or an artisanal winemaker brings to wine. The fresh fish here are nonpareil, and the white-aproned men who work here cut them with the precision of surgeons. Only the salt smell of the sea permeates the shop, and the clear-eyed denizens of the briny deep are spread on big beds of ice.

Food Happenings

January: **Super Hunger Brunch,** sponsored by Greater Boston Food Bank; (617) 427-5200. Around four dozen top restaurants offer special brunches one weekend to benefit the hunger alleviation programs of the Greater Boston Food Bank.

January/February: **Boston Wine Expo,** Seaport World Trade Center, 1 Seaport Lane, South Boston; (877) 946-3976; www.wine-expos.com. Ever dream of being a wine buyer? Seminars, cooking demonstrations, and, of course, tastings headline the largest consumer event of its kind in New England.

March: **Winter Restaurant Week,** Boston; www .bostonrestaurantweek.com. More than 100 high-class restaurants from across the city and the region offer special fixed-price menus at lunch and dinner.

June: **Scooper Bowl,** City Hall Plaza, Boston; (617) 632-5008. One of the largest ice-cream festivals in the country kicks off the summer season in style— and benefits the Jimmy Fund at the same time.

Early July: **Boston Harborfest,** various locations; (617) 227-1528. This festival celebrating the maritime history o f Boston wouldn't be complete without a "chowderfest" competition among Boston restaurants and caterers.

Late July: **Festival Betances,** sponsored by Villa Victoria, Plaza Betances, 100 West Dedham St., Boston; (617) 927-1707. Annual Puerto Rican festival emphasizes food, as well as music, dancing, and sports, as residents of the Villa Victoria housing complex re-create an authentic village celebration. It honors Emeterio Betances, an abolitionist and champion of Puerto Rican independence.

July and August: **Religious festivals,** North End, Boston; (617) 635-4455. Big signs proclaim "Mangia!" as Italian-Americans gather to honor the patron saints of their home country and feast on sausages, cannoli, pizza, and Italian ices.

August: **Caribbean-American Festival,** White Stadium, Franklin Park, Boston; (617) 635-4455. The Saturday "street feast" at Peabody Circle (the junction of Franklin and Blue Hill Avenues) is the heart and soul of this celebration of Caribbean cultures. Expect curried goat, conch fritters, fried plantains, jerk chicken, pigeon peas and rice, and Bahamian *coco*—a dish of codfish and coconut milk.

August: **Summer Restaurant Week,** Boston; www.boston restaurantweek.com. More than 100 high-class restaurants from across the city and the region offer special fixed-price menus at lunch and dinner.

Late September: **What the Fluff? Festival,** Union Square, Somerville; (617) 625-6600, extension 2985; www.somervillearts council.org. A cooking contest and colorful events celebrate the invention of Marshmallow Fluff in Somerville.

CHOCOLATE SEASON

From September to June, when the climate cools enough to work with chocolate, the pastry chefs of the Langham Hotel roll out the **Deluxe Chocolate Bar** on Saturdays from 11:00 a.m. to 3:00 p.m. The all-chocolate buffet is a true feast of cakes, candies, tarts, tortes, cookies, and other pastries. **Langham Hotel,** 250 Franklin St., Boston, MA 02110; (617) 451-1900; www.langhamhotels.com.

October: **Boston Vegetarian Food Festival,** held at Reggie Lewis State Track Athletic Center, 1350 Tremont St., Roxbury, sponsored by the Boston Vegetarian Society; (617) 262-4300. Organized to promote "vegetarian and earth-friendly eating," this popular festival features about eighty vendors offering samples of everything from vegan chocolate peanut butter brownies to soy cheesecake and hemp-sprouted bread to seaweed caviar.

October/November: **Church bazaars.** Bostonians of Armenian, Lebanese, and Greek descent know that church bazaars are the best place to find the foods that their grandmothers used to make. You're also likely to rub elbows with dedicated foodies at some of the most popular fairs, including St. James Armenian Apostolic Church (465 Mount Auburn St., Watertown, MA 02472; 617-923-8860); St. George Orthodox Church (Emmonsdale Rd., West Roxbury, MA 02132; 617-323-9861), Our Lady of the Cedars of Lebanon (61 Rockwood St., Jamaica Plain, MA 02130; 617-522-0225), and St. Stephen's Armenian Apostolic Church (bazaar held at Armenian Cultural and Educational Center, Nichols Ave., Watertown, MA 02472; 617-924-7562).

December: **Cambridge School of Culinary Arts Holiday Bake Sale,** 2020 Massachusetts Ave., Cambridge, MA 02140; (617) 354-2020; www.cambridgeculinary.com. Bake sale of creations by current faculty and students (including gingerbread birdhouses) and items donated by CSCA alumni and area businesses. All proceeds benefit Share Our Strength, a not-for-profit organization dedicated to ending childhood hunger in America.

Individual Molten Chocolate Cakes

Pastry chef extraordinaire Delphin Gomes is director of the Professional Pastry Program at the Cambridge School of Culinary Arts. He conquers the central problem of molten chocolate cake—burnt edges and uncooked centers—by making individual servings in 3¼-inch rings set on parchment paper. This recipe makes rich little chocolates that explode with flavor. Gomes says that you can also add hints of other flavorings. You could try adding 1 teaspoon of ground ginger, cinnamon, grated lemon peel, grated orange peel, or anise extract when you add the flour to the sugar blend. Like most pastry chefs, Gomes measures ingredients by weight, not volume.

13 ounces semisweet chocolate
14 ounces unsalted butter
   (3¾ sticks)
8 eggs, plus 8 egg yolks

21 ounces sugar
7 ounces all-purpose flour
Flavoring (optional)

1. Preheat oven to 375°F.

Learn to Cook

Boston Center for Adult Education, 122 Arlington St., Boston, MA 02116; (617) 267-4430; www.bcae.org. Serious home cooks can opt for brush-up classes focused on specific types of dishes such as risottos, Chinese appetizers, or party desserts. Those with even

2. Melt chocolate and butter in a double boiler. Do not let them exceed 120°F.
3. In a separate bowl, blend together eggs, yolks, and sugar. Do not overmix.
4. Fold flour and, if you wish, your flavoring of choice into sugar mixture. Then add the chocolate-butter mixture; mix well.
5. Grease about two dozen 3- to 4-inch-diameter molds or rings with butter and dust with flour, shaking off excess. Place rings on a baking sheet lined with parchment paper. Fill rings three-quarters full with batter.
6. Bake for approximately 12 minutes, until top just begins to crack. Serve immediately.

Makes 6–8 cakes

Cambridge School of Culinary Arts
2020 Massachusetts Ave.
Cambridge, MA 02140
(617) 354-2020
www.cambridgeculinary.com

grander aspirations can sign up for extended courses to explore, say, Thai, Indian, or Italian cuisine in more depth.

Boston University Food, Wine, and Art Programs, 808 Commonwealth Ave., Boston, MA 02215; (617) 353-9852; www.bu .edu/foodandwine. The university offers a graduate degree in gastronomy as well as a certificate program in culinary education, but the main attraction for the general public is the series of nearly one hundred food and wine seminars. They could range from a tasting of ports or a sustainable harvest dinner to salting, smoking, and curing techniques for classical charcuterie.

Cambridge Center for Adult Education, 42 Brattle St., Cambridge, MA 02138; (617) 547-6789; www.ccae.org. Acknowledging the significant social aspect of cooking classes, CCAE bills its Friday-night cooking series as a place to "meet new people"—over a plate of paella, roast duck, coq au vin, or Korean *lajogi*. Course offerings focus on cuisines of the world as well as more practical matters, such as cooking basics, cooking with natural foods, or creating sandwiches and salads. Once you've mastered the food, tasting sessions of wines, beers, ports, cognacs, and even "bargain bubblies" will help you figure out what to pour.

Cambridge School of Culinary Arts, 2020 Massachusetts Ave., Cambridge, MA 02140; (617) 354-2020; www.cambridgeculinary .com. This professional school offers sixteen-week culinary arts

certificates for professional cooks as well as a thirty-seven-week curriculum for aspiring chefs. It also runs dozens of classes for the home cook and for restaurant staffers looking to expand their repertoire or bone up on special skills. Some of the most popular classes are one-day sessions dealing with regional cuisines, as well as courses on breadmaking, pastry, and knife skills. Recreational classes taught by master pastry chef Delphin Gomes fill up quickly.

Celebrity Chefs Culinary Program, Fairmont Copley Plaza Hotel, 138 St. James Ave., Boston, MA 02116; (617) 267-5300; www.fairmont.com. Saturday-afternoon programs from mid-January through mid-February let you glean some of the secrets of top chefs without getting your hands dirty. Local, regional, and national chefs prepare their specialties, which participants sample along with wines matched to the foods. Even if you attend only one class, you'll be presented with a bound copy of all the recipes and techniques for the entire series. If you'd like to make a weekend of it, the hotel offers special lodging packages.

Dave's Fresh Pasta, 81 Holland St., Somerville, MA 02144; (617) 623-0867; www.davesfreshpasta.com. The pasta shop offers ongoing classes in making different kinds of pasta and pasta sauces. Students taste as they cook, and they can sample the shop's wines.

Les Zygomates, 129 South St., Boston, MA 02111; (617) 542-5108; www.winebar.com. This stylish wine bar–bistro is known for its great wine list and the opportunity to design your own tasting flights. For those who want to go beyond having a couple of glasses

Chefs' Secrets

Home cooks are fortunate that chefs at some of Boston's best and most interesting restaurants have their own cookbooks. After you've dined in their establishments and swooned over some of the dishes, you can pick up copies of their books and try to replicate those flavors at home.

East Coast Grill, 1271 Cambridge St., Cambridge, MA 02139; (617) 491-6568; www.eastcoastgrill.net; $$. Chris Schlesinger, the master of grilling meat and fish, cooks with drama in the open kitchen of this unpretentious Inman Square landmark known for barbecue, soulful side dishes, and extreme spice. Limited reservations, so arrive early to get in line. Schlesinger's many books include *Thrill of the Grill, Big Flavors of the Hot Zone,* and *Let the Flames Begin.*

Elephant Walk, 2067 Massachusetts Ave., Cambridge, MA 02140; (617) 492-6900; also 900 Beacon St., Boston, MA 02215; (617) 247-1500; www.elephantwalk.com; $$. Cambodian cooking, as practiced by chef-owner Longteine de Monteiro, is Asia's original fusion food, blending traditions from Malaysia, India, and China with a strong influence of French technique for stupendous results. The bamboo forest decor of the restaurants is transporting, and de Monteiro's *The Elephant Walk Cookbook* neatly matches perfect fusion dishes with an informative tour of colonial Cambodian haute cuisine.

Hamersley's Bistro, 553 Tremont St., Boston, MA 02116; (617) 423-2700; www.hamersleysbistro.com; $$$. Some credit Gordon Hamersley's South End restaurant with opening the door to the neighborhood's renaissance two decades ago. The spot still makes some of the region's best American food with a French country accent. And Hamersley gives away the secrets of his signature roasted garlic and lemon chicken in *Bistro Cooking at Home.*

Henrietta's Table, Charles Hotel, 1 Bennett St., Cambridge, MA 02138; (617) 661-5005; www.henriettastable.com; $$–$$$. Chef Peter

Davis has long championed local food producers at his New American restaurant, and he finally came out in the open with a splendid cookbook/sourcebook called *Fresh & Honest: Food from the Farms of New England and the Kitchen of Henrietta's Table.*

Jasper White's Summer Shack, 149 Alewife Brook Parkway, Cambridge, MA 02140; (617) 520-9500; also 50 Dalton St., Boston, MA 02115; (617) 867-9955; $$. As a godfather of fine dining in Boston, White surprised everyone when he opened the first Summer Shack in 2000, but he's stuck with casual, fun seafood-based dining ever since. His *Lobster at Home* (1998) remains the Bible for cooking that crustacean, but his 2007 *Summer Shack Cookbook* is the definitive treatment of shore food.

Oleana, 134 Hampshire St., Cambridge, MA 02139; (617) 661-0505; www.oleanarestaurant.com; $$$. Ana Sortun's Mediterranean cooking tends to favor the Arabic side of that sea, and she's especially deft at handling the aromatic spices of the Near East. Her cookbook, *Spice: Flavors of the Eastern Mediterranean,* is organized by groups of spices and herbs.

Olives, 10 City Square, Charlestown, MA 02129; (617) 242-1999; www.toddenglish.com; $$$. Todd English has actively sought and attained a national reputation as a great chef, combining hearty northern Italian cuisine with some of the best of the American South and New England fish cookery. "Big" and "bold" are the bywords here. He has many restaurants around the country, but Olives remains his home kitchen. English's cookbooks include *The Figs Table,* emphasizing simpler and more rustic dishes, and *The Olives Table* and *The Olives Dessert Table,* where he details some of his more complex contributions to the New American culinary scene.

Pho République, 1415 Washington St., Boston, MA 02118; (617) 262-0005; www.phorepublique.net; $$. Didi Emmons has carved out a niche for what might be called "light gourmet" at her South End French-

Vietnamese restaurant. Her menus are invariably vegetarian friendly, reflecting the chef's special dietary interests. Even carnivores will find much to like in her books, *Vegetarian Planet* and *Entertaining for a Veggie Planet*.

Rialto, Charles Hotel, 1 Bennett St., Cambridge, MA 02138; (617) 661-5050; www.rialto-restaurant.com; $$$. Jody Adams cooks the way Ella Fitzgerald sang—with bravura, sass, color, warmth, and exquisite taste. And like Ella, she has fun doing it. Her culinary palate favors the flavors of the Mediterranean basin, especially southern France and Italy. Her cookbook, *In the Hands of a Chef,* is less a recipe book than a full-fledged course in how to cook with your whole body and mind, complete with detailed and useful instructions on technique.

at the bar, Les Zyg offers Tuesday-night wine tastings led by sommelier Geoffrey Fallon, sometimes coupled with cooking demonstrations by chef-owner Ian Just. Like the bistro itself, the sessions are relaxed and unpretentious, focusing on the simple pleasures of good food and wine.

Stir, 102 Waltham St., Boston, MA 02118; (617) 423-7847; www.stir boston.com. Chef Barbara Lynch and wine guru Cat Silirie head the instructional team for one- and two-day workshops, tastings, and dinners in the tiny demo kitchen next to Plum Produce in the South End. If you'd rather appreciate other people's cooking skills than hone your own, Stir also holds regular book club dinners with lively discussion over a small meal inspired by the book.

B&G Oysters, 550 Tremont St., Boston, MA 02118; (617) 423-0550; www.bandgoysters.com; $$–$$$. Chef Barbara Lynch gained the culinary world's admiration with her fine dining restaurant, No. 9 Park, but she's made a world of new friends with the casual seafood and raw bar hangout B&G Oysters in the South End. There are always a dozen or so oyster varieties available (many of them local), and such entrees as skate wing served with semolina cake and pea tendrils are not exactly slouches, either. The highly selective list of about seventy wines was picked to complement the oysters and the Mediterranean seafood.

Barking Crab, 88 Sleeper St., Boston, MA 02210; (617) 426-2722; www.barkingcrab.com; $$. When the Barking Crab first opened, it sat on a forlorn stretch of harbor shoreline, surrounded by crumbling warehouses, a crumbling bridge, and windy parking lots. Fort Point Channel is becoming gentrified as part of the Boston Seaport District, but the fish shack is sticking to its simple roots. The small building is open in all seasons, but summer is best because you can dine outdoors at picnic tables, using the heavy rock on each table as a crude mallet for smashing crab and lobster shells. Boston remains a fishing port, and Barking Crab buys some of everything from the catch landed only blocks away at Fish Pier. You can always

New England Lobster Bake

Chef Peter Davis, of Henrietta's Table at the Charles Hotel in Cambridge, is a champion of farmers, fishermen, and other local food producers and he draws a little on several different purveyors for this authentic lobster bake.

8 medium red-skinned potatoes	2 pounds steamer clams
4 pieces of cheesecloth, cut into 18-inch squares	Fresh seaweed, to cover bottom of pan
4 1½-pound live lobsters	1 pound butter (4 sticks/2 cups)
4 ears of corn, unhusked	2 lemons, halved

1. Preheat oven to 350°F.
2. Boil the potatoes for 5 minutes, then allow them to cool.
3. On a piece of cheesecloth, place 1 lobster, 1 ear of corn, 2 parboiled potatoes, and ½ pound of clams. Fold the cheesecloth to form a sack and tie shut. Repeat with the remaining ingredients to form 4 sacks.
4. Place the seaweed in the bottom of a heavy-bottomed pan large enough to hold the 4 lobster sacks. Add 1 cup water. Place the sacks on top of the seaweed and cover the pan with aluminum foil.
5. Place the pan over a hot stove or char-grill for 10 minutes. Remove and put into the oven for about 15 minutes, or until the lobster is cooked (antennae separate easily when pulled).
6. While the sacks are cooking, melt the butter over low heat.
7. Remove the sacks from the pan and serve with melted butter and lemon halves.

Serves 4

Henrietta's Table

Charles Hotel
1 Bennett St.
Cambridge, MA 02138
(617) 661-5005
www.henriettastable.com

count on steamed or broiled lobster, steamed clams, stuffed qua-hogs, fried flounder, and baked scrod. During the summer, tuna and swordfish run off the coast and day boats bring back huge halibut. Order the tuna or sword grilled; the halibut baked. Many a mellow afternoon can be passed over a bucket of clams and a pitcher of a local microbrew while admiring the Financial District skyscrapers. Open daily for lunch and dinner.

Casablanca, 40 Brattle St., Cambridge, MA 02138; (617) 876-0999; www.casablanca-restaurant.com; $$. The Brattle Theatre, located in the same building, is often credited with setting off a nationwide revival of interest in Humphrey Bogart films shortly after the actor's death. This restaurant pays a not-too-subtle homage to Rick's Café, complete with large murals colorfully reinterpreting black-and-white scenes from the restaurant's movie namesake. The large and often boisterous bar in the rear (enter through the dining room or by a separate entrance behind the theater) is a time-honored watering hole for Cambridge authors, journalists, and other literati—a cast of characters in no short supply. Although legendary for its ham-burgers, Casablanca has steered a course toward Morocco, serving Mediterranean cuisine with a North African interpretation, espe-cially on the tapas menu. Some of the best bets for dinner include seared duck breast and duck confit, pan-fried diver scallops with pistachios, and monkfish with *merguez* (lamb) sausage and brussels sprouts. Open Monday through Saturday for lunch, Sunday for brunch, daily for dinner.

Craigie on Main, 853 Main St., Cambridge, MA 02139; (617) 497-5511; www.craigieonmain.com; $$$–$$$$. Some restaurant people think chef-owner Tony Maws something of a madman because he doesn't prepare the menu of the day until all fifteen to twenty orders of mostly local, all-organic meat, fish, and produce have been delivered. Chances are that even he won't know what's on the evening menu until after lunch. Maws trained in Burgundy, and he brings that hearty country French approach (including a penchant for organ meats and extensive charcuterie) to regional ingredients. Diners on a budget welcome the daily three-course fixed-price menu, which Maws often uses to introduce people to unfamiliar dishes. Open Tuesday through Sunday for dinner.

The Daily Catch, 323 Hanover St., Boston, MA 02109; (617) 523-8567; www.thedailycatch.com; $$. Also known as the Calamari Cafe, this itty-bitty storefront restaurant often has lines down the street as people wait patiently for one of the twenty seats. The menu is almost entirely fresh seafood and pasta, prepared in the open kitchen that takes up a quarter of the room. The food comes straight from the stove to the table, right in the sauté pan it was cooked in. You'll know you're in the right place when you open the door and the twin aromas of fresh seafood and fried garlic come wafting out. Open for lunch and dinner daily.

EVOO Restaurant, 118 Beacon St., Somerville, MA 02143, (617) 661-3866, www.evoorestaurant.com, $$$-$$$$. Peter McCarthy quit the high-profile chef rat race more than a decade ago to open this smart neighborhood American bistro where most of what comes out of the kitchen came out of local fields or waters only hours before. Menu credits for succulent vegetables, meat, and fish are almost as extensive as film credits. Diners on a budget can avail themselves of the daily $35 three-course menu. Open Monday through Saturday for dinner.

Imperial Seafood Restaurant, 70 Beach St., Boston, MA 02111; (617) 426-8439, $. Dim sum aficionados argue endlessly over who has the best in Chinatown, but Imperial Seafood is hands-down the weekend favorite. The place is tiny, but seems to have taken over the skilled dim sum staff from affiliated East Ocean City when that restaurant dropped its breakfast service. Don't speak Cantonese? That's the beauty of dim sum—just point and indicate how many orders with your fingers. Open for breakfast, lunch, dinner, and late night daily.

Locke-Ober, 3 Winter Place, Boston, MA 02108; (617) 542-1340; www.lockeober.com; $$$$. When star chef Lydia Shire acquired this landmark restaurant in 2001, she went to great lengths to restore the gleaming woodwork, the painted tin ceiling, and the raft of pol-ished silver that have been hallmarks of this fine-dining destination since the 1890s. Her restoration also brought back Locke-Ober's dig-nity and gave it a menu worthy of its once-stellar reputation, from the days when Enrico Caruso used to pop into the kitchen to cook his own sweetbreads and Orson Welles swallowed legendary numbers of raw oysters. Boston Brahmins still come to lunch with their financial advisors (probably on Shire's hard-to-hold but delicious lobster club sandwich), but gourmets also jet in from around the country to see how Shire has reinterpreted classic haute cuisine for the twenty-first century, with dinner entrees such as crisped sweetbreads with braised bacon and salsify. A few hidebound traditionalists are aghast that the resurrection of Locke-Ober occurred at the hands of a female chef—women weren't even allowed in the dining room until 1970. Perhaps revenge is the sweetest dish of all. Open for lunch Monday through Friday, for dinner Monday through Saturday.

Maurizio's, 364 Hanover St., Boston, MA 02113; (617) 367-1123; www.mauriziosboston.com; $$. The Italian North End is full of wonderful little restaurants serving all strains of regional Italian cuisine. Many of these trattorias have become trendy destinations, while others attract long lines based on listings in the more popular

guidebooks. But Maurizio's is quite possibly the best restaurant in the neighborhood and still one of the most reasonably priced. The chef-owner, Maurizio Loddo, originally hails from Sardinia, an island overrun by many conquerors who left touches of their cuisine behind. Loddo is a genius with fish and often invents dishes based on what impressed him that morning at the fish market. The restaurant is one of the few in the neighborhood to take reservations; try to snag one of the tables closest to the kitchen to watch Loddo work with balletic grace. Open nightly for dinner, Saturday for lunch, Sunday for brunch.

Oak Room, Fairmont Copley Plaza Hotel, 138 St. James Ave., Boston, MA 02116; (617) 267-5300; www.theoakroom .com; $$$$. The baroque woodwork and carved ceilings of the Oak Room date from the Edwardian era, when the hotel was built to be the showpiece of Boston. Befitting its baronial appearance, the restaurant is an unrepentant steak house where perfectly grilled steaks, delectable roasts, and large slabs of grilled fish head the menu. Before dinner, indulge in a perfect, icy-cold martini and make jumbo shrimp cocktail your starter. Open daily for breakfast, lunch, and dinner.

Porter Exchange Building, 1815 Massachusetts Ave., Cambridge, MA 02140; $. The Art Deco brick exterior of this former Sears & Roebuck does not even hint at the bustle inside, where a group of casual eateries so resemble a Japanese street market that they attract homesick students from Greater Boston's many universities.

Sample noodle soups (with miso broth, Chinese vegetables, and pork, for example) at Sapporo Ramen, sushi and sashimi at Kotobukiya, and rice bowls with chicken, beef, or pork at Asian Barbecue. Or try your hand at cooking thin slices of pork in hot broth at Tampopo, which specializes in the Japanese hot pots known as shabu-shabu. Then stop at Tapicha for a "pearl drink." Pick a tea (black, green, or chai); add flavorings such as mango, peach, or lychee; and then ask the server to throw in "bubbles" of tapioca or coconut jelly. Open daily for lunch and dinner.

Redbones Barbecue, 55 Chester St., Somerville, MA 02144; (617) 628-2200; www.redbones.com; $. Almost as exotic as the Japanese street food at nearby Porter Exchange, Redbones serves the most authentic Austin-style (that's Texas, y'all) barbecue one finds in these chilly parts. Pork and beef ribs, brisket (burnt ends available, if you ask nicely), chicken, and Texas-style pulled pork (with sweet, not vinegar, sauce on the side) share the menu with beer-sopping hush puppies and fried catfish fingers. The decor is strictly Texas roadhouse, and the background music is usually country blues, circa 1935. At least two dozen microbrews available on tap help ease down the heaping plates of meat. Parking is nigh unto impossible, so take the Red Line to Davis Square. Open daily for lunch and dinner.

Santarpio's Pizza, 111 Chelsea St., Boston, MA 02128; (617) 567-9871; www.santarpios pizza.com. Practically hidden under an East Boston highway ramp to Logan Airport, Santarpio's is one of the shrines of authentic Neapolitan-style pizza in the United States. Even Neapolitans love the pizza, and everyone loves the boxing-bar decor. Stick with the Italian cheese and garlic, and pay a little more for extra garlic. Open daily for lunch and dinner.

Upstairs on the Square, 91 Winthrop St., Cambridge, MA 02138; (617) 864-1933; www.upstairsonthesquare.com; $$–$$$. Deborah Hughes and Mary-Catherine Diebel created such a memorable Harvard Square landmark at Upstairs at the Pudding that Harvard's refusal to extend their lease became a cause célèbre among alumni gourmets. In 2002, however, Hughes and Diebel opened this new edition on John Winthrop Square and boosted their cushy whimsy to new extremes. The zebra carpet in the first-level Monday Club Bar and the leopard carpet in the top-level Soirée Room may be the most sedate aspects of the decor. The bold splashes of color look like an explosion at a wrapping paper factory—Gustav Klimt would love the patterned pink and gold of the upstairs room, in particular. But sophisticated comfort food remains Upstairs's forte, with casual dishes such as chèvre pasta pillows with squash, sage, and brown butter in the Monday Club or a duet of veal osso buco and schnitzel in the more formal Soirée. Monday Club open Monday through Saturday for lunch, Sunday for brunch, daily for dinner. Soirée open Tuesday through Saturday for dinner.

Boston Beer Company, 30 Germania St., Jamaica Plain, MA 02130; (617) 482-1332; www.samadams.com. Boston Beer Company is the 800-pound gorilla of small breweries, the maker of the relentlessly promoted Sam Adams line of beers. While major production is farmed out to contract brewers across the country, new brews are developed at the original Jamaica Plain facility, which also offers tours ($2 suggested contribution to local charities and Youth Enrichment Services). Tours run on Monday, Thursday, and Saturday from 10:00 a.m. to 3:00 p.m. and Friday from 10:00 a.m. to 5:30 p.m. For extra tour hours in the summer or additional tour information, call (617) 368-5080. Sam Adams beers are available in Boston pretty much wherever beer is sold.

Boston Beer Works, 61 Brookline Ave., Boston, MA 02215; (617) 536-2337; also 112 Canal St., Boston, MA 02114; (617) 896-2337; www.beerworks.net. These cavernous brewpubs produce small batches of many beer types, ranging from IPAs to fruit-flavored wheat beers to heavy porters. Both have pretty good restaurants, with an emphasis on pastas, barbecue, salads, and a very hearty mixed-grill plate that will feed one linebacker or an entire table of sports fans.

Cambridge Brewing Company, One Kendall Square, #100, Cambridge, MA 02139; (617) 494-1994; www.cambrew.com. Established in 1989, CBC is the area's longest-operating brewery restaurant. Brewmaster Will Meyers is the kind of brewer that hops-heads call a Beer Hero. In other words, he tends to make five-gallon batches of bold, idiosyncratic beers (espresso-laced porter, golden ale flavored with handpicked heather) to flesh out the basic line. Standard beers include a golden ale, an American-style pale ale, a robust porter, and an American amber. On Tuesday nights Meyers breaks out a new firkin of English-style cask-conditioned ale (often gone by the next day).

Harpoon Brewery, 306 Northern Ave., South Boston, MA 02210; (617) 574-9551; www.harpoonbrewery.com. Some area bars, especially in South Boston, have Harpoon's ales on draft, but everyone sells them by the bottle. The standard amber is a fruity brew, while the copper-colored IPA has a delicately floral nose. Real hops fans gravitate toward the English-style bitter. Seasonal drinks include an Irish-style red ale in early spring (Hibernian Ale), a complex and malty Octoberfest, and Harpoon Summer Ale (a light-bodied, clear ale in the Kölsch style). You can stop by the brewery store Tuesday through Friday from 11:00 a.m. to 5:30 p.m. and Saturday from 11:00 a.m. to 5:00 p.m. to purchase T-shirts, hats, pint glasses, key chains, vests, sweatshirts, long-sleeved T-shirts, and golf shirts, as well as to get your growlers refilled. Recognizing that most folks take brewery tours to get to the tasting, Harpoon has dispensed with the walk-through and offers tastings Tuesday through Thursday at 4:00 p.m., Friday at 2:00 and 4:00 p.m., and Saturday at noon, 2:00, and 4:00 p.m.

O Come Ye Back

Of all the green-tinged cities of America, Boston has the highest percentage of residents of Irish descent, and both the Irish-American bar and the Irish pub are institutions here. The most venerable of the lot is Doyle's in Jamaica Plain. It was founded in 1882, and every mayor since Rose Kennedy's father, "Honey Fitz" Fitzgerald, has made it an essential campaign stop. Every Thursday (and on St. Patrick's Day), you can order corned beef and cabbage. The other Irish pubs listed below are comparative newcomers, dating from the second half of the twentieth century. In each you can expect Guinness and/or Murphy's on draft (usually along with Harp, Newcastle, and the local brews of Sam Adams, Harpoon, and Tremont Ale), and a menu strong on such pub staples as shepherd's pie and bangers and mash. Most offer entertainment as well, which can range from Irish fiddlers to head-banging rock and roll in the manner of Dublin's Northside.

Doyle's, 3484 Washington St., Jamaica Plain, MA 02130; (617) 524-2345; www.doyles-cafe.com.

Druid Restaurant, 1357 Cambridge St., Cambridge, MA 02139; (617) 497-0965; www.druidpub.com.

The Field Pub, 29 Prospect St., Cambridge, MA 02139; (617) 354-7345; www.thefieldpub.com.

Kinsale Irish Pub & Restaurant, 2 Center Plaza, Boston, MA 02108; (617) 742-5577; www.classicirish.com.

Phoenix Landing, 512 Massachusetts Ave., Cambridge, MA 02139; (617) 576-6260.

The Playwright, 658 East Broadway, South Boston, MA 02127; (617) 269-2537; www.theplaywrightbar.com.

The Plough & Stars, 912 Massachusetts Ave., Cambridge, MA 02139; (617) 576-0032.

John Harvard's Brew House, 33 Dunster St., Cambridge, MA 02138; (617) 868-3585; www.johnharvards.com. Unlike other area brewpubs, John Harvard brews both pale golden light lagers and somewhat more aggressive ales, including copper-colored IPA, English-style nut brown ale, and a stout that's dark as a coal mine. With ten lines running at the original location (there are now branches around the eastern United States), the beers change with some frequency. The Harvard Square operation, however, almost always has a crisp wheat beer on tap. Do not be taken in by some of the extravagant and fanciful claims—the recipes were neither written by William Shakespeare nor brought to these shores by the Rev. John Harvard, for whom the nearby school is named. It is possible, however, that the first brewery of the Massachusetts Bay Colony sat either on this spot or very near it.

Southeastern Massachusetts

Many Bay Staters don't even think of Norfolk, Bristol, and Plymouth Counties when their attention turns to food, considering the region between Boston and Cape Cod a ring of southern suburbs followed by a long stretch of highway to reach the bridges to the Cape. Yet this area embraces the great fishing port of New Bedford—one of America's richest—as well as boulder-strewn peninsular farms where vegetables seem to spring up with no more effort than calling their names.

It is also a region of substantial cultural diversity. Devotees of the Food Channel may know that star chef Emeril Lagasse rose to fame in New Orleans, but his roots are in the Fall River French community, and he frequently makes reference to the French-Canadian traditions he learned in the family kitchen. Even more dramatic is the culinary influence of the Portuguese, who have made up a substantial segment of New Bedford's fishing fleet since the early-nineteenth-century whaling days. It is said that the Portuguese have 365 ways to cook codfish, or *bacalhau*, one for every day of the year; you can taste many of them in area restaurants.

Despite the population pressures imposed by the proximity to Boston (which gets closer every day through improved public transportation), much of southeastern Massachusetts remains farmland and orchards. The acidic but sandy peat bogs of Plymouth County produce much of the nation's cranberry crop. The alluvial loam of Westport's peninsulas yields an almost embarrassing abundance of crops, from spring lettuce to fall pumpkins. Gentle microclimates abound, especially among the towns that border on Buzzards Bay, permitting the cultivation of European wine grapes and other crops that normally require a growing season longer than most of the state provides.

Even apart from the deep-sea harvest of flaky fish and sea scallops that the monster fishing boats bring into New Bedford, you'll discover that enterprising clam and oyster diggers and mussel gatherers not only stock the restaurants and fish shacks of the area, but many of them also set up impromptu roadside stands to unload their extra catch. The estuaries of Buzzards Bay rival the North Shore for their extensive flats.

While much of the southeastern Massachusetts bounty is siphoned off to the restaurants of Boston and New York, many small farmers and fishermen have turned to direct retailing to gain an economic edge in businesses with traditionally thin margins. Look for the symbol of the Southeastern Massachusetts Agricultural Partnership (SEMAP) at farm stands, stores, and restaurants. These are businesses that support local producers, guaranteeing the freshest food and a sustainable harvest.

Cape Cod Specialty Foods, 11 Cranberry Highway, Sagamore, MA 02561; (508) 888-7099; www.bogbeans.com. Bog Beans pop up in gift shops and candy stores across southeastern Massachusetts. They're among the best chocolate-dipped dried cranberries available. Our nod goes to the "Dark 'n' Raspberry," which are coated in raspberry-scented dark chocolate. Recognizing a good thing, the company also makes chocolate-covered blueberries, espresso beans, and butter-toffee peanuts. All the products are available by mail order.

Cranberry Hill Farm, 103 Haskell Rd., Plymouth, MA 02360; (508) 888-9179; www.organiccranberries.com. This farm's six acres of cranberry bogs have been certified organic since the mid-1990s, making them a setting where birds, frogs, crayfish, and dragonflies thrive. Growing cranberries organically means constant weeding, cultivating, and bug-picking, but the resulting fruit is worth the work. Bob and Kristine Keese don't encourage farm visits but do take orders large and small for fresh or sweet dried cranberries over the phone, by mail, or by e-mail (cranhill@capecod.net). See the Web site for current prices.

Equal Exchange, 50 United Dr., West Bridgewater, MA 02379; (774) 776-7400; www.equalexchange.com. Founded in 1986, Equal Exchange has become the largest seller of certified fair-trade coffee in the United States. The company, which itself is a workers' cooperative, deals directly with small coffee farmers in Latin America,

Asia, and Africa. More to the point, the coffees are as good as they are socially conscious. Many health food stores and some supermarkets carry Equal Exchange coffees in their bulk bins. You can also order ten-ounce, twelve-ounce, two-pound, and five-pound packages via the Web site. If you're not a coffee fan, the company also carries organic tea, chocolate, and hot cocoa mix.

Gaspar's Sausage Company Factory Outlet, 384 Faunce Corner Rd., North Dartmouth, MA 02747; (508) 998-2012 or (800) 542-2038; www.linguica.com. Since the late 1920s, Gaspar's has been the largest producer of smoked Portuguese sausages in the country. The line emphasizes *linguiça* and *chouriço* spiced pork sausages (pronounced "ling-GWEE-sah" and "shoor-REES") made by Portuguese Americans in southeastern Massachusetts. The *chouriço*, which is noticeably hotter than the *linguiça,* is often used in casseroles and fried dishes, while *linguiça* is frequently grilled and served on a bun. A *morcela* (blood sausage) is also available seasonally. Look for Gaspar's products in Portuguese markets or visit the factory store.

Great Hill Dairy, 160 Delano Rd., Marion, MA 02738; (888) 748-2208; www.greathillblue.com. Specialization can pay off in the cheese business. This dairy on the shores of Buzzards Bay, long known in agricultural circles for its Guernsey herd, concentrates on a single cheese: Great Hill Blue. Made from raw, unhomogenized milk, the blue-veined yellow curd ranks among America's top blue cheeses. Production is limited, but you'll find Great Hill Blue in some health food and gourmet stores, at specialty cheesemongers,

Kale Soup

This classic Portuguese soup recipe, provided by Bob Gaspar of Gaspar's Sausage Company, mates kale, cabbage, and Portuguese sausage for a hearty fall or winter meal.

1½ pounds *linguiça or chouriço*
½ pound shredded shank meat
   or chuck roast (optional)
2 teaspoons crushed red pepper
1 medium onion, sliced
2 teaspoons salt

2 bunches of kale, shredded, or
   4 boxes of frozen kale
1 head of cabbage, shredded
1–2 cans kidney beans
6 potatoes, peeled and diced

1. Place *linguiça* or *chouriço* (and shank meat or chuck roast, if using) in a large stew pot or Dutch oven.
2. Add red pepper, onion, and salt. Add water to cover. Bring to a boil and simmer until meat is almost done (about 30 minutes).
3. Add kale, cabbage, and kidney beans to broth.
4. When kale is about half-cooked (about 10 minutes), add potatoes and cook an additional 30 minutes.

Serves 8

**Gaspar's Sausage Company
Factory Outlet**

**384 Faunce Corner Rd.
North Dartmouth, MA 02747
(508) 998-2012 or (800) 542-2038
www.linguica.com**

That First Cup

With its orange and purple decor, the busy shop looks like all the others in the Dunkin' Donuts chain—except for the small plaque inside the door proclaiming, "On this site the original Dunkin' Donuts opened its doors in May 1950." When Dorchester native and eighth-grade dropout William Rosenberg set up shop in a former awning store, he charged a nickel for a donut and ten cents for the cup of coffee to dunk it in. His simple formula proved a huge success. According to corporate headquarters, Dunkin' Donuts is the largest retailer of coffee-by-the-cup in the United States, serving almost a billion cups a year. On an average day, Dunkin' sells about thirty cups per second.

Dunkin' Donuts
543 Southern Artery
Quincy, MA 02169
(617) 472-9502
www.dunkindonuts.com

and on the menus of a few restaurants. The dairy is not open to the public, but you can order directly through the Web site.

Maria & Ricardo's Tortilla Factory, 320 Turnpike St., Canton, MA 02021; (781) 828-0848; www.harbar.com. This company started out supplying corn tortillas to Boston's Mexican restaurants and became so successful that it had to move to much larger facilities. Now it produces enough white and blue corn tortillas (as well as whole wheat and white flour tortillas) to make them available in the refrigerated food sections of eastern Massachusetts health food stores and in Hispanic grocery stores.

Newland Farm, 145 Newland St., Norton, MA 02766; (508) 285-3169. Earl and Ethel Willcott keep a herd of approximately 1,000 emus, which grow up to 6 feet tall in a year. They sell emu-oil skin care products, as well as a full line of emu steaks, ground meat, and sausages. The low-fat, low-cholesterol red meat is prized by many gourmet restaurants, and the Willcotts also provide recipes for home cooks. Call for hours to visit the farm to purchase meat and other products.

Peaceful Meadows Farm, 60 Bedford St. (Route 18), Whitman, MA 02382; (781) 447-3700; www.peacefulmeadowsicecream.com. The barn at the nearly century-old dairy farm is often open to the public (call ahead), but the easiest way to sample Peaceful Meadows' premium ice cream is to visit the stand at Village Landing in Plymouth (170 Water St.; 508-746-2362) throughout the year. Peaceful Meadows makes all the traditional flavors, as well as the usual cookie and candy mix-ins. The best compromise between old and new styles might be Buttercrunch, which contains bits of butterscotch candy in butterscotch ice cream.

Rainbow Turkey Farm, 199 Homestead Ave., Rehoboth, MA 02769; (508) 252-4427. Judy and Tom Mello raise about 500 turkeys each year for the Thanksgiving and Christmas holidays. Call a few days before you need a bird and you'll be able to pick it up, freshly dressed, at the farm.

Spring Valley Natural Spring Water Co., 1941 GAR Highway (Route 6), Swansea, MA 02777; (508) 379-9842. Bottle your own natural spring water from one of the few free-flowing natural discharge springs in southeastern Massachusetts. The certified spring is naturally filtered through bedrock and has been a source of drinking water in the area since the early settlers. There's a coin-operated dispenser station on site, open around the clock.

Willow Tree Poultry Farm, 997 South Main St., Attleboro, MA 02703; (508) 222-2479; www.willowtreefarm.com. Specialists in making premium all-white-meat frozen chicken pies and fresh all-white-meat chicken salad, Willow Tree boasts products sold throughout New England. The retail store at the farm factory, open daily, has those products as well as fresh chicken, capons, turkeys, and geese (order capons, turkeys, and geese a day ahead) and a range of other grocery products, including cold cuts, salads, and fresh pies.

Almaeedeh International Market, 690 Hancock St., Quincy, MA 02170; (617) 773-2285. Open since 1998, this little Middle Eastern market seems unassuming from the outside, but it's jam-packed with delicacies from Pakistan, India, Greece, Turkey, Lebanon, and Iran. Some of the unusual items include Beirut syrups (rose, tamarind, and blackberry), bulgur in several graded kernel sizes, semolina, real basmati rice, dried and canned fava beans, Moroccan green olives, French feta cheese, Turkish coffee, dried lemons, figs, prunes, dates, curry and spice mixes from Pakistan, bulk fennel seeds and lentils, and a selection of canned goods that includes grape leaves, hummus, and baba ghanoush. An even better reason to visit is the market's halal butcher shop, which has humanely slaughtered lamb, goat, and beef daily. It's the ideal place to purchase a whole or half kid or lamb, as well as legs, chops, roasts, and organ meats.

Amaral's Bakery, 241 Globe St., Fall River, MA 02720; (508) 674-8988; www.amaralsbakery.com. You'll find Amaral's Portuguese sweet bread, biscuits, and muffins (sort of like English muffins but sweeter and more substantive) in little shops all over eastern Massachusetts, wherever there is a substantial Portuguese or Brazilian population. But if you go directly to the bakery (open Monday through Friday from 5:00 a.m. to 4:00 p.m. and Saturday from 5:00 a.m. to 3:00 p.m.), you can get the sweet bread rings fresh from the ovens where the Amaral family has been making them for more than a half century.

The Butcherie II, 15 Washington St., Canton, MA 02021; (781) 828-3530. Looking for potato latkes like your bubbie used to make? Beef knishes? Carrot kugel? You'll find them in the refrigerated cases at The Butcherie, a one-stop kosher grocer for the suburbs south of Boston. That same section also offers several brands of New York half-sour pickles, along with ready-to-heat chicken noodle soup, split pea soup, hearty cabbage soup, tzimmes, potato kugel, five-vegetable knishes, mushroom knishes, and scallion latkes. The shelves are filled with canned goods and dry goods from Israel and the large kosher foods companies of New York and New Jersey. Empire-brand kosher poultry is available, as are whole corned briskets and tongues.

Butler's Colonial Donut House, 1448 Grand Army Highway, Somerset, MA 02726; (508) 672-0865. The owners and location may have changed, but Butler's continues to create what many doughnut aficionados consider the best in New England. The ethereal pastries are made with a yeast-raised dough, then filled with jelly or plain or mocha hand-whipped cream. Our favorite is the Long John—a long tubular doughnut split to sandwich whipped cream and blackberry jelly.

Cape Cod Chowder Company, 173 Wareham Rd., Marion, MA 02738; (508) 748-3870; www .capecodchowder.com. Formerly known as the Daniel Webster Inn's Cape Cod Chowders, these all-natural fresh and frozen chowders come in twelve-ounce, ready-to-heat (no diluting required) packages. Choices include lobster bisque and lobster, clam, and corn chowders. Institutional-size packages are also available for mail-order.

Dorothy Cox's Chocolates, 115 Huttleston Ave., Fairhaven, MA 02719; (508) 996-2465; www.dorothycox.com. This family-owned and -operated business has been creating gourmet chocolates for more than three-quarters of a century; one of the current owners is, in fact, the namesake of her grandmother. The company produces 110 varieties of chocolate candies, but it is best known for its buttercrunch, made with equal quantities of butter and sugar. The company claims to have introduced chocolate-covered dried cranberries and it certainly makes some of the best. Located east of town, heading toward the Bourne Bridge, it's an ideal spot to stop and load up on sweets for a Cape vacation. Call during slower seasons to see if tours are being offered.

Gypsy Kitchen, 1241 Hancock St., Quincy, MA 02169; (617) 847-1846; www.drhot.net. Formerly a sauce stand in Boston's Quincy Market, Gypsy Kitchen has expanded its horizons and its product lines in this handsome downtown Quincy storefront. It's still a prime resource for all varieties of hot sauce from around the globe, but it now carries many other spices, coffees, and gift baskets, as well as imported cheeses and wines from France, Italy, Spain, and California. Fresh European-style breads are available on Friday and Saturday.

How on Earth, The Store, 62 Marion Rd. (Route 62), Mattapoisett, MA 02739; (508) 758-1341; www.howonearth.net. The motto at the nonprofit How on Earth project of the Marion Institute is "Know your farmer, know your food." The Store carries local produce, mostly from Lucky Field Organics in Rochester and Round the Bend Farm in Dartmouth. (It's also the pick-up point for Lucky Farm CSA shareholders.) Some products, of course, come from other southeastern Massachusetts farms or entrepreneurs, including pies and other baked goods, quiches, pastries, honey, and jams. The Store also carries organic lamb and pork from western Massachusetts. Tuesday through Saturday, The Store offers freshly prepared lunch entrees.

Kenny's Salt Water Taffy, Town Pier, 82 Onset Ave., Onset (Wareham), MA 02532; (508) 295-8828. Kenny's is the quintessence of summer at the beach. It makes dozens of flavors of saltwater taffy, each piece twisted neatly in waxed paper. Taffy covers two-thirds of the meager counter, but you can also order classic beach food at the window on the right: burgers, fried fish sandwiches, hot dogs, and french fries. Offering limited parking, Onset Beach is one of the least crowded strands at the west end of the Cape Cod Canal.

New Bedford Linguiça Company, 56 Davis St., New Bedford, MA 02746; (508) 992-9367. You'll have to look carefully to find the nondescript entrance to this sausage factory behind Amaral's Market (see below) off Bellevue Ave., but it's worth the hunt for the superb sausages that the elderly Portuguese ladies of New Bedford swear by. The retail operation is bare bones: a couple of signs, a refrigerator case, and a cash register. One sign explains, for example, that the *chouriço* is available as "very hot or a little hot." Products include the two types of *chouriço* links, *linguiça, linguiça* franks or patties, hot *linguiça,* ground *chouriço,* and *morcela,* a blood sausage made only from October through May.

O'Brien's Bakery, 9 Beale St., Quincy, MA 02170; (617) 472-4025. This Wollaston-center Irish bakery—shamrocks everywhere—makes a lot of standard fare such as cookies, doughnuts, and cakes. But the big draw at the holidays (including March 17) are owner Brian Jackal's soda breads, made with or without caraway seeds. Chances are you'll have to stand in line to get one.

Sid Wainer & Sons Specialty Produce and Specialty Foods, 2301 Purchase St., New Bedford, MA 02746; (800) 249-0447; www.sidwainer.com. This remarkable company distributes imported and locally grown gourmet products all around the country. Fortunately,

TOLL HOUSE: THE FIRST CHIP

In 1997 the Massachusetts legislature designated the chocolate chip cookie the official cookie of the Commonwealth, despite strong lobbying on behalf of the Fig Newton. In the 1930s, Ruth Wakefield made culinary history when she added pieces of a cut-up Nestle chocolate bar to some butter cookies she was baking for guests at the Toll House Inn, which Ruth and husband Kenneth ran in an eighteenth-century toll house outside of Whitman. The "toll house" cookies were an immediate hit, and Ruth eventually allowed Nestle to publish her recipe in return for a lifetime supply of chocolate (and other considerations—stock in the company, we hope). To make it even easier for cooks to whip up a batch, Nestle introduced prechopped Semi-Sweet Chocolate Morsels (with the recipe on the bag) in 1939 and set the cookie on the road to becoming the country's favorite.

they also have this retail market. Forget your mother's advice to never visit a grocery store on an empty stomach. We fast for a day before we hit Sid Wainer, where the shopping experience is a smorgasbord that's as filling as it is educational. On a single Saturday morning, we could sample grilled black olives; roasted yellow, green, and red tomatoes; organic red rice salad; goat cheddar, Manchego, farmhouse cheddar, Pont l'Évêque, and Camembert cheeses; smoked duck breast; artichoke paste from Italy; banana walnut coffee cake from Cape Cod; soft amaretti from Italy; Italian baby fig compote; figs in syrup; pumpkin chestnut whole grain soup made with Zuppa Saracena grain mix; chive, red pepper, and wild berry soft unripened goat cheeses; two Spanish olive oils from Arbequina olives; two Tuscan olive oils; two aged balsamic vinegars from Modena; and anise, raspberry, tangerine, lavender, and lemon honeys. The staff chefs and bakers prepare foods in the demonstration kitchen to show you how to use the products. Walk in at the holiday season and you might see a chef whipping up stuffing with truffles or blue Hubbard squash with fennel.

Wasik's Cheese Shop, 61 Central Ave., Wellesley, MA 02482; (781) 237-0916; www.wasiks.com. The five members of the Wasik family (and their employees) understand that cheese is a live product that keeps changing over time. The 3,000-square-foot refrigerated cellar allows the family to buy artisanal cheeses and age them until they reach their flavor peak. Although the shop sells through its Web site, you really have to go in to peruse the cheese board, which lists varieties under their countries of origin. Besides, it's impossible to do a virtual tasting, and the Wasiks are generous with their tastes. Not only will you find some of New England's top artisanal cheeses, but you can get deep orange aged Dutch Gouda, nutty two-year-old Comté Gruyère from the French Alps, and farmstead cheddars from England, Wales, and Scotland. The shelves and refrigerator cases also hold the appropriate complements: olives, cornichons, crackers, pâtés, and terrines.

The Southeastern Massachusetts Agricultural Partnership (SEMAP) links farmers, educators, and conservationists to promote farm businesses in Bristol, Plymouth, Barnstable, Dukes, and Nantucket Counties. The partnership's slogan—"Be Farm Friendly. Buy Local."—may not be the catchiest, but it's good advice. SEMAP publishes a harvest guide to farms and their products and a list of farmers' markets. The publications are available at many farm stands and tourist offices and on the Web at www.farmfresh.org. For more information, call SEMAP at (508) 295-2212, extension 50.

Attleboro Farmers' Market, Gilbert Perry Square, Attleboro. Saturday from 8:00 a.m. to noon, July to October.

Brockton Farmers' Market I, Brockton Fair Grounds, Brockton. Saturday from 9:00 a.m. to noon, mid-July to mid-October.

Brockton Farmers' Market II, City Hall Plaza, Brockton. Friday from 10:30 a.m. to 1:30 p.m., mid-July to October.

Buzzards Bay Farmers' Market, Main St., Buzzards Bay Village. Friday from 10:00 a.m. to 2:00 p.m., July through October.

Cohasset Farmers' Market, Cohasset Common, Main St., Cohasset. Thursday from 2:30 to 6:30 p.m., June to October.

Fall River Farmers' Market I, Kennedy Park, Fall River. Saturday from 7:30 a.m. to 12:30 p.m., May through November.

Fall River Farmers' Market II, Ruggles Park, Fall River. Wednesday from 9:00 a.m. to 1:00 p.m., June through October.

Hingham Farmers' Market, Bathing Beach parking lot, Route 3A, Hingham. Saturday from 10:00 a.m. to 2:00 p.m., mid-May to late October.

Mansfield Farmers' Market, parking lot, 80 North Main St., Mansfield. Thursday from 2:00 to 6:00 p.m., mid-July to October.

Middleboro Farmers' Market, Town Hall lawn, Route 105, Middleboro. Saturday from 9:00 a.m. to 1:00 p.m., mid-June to late October.

Milton Farmers' Market, Wharf Street park off Adams St., Milton Village. Thursday from 1:00 to 6:00 p.m., late June to mid-October.

New Bedford Farmers' Market, Brooklawn Park (Ashley Blvd. side), New Bedford. Monday from 2:00 p.m. to dusk, July to late October.

New Bedford Clasky Common Farmers' Market, Pleasant and Pearl Streets, New Bedford. Saturday 9:00 a.m. to 1:00 p.m., mid-July to late October.

New Bedford Wings Court Farmers' Market, Purchase and Union Streets, New Bedford. Thursday from 2:00 to 7:00 p.m., mid-July to October.

North Easton Farmers' Market, the Sheep Pasture, 261 Main St., North Easton. Tuesday from 2:00 to 6:00 p.m. and Saturday from 10:00 a.m. to 2:00 p.m., mid-May to mid-October.

Norwood Farmers' Market, municipal parking lot, Nahatan and Cottage Streets, Norwood. Tuesday from 1:00 to 6:00 p.m., late May to late October.

Quincy Farmers' Market, John Hancock municipal parking lot, Quincy center. Friday from 11:30 a.m. to 5:00 p.m., June to late October.

Rochester Farmers' Market, Plumb Corner Market Parking Lot, Rounseville Rd. and Constitution Way, Rochester Center. Saturday from 8:00 a.m. to noon, mid-May to late October.

Taunton Farmers' Market, Town Green, Taunton. Thursday from noon to 5:00 p.m., mid-July through October.

Ashley's Peaches, 1461 Main St., Acushnet, MA 02743; (508) 763-4329. The stand opens at noon daily from late July through mid-October, but it's best to call ahead because Ernest and Diane Ventura pick peaches each morning and sell them the same day. If none are ripe, the stand will not open. To try to ensure a steady supply and a long season, this family farm, now in its fifth generation, grows more than thirty varieties of peaches, as well as nectarines, a few varieties of apples, and tomatoes and pumpkins. Although it's hard to imagine anything better than a fresh-picked peach, you'll also find jams and jellies, peach cobblers, apple pies, and muffins.

Dowse Orchards, 98 North Main St. (Route 27), Sherborn, MA 01770; (508) 653-2639; www.dowseorchards.com. The motto at Dowse is "America's best crunchin' apples since 1778," but the family has been pressing cider from the apples "only" since 1853. About 35 acres of the farm are planted in apples, and several acres more grow vegetables, flowers, and Christmas trees. The Dowse family also keeps chickens and sells free-range eggs at the farm stand, which is open from May until Christmas Eve, beginning with lettuces and garden plants in the spring and wrapping up with the last of the apples (mostly older varieties like Spencer, Baldwin, and Stayment Winesap), pumpkins, and trees in the fall and early winter.

Four Town Farm, 90 George St., Seekonk, MA 02771; (508) 336-5587. Located at the border of Massachusetts and Rhode Island, where the acreage edges into four different municipalities, Four Town has extensive fields of flowers for picking as well as strawberries, raspberries, and pumpkins. The farm stand has baked goods, soups, pies, vegetables, cider, and apples. Open daily mid-April through Christmas. Call for pick-your-own days and hours.

Noquochoke Orchards, 594 Drift Rd., Westport, MA 02790; (508) 636-2237. George and Sue Smith are the stewards of this eighty-acre family farm, where some of the best qualities of southeastern Massachusetts agriculture are manifest. The orchards are a regional treasure, producing (at last count) ninety-eight varieties of apples, covering the entire harvest season with both cooking and eating varieties, along with nine different pears, sixteen different peaches, and four kinds each of plums, apricots, and quinces. Although the orchards demand the lion's share of the Smiths' efforts, they also grow strawberries, elderberries, sweet corn, squash, tomatoes, and the local heirloom root vegetable, the Westport Macomber (see sidebar). The Smiths hand-wash their cider apples before pressing, then sterilize the cider with ultraviolet light, thereby avoiding the cooked taste of most stable fresh ciders. The farm stand is open weekends August through November, and the Smiths usually welcome visitors on weekdays as well, although you'll have to sort through the harvesting bins in the barn instead of selecting from the farm stand display.

Westport Macomber

The growing movement to "eat local" has sparked interest in the intensely local Westport Macomber. This cross between a radish, turnip, and cabbage was developed on a farm that had been in the Macomber family since the seventeenth century. In 1876 brothers Adin and Elihu Macomber planted radishes next to rutabagas (themselves a cross between a cabbage and a turnip) to allow for cross-pollination. The resulting vegetable—with its white flesh, sweet flavor, and aroma of horseradish—became known, logically enough, as the Westport Macomber. Harvested in October and November, macombers have become popular with local chefs. You might find them used in soups or baked goods or mashed (alone or with carrots or potatoes). If you want to try them yourself, Kerry Downey Romaniello, the executive chef at Westport Rivers Vineyard and Winery, advises buying macombers that are solid and fairly dense. Wash and peel them before boiling. She notes that many aficionados believe that macombers are best after the first frost.

Oakdale Farm, 59 Wheaton Ave., Rehoboth, MA 02769; (508) 336-7681. Richard and Mary Pray's fields and greenhouses yield corn, summer and winter squashes, tomatoes, collards, lettuces, and dozens of types of culinary and medicinal herbs. Their retail shop sells dried herbs and herb and flower flats, as well as candles, wreaths, and other decorative craft items. Many of the crops are pick-your-own, including the fresh herbs. Open April through December. Call for days and hours.

Pine Hall Farm, 588 Middle Rd., Acushnet, MA 02743; (508) 995-0041. Pine Hall offers pick-your-own blueberries and dry-harvest cranberries in season—July and August for the blueberries, August and September for the cranberries. A few blueberry areas are wheelchair accessible. Open mornings only in season.

Sampson Farm, 222 Old Bedford Rd., Westport, MA 02790; (508) 674-2733. People unfamiliar with southeastern Massachusetts are often surprised to discover how many farmers grow potatoes. Jerome Sampson has seventy of his hundred acres in potatoes, and while he sells most of the crop to the wholesale market, he also maintains a small retail stand. Open mid-July to October, Monday through Friday 3:00 to 6:00 p.m., Saturday 9:00 a.m. to 5:00 p.m., and Sunday 10:00 a.m. to 5:00 p.m.

Spring Meadow Farm, 109 Marion Rd., Mattapoisett, MA 02739; (508) 758-2678. Monika Weldon and husband Peter Belanger grow raspberries, blackberries, and strawberries on this small berry farm certified as organic by the Northeast Organic Farms Association. The warm exposure on Buzzards Bay means strawberry picking begins the last weekend in May. Open Wednesday, Saturday, and Sunday in season.

Wilted Spinach Salad with Dried Cranberries, Pecans, and Feta

Make this salad in the fall or spring, when local spinach is tender and tasty. Tossing the salad with hot olive oil causes it to wilt just enough to soften and bring out a bright green color in the spinach. We like the cranberries in this recipe, which is supplied by the Cape Cod Cranberry Growers' Association, because they provide a nice, tart accent without dominating the salad.

1 small red onion
8–9 cups spinach leaves, washed and patted dry
½ cup coarsely chopped toasted pecan halves
4 ounces feta cheese, crumbled
¼ cup dried cranberries
1 tablespoon chopped fresh mint leaves
2 tablespoons sherry vinegar

Pinch of salt
6 tablespoons olive oil
Freshly ground black pepper

Garlic Croutons
12 thin slices baguette or other artisanal bread
Olive oil
1 large clove garlic

1. Quarter and thinly slice the red onion. Place the slices in cold water and allow to soak for 30 minutes. Drain and pat dry.
2. Meanwhile, make the croutons. Brush the bread slices with olive oil. Toast the slices in a 375°F oven until nicely browned. Peel the garlic clove and smash it. Remove the bread slices from the oven and rub with the garlic. Set the croutons aside.
3. Place the soaked onion slices, spinach, pecans, feta, cranberries, mint, and vinegar in a large mixing bowl. Toss together with a large pinch of salt.
4. In a saucepan, heat the olive oil to just below smoking. Pour the hot oil over the salad in the bowl, tossing well as you do. Taste, then correct the seasoning with salt, pepper, and vinegar. Serve with croutons.

Serves 6

CRAZY ABOUT CRANBERRIES

Cranberries have a long history in Massachusetts. Native Americans ate fresh cranberries and also combined them with cornmeal to make bread or with dried deer meat and fat to make that precursor of the energy bar, pemmican. A recipe for cranberry sauce appears in a 1663 Pilgrim cookbook, but the berries didn't really become popular until the late nineteenth century, when enough sugar was imported from the West Indies to balance their natural astringency.

Today, Massachusetts produces nearly half of all cranberries grown in the United States, and most of the state's cranberry bogs are located in the swampy flatlands of Plymouth County. If you're driving around southeastern Massachusetts in October, turn off the main road to be treated to the stunning sight of bright red cranberries floating on deep blue water as they wait to be harvested.

You might want to time your visit for the mid-October **Cranberry Harvest Festival** at Edaville USA (off Route 58, South Carver; 508-295-5799). You'll probably have a chance to watch farmers operate big "egg beaters" that separate the berries from the vines so that they float to the surface of the water and can be gathered and suctioned into waiting trucks.

For a more low-key cranberry encounter, stop by **Flax Pond Cranberry Company** (1 Robbins Path, Carver, MA 02330; 508-866-2162) in the afternoon from late September to late October. You'll turn down a packed-sand road and pass old, weathered buildings where ancient pickup trucks are parked out front. Farther in are massive rectangular bogs. Jack and Dot Angley talk a bit about cranberry growing and demonstrate the "dry" method of cranberry harvesting. Visitors can try their hand at screening berries on an antique separator and can sample cranberry juice and raw berries "if they dare." There's even a small gift shop.

Ward's Berry Farm, 614 South Main St., Sharon, MA 02067; (781) 784-6939. Fields are open Thursday through Tuesday for pick-your-own strawberries, blueberries, and raspberries. The farm stand also has farm-grown vegetables and baked goods—including Ann Ward's legendary (and huge) blueberry muffins in season.

Fishmongers

Amaral's Market, 488 Belleville Ave., New Bedford, MA 02746; (508) 996-1222. Portuguese life in America is distilled at this excellent market that specializes in fresh and frozen fish. The cases of fish on crushed ice take up a large corner of the store, and here you'll find fish that never make it to the Anglo markets, such as chinchards (North African horse mackerel that are usually grilled) and large herring, as well as some that do, such as sea bass, haddock, hake, fresh squid, perch, pollack, and sea bream. Look into the frozen food cases and the selection expands to include frozen octopus (whole and sectioned). Several brands of salt cod (*bacalhau*) are also available. This is one of the rare places where you can find freshly rendered cooking lard (a huge improvement over the usual waxy grease sold as lard) and a refrigerator case where chocolate chip cookie dough is sold next to blood sausages. Amaral's also carries Martin's cheese, a Portuguese-style fresh cheese made locally. Open daily.

Cape Quality Seafood, 657 Dartmouth St., Dartmouth, MA 02748; (508) 996-6724. Here's another outstanding fish market that caters to the more Catholic tastes of the ethnic populations of southeastern Massachusetts. It's one of the few spots where you'll find periwinkles next to littleneck, steamer, and chowder clams. Cape Quality also sells large (five- to seven-pound) lobsters, shucked-out lobster tails and claws, and the full range of finfish caught by local fishermen. Many ready-to-heat items are available, including stuffed quahogs. If you want to sit down and eat, there are several booths (separate entrance) where broiled, baked, steamed, and fried fish and shellfish are served, along with a few grilled steaks. Open Tuesday through Sunday.

Westport Lobster Company, 915 Main Rd., Westport, MA 02790; (508) 636-8500. While it might seem peculiar to find a fishmonger along a main road, keep in mind that this end of Westport is a thin peninsula and fishing boats are moored not more than a hundred yards away. The unassuming brown-shingled 1875 former stable fairly brims over with the ocean's bounty. Deep-sea fish such as swordfish and tuna are usually available, as are more coastal cod, flounder, and haddock. Fresh shellfish varieties include quahogs, littlenecks, mussels, steamer clams, and oysters. As the name suggests, there's never a shortage of lobster (or crabs, for that matter). Westport Lobster also smokes salmon, trout, mussels, haddock, and scallops. Open Tuesday through Sunday.

Grist Mill Corn Bread

If you've ever wondered about the origins of the phrase "nose to the grindstone," stop in at the Jenney Grist Mill in Plymouth for a graphic demonstration. The 1970 mill is a re-creation of the original one built on this site in 1636, which was in continuous operation until destroyed by a fire in 1847. Today the owners grind organic corn from Champlain Valley, New York. Meal can be purchased in the gift shop, which is open April through Thanksgiving (call for hours) or by mail order the rest of the year.

Gray's Grist Mill

**638 Adamsville Rd.
Westport, MA 02790
(508) 636-6075
http://graysgristmill.com**

**Jenney Grist Mill
Museum**

**Up from Town Brook,
off Summer St.
Plymouth, MA 02760
(508) 747-4544**

Gray's Grist Mill in Westport has been producing Rhode Island Jonny Cake Meal since 1878. The mill sits close to the Rhode Island border and uses an heirloom variety of white cap flint corn grown on a local farm. You can buy it at the gift shop at the site. The mill is open year-round, daily from spring through fall; call for off-season hours.

This recipe from the Jenney Grist Mill makes a classic New England–style corn bread with a hint of sweetness and a nice crunch to the crust if cooked in a cast-iron pan.

1 cup cornmeal	½ teaspoon salt
1 cup all-purpose flour	1 cup milk
5 tablespoons sugar	1 egg
4 teaspoons baking powder	¼ cup vegetable oil

1. Preheat oven to 425°F. Place dry ingredients in a bowl and mix.
2. Put milk, egg, and vegetable oil in a small bowl; beat until smooth. Add to dry ingredients.
3. For bread, pour batter into a greased 8-inch square pan and bake for 20 to 25 minutes. For muffins, pour into a lined muffin tin and bake for 15 to 20 minutes. Muffins are done when cake tester comes out clean.

Makes 12 muffins or 1 loaf

Woods Seafood Market & Restaurant, Town Pier, Plymouth, MA 02360; (508) 746-0261. With all the emphasis on turkeys, it's easy to forget that Plymouth was founded first and foremost as a fishing village. Woods continues the tradition in style from a large gray building on Town Pier. One end is the fish market, which carries the usual fresh Cape Cod Bay fish (flounder, cod, haddock), several deep-sea fish (tuna, swordfish, shark), mussels, sea and bay scallops, and all variety of clams. Crustaceans, of course, abound, with both large and small lobsters available. If you feel the need to eat your fish immediately, place an order at the take-out window and carry your sandwiches or fried plates to booths or tables in a large glassed-in room overlooking the ocean.

Food Happenings

Mid-June: **Summertime Polish Feast,** sponsored by Our Lady of Perpetual Help Church and held at 235 North Front St., New Bedford, MA 02746; (508) 992- 9378. Tents on the lawn of the church offer arts and crafts and live entertainment, but the real focus is on authentic Polish food. On Sunday there's also a polka mass.

July: **Pilgrim Breakfast,** Harlow Old Fort House, 119 Sandwich St., Plymouth, MA 02360; (508) 746-0012; www.plymouthantiquarian society.org. Servers in Pilgrim-era costume deliver cod cakes, homemade baked beans, corn bread, muffins, and juice to diners at outdoor tables on the lawn. Strolling entertainers sing, tell riddles, and generally make merry, seventeenth-century style.

Mid-July: **Annual Clambake,** sponsored by the Lloyd Center for the Environment and held at Demarest Lloyd State Park, 430 Potomska Rd., Dartmouth, MA 02748; (508) 990-0505, extension 13. This environmental research and education organization serves up "an old-fashioned, mouthwatering clambake with all the fixings" to raise funds to support its programs. It's a bit of a splurge but supports a worthy cause.

Early August: **Feast of the Blessed Sacrament,** sponsored by the Clube Madeirense S.S. Sacramento and held at Madeira Field, Belleville Ave. and Earle St., New Bedford, MA 02746; (508) 992-6911; www.portuguese feast.com. Four Madeiran immigrants who wanted to re-create the religious festivals that were so common in the villages of their home island founded the Feast of the Blessed Sacrament in 1915. Today its organizers claim it is the world's largest Portuguese feast and the largest ethnic festival in New England. More than 300,000 people attend for the continuous live entertainment and the Portuguese food specialties, including *carne de espeto* (a form of barbecue), stewed codfish, marinated fresh tuna, *carne guisada* (stewed beef), stewed rabbit, fresh fava beans, sausages, and fried pastries.

Pilgrim Breakfast Fish Cakes

One of Plymouth's best traditions is the annual Pilgrim Breakfast, which has taken place at the Harlow Old Fort House in Plymouth in early July for almost seventy years (see Food Happenings). Guests sit outdoors at big tables and are served family style. The highlight of the meal is "big, fat juicy fish cakes," says Donna Curtin, director of the Plymouth Antiquarian Society. Part of the secret is that they're fried twice. Here's the Society's recipe as served for many years.

1 pound pollock fillets
1 pound codfish fillets
2 medium Red Bliss potatoes,
    peeled and cubed
1–2 tablespoons milk
1 tablespoon olive oil, plus 1
    quart for frying
1 large onion, minced
1 tablespoon Old Bay Seasoning

½ teaspoon white pepper
½ teaspoon salt
½ teaspoon sugar
1 teaspoon garlic powder
½ teaspoon baking powder
2 cups corn flour or commercial
    clam fry mix
1 cup crushed cornflakes

1. Cube pollock and codfish and place in large pot. Add water to cover. Bring to boil, reduce heat, cover, and simmer until fish begins to fall apart. Remove fish with slotted spoon or spatula. Let fish cool.

2. Add potato cubes to fish water, cover, and simmer 10 minutes or until tender. Drain potatoes and whip with electric mixer, adding milk as necessary to gain volume and make smooth.

3. While potatoes are whipping, heat 1 tablespoon
   olive oil in a 10-inch frying pan and sauté onion
   until browned. Remove from heat and drain onions
   on paper towels.
4. Mash cooled fish into flakes and add to potatoes.
   Continue whipping as you add Old Bay Seasoning,
   white pepper, salt, sugar, garlic powder, and baking powder.
   Let cool.
5. Stir onions into fish-potato mixture and shape into 12 fish cakes.
6. Heat remaining 1 quart olive oil to 375°F in a 4-quart pot.
7. Dredge fish cakes in corn flour and deep-fry, a few at a time. Remove
   to cookie sheet to cool. (At this stage, fish cakes can be wrapped
   tightly and frozen for up to 2 weeks or refrigerated overnight before final
   cooking.)
8. Add crushed cornflakes to remaining corn flour to make sweeter,
   crunchier breading mix.
9. Reheat the 1 quart olive oil to 375°F.
10. Dredge fish cakes in corn flour–cornflake mixture and deep-fry
    until golden brown.

Serves 6

Early September: **Bourne Scallop Fest,** Buzzards Bay Park, Main St., Buzzards Bay, MA 02532; (508) 759-6000. Buzzards Bay is renowned for its scallops, and this long-standing annual celebration of the harvest features grilled, fried, and baked scallop dishes along with crafts, entertainment, a parade, and children's games.

Late November: **Thanksgiving Dinner at Plimoth Plantation,** Route 3A, Plymouth, MA 02362; (508) 746-1622; www.plimoth.org. Our modern Thanksgiving grows out of several earlier traditions, including the harvest festival, the commemoration of the Pilgrims' landing at Plymouth, and their Thanksgiving feast the following spring. Thanksgiving as we celebrate it today developed in the Victorian period, as an elaboration of the day of national Thanksgiving first proclaimed by Abraham Lincoln in 1863. The living history museum Plimoth Plantation offers several versions of Thanksgiving dining, each of which makes a nod to the changing traditions around the holiday. The "Victorian Thanksgiving Dinner" is a sit-down feast in Victorian dress with period singers. The museum also offers a classic Thanksgiving dinner buffet menu as well as a la carte dining without reservations on Thanksgiving Day. The buffet and Victorian dinners tend to sell out by mid-October.

Learn to Cook

Johnson & Wales Inn, 213 Taunton Ave., Seekonk, MA 02771; (508) 336-8700 or (800) 232-1772. The renowned Johnson & Wales University culinary arts school in Providence, Rhode Island, maintains this inn as a teaching facility for student training. With its eighty-six rooms—twenty-one of which are two-room suites—it makes an excellent base for exploring southeastern Massachusetts. If the bounty of the area inspires you to sharpen your culinary skills, you can sign up for one of the inn's "Now We're Cooking" packages, which include a three- to four-hour recreational cooking class at the Johnson & Wales campus along with overnight lodging and a $50 certificate toward dinner at Audrey's, the inn's contemporary fine-dining restaurant. Both weekday and weekend classes are available, and course offerings change quarterly.

Landmark Eateries

The Back Eddy, 1 Bridge Rd., Westport, MA 02790; (508) 636-6500; www.thebackeddy.com; $$. Founded by legendary grill chef Chris Schlesinger, this casual bistro overlooking the town harbor is famous for its use of local products: native produce, locally harvested seafood, and regional cheeses, wine, beer, and breads. Some of the summer dishes celebrate the goodness of the season with

Scallion-Crusted Cod with Mango Salsa

Blue Ginger chef Ming Tsai says that this recipe highlights the affinity that Bostonians have for codfish (witness the five-foot-long wooden cod hanging in the State House). The crunchy scallion crust combined with the spicy mango salsa adds his signature East-West touch to this noble fish. The recipe is reprinted with permission from Simply Ming *(Clarkson Potter, 2003; recipe copyright Ming Tsai).*

4 6- to 8-ounce center-cut cod fillets, boned and skinned

Salt and black pepper to taste

2 cups panko or your favorite bread crumbs (panko can be found in most Asian markets and many specialty stores)

½ cup sliced scallions

1 egg, gently mixed with 1 tablespoon water to form an egg wash

Grapeseed or canola oil

1 cup Mango Salsa (recipe follows)

¼ cup chopped cilantro, plus 1 tablespoon for garnish

1. Preheat oven to 400°F.
2. Season the cod with salt and pepper on both sides.
3. On a plate, mix the panko and scallions. Lightly brush the seasoned fillets with the egg wash and dredge in the panko.
4. In a sauté pan over medium heat, coated lightly with 2 tablespoons oil, cook the fillets until first side is browned. Gently flip fillets and transfer to the oven, cooking until the other side is brown and fish is cooked through, about 6 to 8 minutes.
5. Meanwhile, mix the salsa with the cilantro.

6. Spoon a thin layer of salsa in the center of four plates, forming circles slightly larger than the fillets. Top salsa with hot fillets and garnish with cilantro.

Spicy Mango Salsa

To dice mango, peel first whole, then slice along the seed starting from outside in to make mango slices. Stack for julienne, then dice. Tsai recommends rolling the lime on a hard surface to soften it before juicing.

**1 large ripe mango, peeled and cut into
¼-inch dice**
1 small red onion, cut into ¼-inch dice
**1 red jalepeño pepper, stemmed and
minced**
1 tablespoon minced ginger
**1 teaspoon sambal (Asian chile paste) or
6 shakes of Tabasco sauce**
2 tablespoons fresh-squeezed lime juice
Salt and black pepper to taste

In a large bowl, gently mix together the mango, onion, jalepeño, ginger, sambal, and lime juice. Season to taste with salt and pepper.

Serves 4

Blue Ginger

**583 Washington St.
Wellesley, MA 02482
(781) 283-5790
www.ming.com/blueginger.htm**

sheer exuberance—pasta with roasted fresh corn, chopped tomatoes, and julienned basil, for example. The wood grill is pressed into service in most preparations, though, with grilled seafood and barbecue making up the bulk of the menu. Dinner is served daily, lunch on weekends.

Blue Ginger, 583 Washington St., Wellesley, MA 02482; (781) 283-5790; www.ming.com; $$$. Chef and owner Ming Tsai, Food Network star and cookbook author, makes Blue Ginger his home base. Unlike many celebrity chefs, he's often cooking at his own restaurant—you'll spot him in the open kitchen most nights. Known for his matchmaking of Asian and European cuisines, Tsai composes dishes where the elements cooperate rather than compete, serving Long Island duck breast in a five-peppercorn sauce, for example, with a leek–taro root hash and braised baby bok choy. Open Monday through Friday for lunch, daily for dinner.

Mimo Restaurant, 1526–1530 Acushnet Ave., New Bedford, MA 02746; (508) 997-8779; $. Take a look at the wine list before you even bother to read the menu and you'll understand that this casual restaurant is serious about Portuguese cuisine. The list of roughly eighty wines is broken down by region of Portugal (Alentejo, Dão, Douro, Ribatejo, Setúbal, Bucelas, etc.). A short list of wines appears, almost as an afterthought, under "United States," and an even shorter list under "Rest of the World." The food ranges even more widely, pulling in some of the former Portuguese colonies (*camarão á Moçambique,* or shrimp Mozambique, for example, and a Brazilian version of stewed salt cod), as well as the classics of the home country (*puerco Alentejana,* or marinated pork cubes in a brown sauce with clams). The lunch menu, by contrast, leans heavily on simple sausage dishes and sandwiches. Open daily for lunch and dinner.

Riva, 116 Front St., Scituate, MA 02066; (781) 545-5881; www.riva restaurant.net; $$. This casual trattoria on Scituate harbor was founded by the Burke family (as in legendary Boston-area chef Jimmy Burke), and it continues the market-driven approach to fine Italian cuisine, employing the incredible local produce, fish, and shellfish. Forget the menu and order from the specials: the lobster pasta of the day, the fish of the day. In the summer, don't miss the bountiful salads or the bruschetta with sliced ripe tomatoes, herbs, and sheep's-milk cheese. In cold weather, few dishes are as welcoming as the  slow-roasted chicken marinated with lemon, garlic, and herbs. Open Wednesday through Sunday for dinner, also for lunch from June through August.

Shawmut Diner, 943 Shawmut Ave., New Bedford, MA 02746; (508) 993-3073; www.theshawmutdiner.com; $. The neon Indian atop the Shawmut glows, his reflection flashing off this large aluminum diner like a clarion call from America's roadside past. This

New Bedford landmark is perpetually jammed in the mornings, but it serves breakfast food all day as well as grilled sandwiches, burgers, hot dogs, and such diner specialties as American chop suey at lunch. Open daily until 2:30 p.m., Friday until 8:00 p.m.

Brewpubs & Microbreweries

Buzzards Bay Brewing Company, 98 Horseneck Rd., Westport, MA 02790; (877) 287-2421 or (508) 636-2288; www.buzzardsbrew .com. Allied with Westport Rivers Winery, this microbrewery sits on a 140-acre family farm. You'll see hops growing along the drive to the three-story barn that houses the brewery and retail shop. Unlike many small breweries, Buzzards Bay makes both ales (top-

fermented beers ready for bottling in two weeks) and lager beers (bottom-fermented at a cooler temperature for three weeks). Year-round brews include Buzzard Lager, made with a Munich malt and German Hallertauer hops; Buzzard Black Lager that includes a Carafa black malt and three types of hops; and a pilsner with sprightly pale and Vienna malts and crisp Hallertauer and Saaz hops. Several seasonal brews are also produced, including an Oktoberfest and a wheat beer. All are available at about 350 stores and restaurants in Massachusetts and Rhode Island and at the brewery. Retail store open Saturday 11:00 a.m. to 5:00 p.m. from April through December (brewery tours every half hour).

Plymouth Bay Winery, 114 Water St., Plymouth, MA 02360; (508) 746-2100; www.plymouthbaywinery. Located just across the street from Plymouth Harbor, this small winery produces a variety of sweet and semisweet wines from cranberries, raspberries, blueberries, and peaches. The company also makes cranberry, raspberry, and blueberry pancake syrups. Free tours and tastings. Open Monday through Saturday 10:30 a.m. to 5:00 p.m. (until 9:00 p.m. late June to Labor Day), Sunday noon to 5:00 p.m. Closed January and February.

Plymouth Colony Winery, 56 Pinewood Rd. (off Carver Rd.), Plymouth, MA 02360; (508) 747-3334; www.plymouthcolonywines .com. Opened in 1982, this winery was a pioneer in making cranberry wines, says winemaker Charlie Caranci, who confesses, "I eat raw cranberries by the fistful." The winery occupies a small yellow building—originally a berry screening house—along

Roast Turkey with Rosemary-Scented Stuffing

Kerry Downey Romaniello is the talented executive chef at Westport Rivers Winery and author of Out of the Earth: A Heritage Farm Coast Cookbook *(Spinner Publications, 2000), from which this recipe is reprinted with permission. Wine is used to season and moisten this stuffing. Romaniello suggests serving the turkey with unsweetened but slightly warmed applesauce, buttered rice or delicately seasoned mashed potatoes, and steamed broccoli or late-season corn.*

Stuffing
1 cup bread crumbs
1 teaspoon fresh rosemary leaves
1 clove garlic
1 small yellow onion, peeled and quartered
¼ cup slivered dried apple or apricot
¼ cup Johannesburg Riesling

6 turns on a mill or a generous pinch black pepper
¼ teaspoon salt

Turkey
2- to 3-pound boneless turkey breast, skin and tender on
1 teaspoon brown sugar
Salt and black pepper

1. Preheat oven to 425°F.
2. Place the bread crumbs, rosemary, and garlic in a food processor with the chopping blade and pulse until the rosemary and garlic are in tiny pieces and thoroughly incorporated into the bread crumbs. Dump the mixture into a small mixing bowl.

3. Drop the onion and dried fruit into the food processor and pulse-chop to small bits, then add to the mixing bowl of crumbs. Stir in the wine and seasonings and combine completely. Set the stuffing aside.

4. Place the turkey skin-side down on a cutting board, with the narrow end pointing toward you. Fold the tender out over the nearest edge, then, with a thin sharp knife, slice a flap from top to bottom, from the center out toward the edge opposite the tender. (The breast can be ordered butterflied from the butcher to save time.)

5. Open the meat up and spread the stuffing in the center, leaving a small border around the edges. Fold the tender back over, then fold the cut side over that. Tuck any extraneous meat or skin in and turn the whole shebang into a small glass baking dish, skin-side up.

6. Rub the skin with the brown sugar and season with salt and pepper. Roast for 30 minutes. Then turn the oven down to 350°F and cook turkey for 45 minutes to 1 hour, until completely cooked. (Meat thermometer inserted into breast should read 165°F.)

7. Allow turkey to sit at room temperature for 15–30 minutes before slicing. Leftovers can be refrigerated for several days if tightly wrapped.

Serves 4–6

**Westport Rivers Vineyard
& Winery**

**417 Hixbridge Rd.
Westport, MA 02790
(508) 636-3423 or
(800) 396-9463
www.westportrivers.com**

the banks of a cranberry bog. If you're lucky, you might visit on the two days in October when they harvest the berries. The winery's flagship is the full-bodied and intensely flavored Cranberry Grande, made solely from cranberries. Caranci produces 1,500 to 1,600 cases of cranberry wine a year. He also makes wines from Cayuga and Baco Noir grapes, and from blueberries, raspberries, and peaches. One interesting wine combines cranberries and honey mead. May through December, open Monday through Saturday 10:00 a.m. to 5:00 p.m., Sunday noon to 5:00 p.m. February through April, open Saturday 10:00 a.m. to 4:00 p.m., Sunday noon to 4:00 p.m. Closed January.

Westport Rivers Vineyard & Winery, 417 Hixbridge Rd., Westport, MA 02790; (508) 636-3423 or (800) 396-9463; www .westportrivers.com. Established in 1986, Westport Rivers makes the best varietal grape wines in Massachusetts, perhaps the best in New England. The winery is justifiably famed for its *méthode champenoise* sparkling Chardonnay, from grapes grown on the farm. In addition to the sparkling wines, Westport Rivers also produces a still Chardonnay, Pinot Noir, Riesling, Pinot Blanc, and a small vintage of Rkatsiteli (a variety native to the country of Georgia). Besides the wines (tastings always available), the winery store carries a few select items for picnicking, including Great Hill Blue cheese, local goat cheese, crackers, and biscotti, as well as glasses, picnic baskets, and corkscrews. On the tours, offered on weekends, you walk from the gray-shingled shop to the brown-shingled winery through a grape arbor that frames views of the vineyards. Executive chef Kerry Downey Romaniello directs special programs at the Long Acre House food and education center. Several festivals and special dinners feature local produce, seafood, beef, and specialty foods. May through December, open Tuesday through Saturday 11:00 a.m. to 5:00 p.m., Sunday and Monday 1:00 p.m. to 5:00 p.m. January through April, open weekends only.

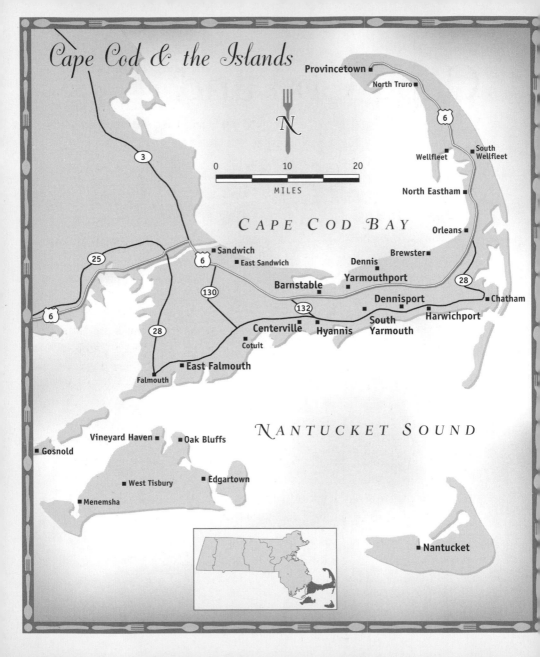

Cape Cod and the Islands

It's obvious from a map that Martha's Vineyard and Nantucket are islands, but so is Cape Cod, separated from mainland Massachusetts by the Cape Cod Canal. The air of impermanence about these land masses is no illusion. Virtually everything you see above water is glacial debris—deposits of rock and grit scraped off the face of New England and left behind when the ice sheets ebbed a hundred centuries ago.

Native peoples did manage to grow corn here for centuries before the English colonists arrived—indeed, their cache of dried corn, pilfered by the Pilgrims in Provincetown, kept some of the Plymouth colonists from starvation over the winter of 1620–21. As European settlers spread onto the Cape and out to the islands in the seventeenth century, they eventually turned to the sea for their living.

And so it is today. Although the few farm stands of the Cape and Islands are nothing short of spectacular, the most prominent thing about the region is not the land, but the ocean. The waters of Cape Cod Bay are no longer so thick with cod that a person could walk from boat to boat on their backs, as some early accounts claimed, but they are rich fishing grounds nonetheless. Sportfishermen speak of striped bass and bluefish runs in these waters as some of the finest in the world, and the halibut and tuna fisheries, especially around the Nantucket shoals, show amazing resilience in an era of otherwise depleted fish stocks.

The real gastronomic success story in the Cape and Islands, however, is shellfishing. Oyster aficionados rank the Wellfleet bluepoint oyster as one of the finest flavored in the world, and the mussel farms on the sandy shoals off Chatham are unparalleled in New England. Order shellfish at the humblest seafood shack on Cape Cod, and you're guaranteed a gourmet treat. Visit town hall for a license, and you can gather your own. It is one of the mysteries of summer that no clams taste as good as the ones you dig yourself and steam on a bed of kelp in a pot of seawater.

This corner of Massachusetts is the state's summer beach playground, attracting hundreds of thousands of vacationers. In America, wherever you find tourists, you also find sweets. Cape Cod is one of the great historical centers for the production of saltwater taffy, and old-fashioned purveyors are still turning out these sticky morsels, each wrapped in a twist of waxed paper. The chocolatiers are comparative latecomers, but they have flourished, and temptation calls on almost every block.

Nantucket Roasters, 15 Teasdale Cir., Nantucket, MA 02584; (508) 228-6862 or (800) 432-1673; www.nantucketcoffee.com. Wes Van Cott has been roasting coffee beans on Nantucket since the spring of 1993, under the slogan, "Don't get burnt, get roasted!" (a sly dig at a certain West Coast roaster often accused of disguising mediocre beans with dark roasts). Look for such rarities as Tanzania peaberry. Roasted beans are available by mail order or through the Web site—or you can taste the goods at the company's coffee shop, **The Bean,** at 29 Center St. in Nantucket (508-228-6215).

Pain D'Avignon, 15 Hinckley Rd., Hyannis, MA 02601; (508) 771-9771; www.french-bread.com. Back in 1992, four friends—three ex-Yugoslavs and a French Canadian—found themselves thrown together on Cape Cod by unpredictable world politics. So they opened an Old World bakery that makes some of the finest breads—try the signature pecan and raisin loaf—in eastern Massachusetts. Dense without being heavy, Pain D'Avignon breads can be the centerpiece of a meal rather than an afterthought. They're widely available at gourmet shops, health food stores, convenience stores, and some supermarkets. The bakery-cafe carries the full line, along with sandwiches, salads, pizza, coffee, pastries, Italian oils and vinegars, French mustards and pâtés,

CRUNCH!

When the Cape Cod Potato Chip Company opened in 1980, it occupied an 800-square-foot kitchen on West Main St. in Hyannis and cranked out 200 bags of chips a day. Now in a state-of-the-art facility near the Hyannis airport, the company makes more than 150,000 bags of chips a day, running through about twenty-eight million pounds of potatoes a year.

The company buys many of its potatoes locally, helping to keep Cape Cod and southeastern Massachusetts farms viable. Machinery relieves most of the drudgery (you try peeling twenty-eight million pounds of spuds . . .) and you can walk down a corridor at the factory to see how potatoes become chips. At the gift shop at the end, pick up some free samples, including experimental products, such as chips made from specific types of potatoes. The company's expanding product line chronicles the public's changing taste in snack foods: popcorn with white cheddar cheese (1987); all-natural popcorn (1989); sour cream and chive, barbecue, and sea salt and vinegar potato chips (1991); reduced fat potato chips (1996); golden russet potato chips (1999); tortilla chips (2000).

Cape Cod Potato Chip Company, 100 Breed's Hill Rd., Hyannis, MA 02601; (508) 775-3358 or (888) 881-CHIP; www .capecodchips.com. Open Monday through Friday 9:00 a.m. to 5:00 p.m.

high-quality cheeses, and organic juices. Bakery-cafe open Monday through Friday 6:30 a.m. to 8:00 p.m., Saturday 8:00 a.m. to 6:00 p.m., Sunday 8:00 a.m. to 5:00 p.m.

Plymouth Tea Co., P.O. Box 907, Chatham, MA 02669; (508) 945-7832; www.plymouthtea .com. Plymouth Tea carries only loose premium or better-grade teas, hand-packing each purchase to ensure absolute freshness. You'll find the whole range of fine teas here, from estate black and green teas to oolong, scented, and white teas, as well as a good selection of herbals such as Cape cranberry and licorice mint. Be warned: You probably won't be able to resist the unusual teapots. Products are available through the Web site.

Specialty Stores & Markets

All Cape Cook's Supply, 241 Main St., Hyannis, MA 02601; (508) 790-8908. This remarkably encyclopedic cooking supply store is divided into two sections. Serious cooks might never get past the initial room of cookware and tools to the second room of giftware. The shop is located about a block from the Nantucket ferry landing, and Nantucketers often swarm into the shop like locusts with platinum cards when the ship comes in. The emphasis here is utility: You can choose among a top-of-the-line professional mandoline for

$200, a couple of good metal mandolines for half that, or a perfectly functional "occasional" plastic mandoline for $15. The shop carries odd sizes of cake pans, baking sheets, tart pans, and pizza pans as well as clam knives, oyster knives, steaming kettles, lobster picks, and a whole wall of kitchen hand tools you didn't know existed but can't live without. Commercial cookware (twenty-gallon stock kettle, anyone?) is also a specialty.

Atlantic Spice Company, Route 6 at Route 6A, North Truro, MA 02652; (800) 316-7965 or (508) 487-6100; www.atlanticspice.com. Open since 1994, this former wholesale herb and spice company carries more than 500 products for cookery and craft, including culinary herbs and spices, spice blends, baking items, shelled nuts and seeds, bulk tea, essential oils, and bins and bins of ingredients for potpourri. Packages tend to be large, but not as large as they were when the operation was primarily wholesale. Medicinal herbs are mostly those also used in cooking or as herbal tea.

Blue Willow Foods & Farm Market, 1426 Route 6 (Post Office Square), South Wellfleet, MA 02667; (508) 349-0900. Half of this tiny shop is devoted to the kitchen where the staff bakes delicious cookies, bars, cakes, and pies and prepares ready-to-cook meals such as crab cakes, Portuguese mussels, marinated steak tips, and grilled scallops with pasta. You can also order coffee and sandwiches to go. During the summer, a substantial farm stand outside overflows with fresh produce from nearby growers.

Cabot's Candies of Cape Cod, 276 Commercial St., Provincetown, MA 02657; (508) 487-3550; www.cabotscandy.com. Owned and operated by third-generation candymakers, this old-fashioned shop makes all its saltwater taffy on the premises. Of the thirty different flavors, molasses peanut butter is the most popular. If you visit during production time, you can see the taffy being wrapped on a sturdy 1920s machine. Cabot's also makes sixteen flavors of fudge and sells a wide variety of chocolates and hard candies.

In a town where contemporary flash and sizzle are the order of the day, Cabot's offers a somehow reassuring window to a more innocent era on old Cape Cod.

Candy Co., 975 Route 28, South Yarmouth, MA 02664; (508) 398-0000. Making a choice here is a little like, well, being a kid in a candy store. The store makes its own barks and nut clusters, but it also sells all the retro small candies of everyone's youth, whether you're seven or seventy years old. When's the last time you saw Licorice All-Sorts, Mary Janes, or Walnettos? Real German Gummis come in a bewildering variety of creepy shapes (bears, worms, frogs). And if you get the itch to make your own chocolates, Candy Co. also carries melting chocolate and molds for Christmas, Easter, and less seasonal themes, such as animals and babies.

Chatham Candy Manor, 484 Main St., Chatham, MA 02633; (508) 945-0825; www.candymanor.com. This family-run business was founded more than a half century ago. The "specialty of the

Manor" is the Turtle, a homemade caramel thick with pecans, walnuts, cashews, or almonds and drenched in milk or dark chocolate. The shop also produces truffles, chocolate-dipped fruits, caramels, and fudge. But on Friday evenings from July through Labor Day weekend, most people come in to pick up a small bag of chocolate creams to eat during the Chatham Band Concerts, which are held in the park next door (beginning at 8:00 p.m.). Among the fancy candy packages, check out the Clambake, which includes a chocolate lobster, a chocolate ear of corn, and candy pebbles and seashells.

Chatham Jam & Jelly Shop, 10 Vineyard Ave., Chatham, MA 02633; (508) 945-3052; www.chathamjamandjellyshop.com. Since 1983 Robert and Carol Cummings have been making preserves at their home on the west side of town, doing all the fruit preparation, cooking, and canning in their kitchen. They pick a number of local fruits, including wild beach plums, cranberries, blueberries, wild blackberries, and wild grapes. In the fall, they travel all over the state to purchase apples, pears, plums, quince, and crabapples directly from the orchards. Products include jams, jellies, marmalades, butters, conserves, and chutneys. The Cummingses keep more than eighty varieties open, so you can taste before you buy.

Cottage Street Bakery, 5 Cottage St., Orleans, MA 02653; (508) 255-2821; www.cottagestreetbakery.com. You might be tempted

to try the almond cream croissants, cranberry almond poppyseed muffins, or
peach date oatmeal muffins. But go
for the Dirt Bomb, a heavenly if messy
muffin, redolent of nutmeg and cinnamon, that sheds sugar even as you try
to break it into manageable pieces. Founder

JoAnna Keeley has retired, but her recipes are lovingly followed
by her successors. Other sweets include bars (lemon, linzer, fig),
cookies (chocolate chip, peanut butter, molasses hermits), breads,
and pies (pumpkin, pecan, apple). At lunchtime the bakery serves
savory soups (Hungarian mushroom, potato leek, pumpkin bisque,
and corn chowder) and sandwiches (roast turkey, boiled ham, and
barbecued chicken).

Dexter Grist Mill, Shawme Pond, Sandwich, MA 02563. Built in
1654, this picturesque mill ground corn for some of the first settlers
in Sandwich. It was restored in 1961 and is open for demonstration
tours June through September. The mill sells freshly ground meal
and updated colonial-era recipes that use it.

Dunbar Tea Shop, 1 Water St. (Route 130), Sandwich, MA 02563;
(508) 833-2485; www.dunbarteashop.com. Located in a circa-1740
carriage house across Water St. from the Dexter Grist Mill, this
tea shop, opened in 1991, has become known as one of America's
finest. The front of the shop carries an extensive line of packaged
and loose teas, teapots, strainers, and tea services. The tearoom is

Honey Pumpkin Tea Bread

This is the taste of fall. If you'd like, you can substitute mashed steamed pumpkin for the canned pumpkin. Enjoy breads like this at the Dunbar Tea Shop with a steaming cuppa.

2 cups all-purpose flour
1 teaspoon baking soda
½ teaspoon salt
½ teaspoon ground cinnamon
½ teaspoon ground ginger
½ teaspoon grated nutmeg
½ cup (1 stick) unsalted butter,
    at room temperature

1 cup honey
1 cup canned pumpkin (not
    pumpkin pie filling)
2 eggs, at room temperature
2 teaspoons lemon juice
1 teaspoon vanilla extract

1. Preheat oven to 350°F. Position rack in center of oven. Generously butter a 9 x 5-inch metal loaf pan and set aside.
2. Sift flour, baking soda, salt, cinnamon, ginger, and nutmeg into a medium bowl. Set aside.

up a few steps, in a wood-paneled former billiard and gentleman's smoking room. Only the fireplace smokes there now, and only in the winter. Additional summer seating is available on the patio and in the shady tea garden for tea, pies, cakes, shortbreads, scones, and tiny sandwiches.

3. In a large bowl, combine butter and honey and beat with an electric mixer at medium speed for 2 minutes or until smooth. Add the pumpkin; beat for 1 minute or until well combined. Beat in eggs one at a time, beating each for 1 minute. Stir in lemon juice and vanilla extract.
4. Add the sifted dry ingredients. With the mixer on low, beat until just incorporated. Increase mixer speed to medium and beat for 2 minutes or until the batter is smooth, scraping down the sides of the bowl as necessary with a rubber spatula.
5. Spread batter in prepared pan. Bake about 65 minutes, or until a cake tester or wooden skewer inserted into the middle of the loaf comes out clean. Cool the bread on a wire rack for 10 minutes, then remove from pan and continue cooling on the rack for 30 minutes before cutting.

Makes 12 slices

Dunbar Tea Shop
1 Water St. (Route 130)
Sandwich, MA 02563
(508) 833-2485
www.dunbarteashop.com

Four Seas Cape Cod, 360 South Main St., Centerville Corners, MA 02632; (508) 775-1394; www.fourseasicecream.com. Cape Cod's oldest ice-cream shop has been operating since 1934 in a small white cottage that was originally a blacksmith shop. Ten small stools line the counter and a half dozen blue and white booths are clustered on

the left side against a wall. Located near Craigville Beach, it's a charming little roadside stop—the forerunner of the Cape's many ice-cream shops, setting the standard for high quality and a wide variety of flavors. Among the more unusual varieties are cantaloupe, penuche (made with brown sugar fudge), coconut, and blueberry frozen yogurt. Four Seas is open daily from the Saturday before Memorial Day weekend through the Sunday after Labor Day.

Hallet's, 139 Route 6A, Yarmouthport, MA 02675; (508) 362-3362; www.hallets.com. Established in 1889, Hallet's was for many years a pharmacy with a soda fountain. The apothecary is gone, but the soda fountain survives, complete with a marble counter and five vintage stools. Belly up to the bar and order ice-cream sodas, malteds, frappes, milk shakes, sundaes, and fountain drinks. You can also purchase breakfast sandwiches and bagels, sandwiches, chowders, and salads. Take a little taste of Hallet's along when you leave: They bottle their own black cherry, sarsaparilla, lemon-lime rickey, birch beer, root beer, and cream sodas.

Marion's Pie Shop, 2022 Main St. (Route 28), Chatham, MA 02633; (508) 432-9439; www.marionspieshopofchatham.com. For a half century this little roadside shop has been providing fabulous baked goods to both loyal locals and amazed vacationers whose motel rooms have microwaves for reheating. Breakfast muffins and coffee cakes are delicious, as are the fruit and pumpkin pies, but the real stars are the savory pies in 6- and 9-inch sizes: chicken (with or without carrots and peas); beefsteak with baby carrots and pearl onions; clams with sautéed onions and clam broth thickened with fresh bread crumbs; hamburger (ground beef and beef gravy); and seafood (lobster, shrimp, scallops, and cod in a sherry-butter-cream sauce). Open daily Memorial Day to Labor Day; call for winter hours.

Murdick's Fudge, 21 North Water St., Edgartown (Martha's Vineyard), MA 02539; (508) 627-8047; www.murdicks.com. Other locations: 5 Circuit Ave., Oak Bluffs, MA 02557; (508) 693-2335; Union St., Vineyard Haven, MA 02568; (508) 693-7344. A box of Murdick's fudge is a tradition for most people who summer on (or even visit) Martha's Vineyard. The company is more than a century old and still uses the same basic recipes of butter, sugar, and all-natural ingredients. Buy by the piece or the box. (A box gets you a handy knife for splitting it up.)

Nantucket Wild Gourmet & Smokehouse, 1223 Main St., Chatham, MA 02633; (508) 945-2700; www.nantucket wildgourmet.com. Born in West Cork, Ireland, Peter O'Donovan came to the Cape as a private chef. He opened Nantucket Wild Gourmet & Smokehouse with marketing guru Marco Protano in 2006. They cold-smoke only line-caught wild fish: king salmon, butterfish, and sushi-grade white albacore from the West Coast and blue-fish and haddock from local waters. Smoked haddock was once a standby in New England cuisine, but it hasn't been readily available for decades. "It blows my mind that more people aren't doing it," O'Donovan says. Certified both kosher and halal, Nantucket Wild Gourmet & Smokehouse uses kosher organic sea salt to prep the fish and pesticide-free wood from Canada to smoke it, often for up to two days at a time. The shop has quickly become a tradition at the Cape's elbow, as vacationers stop on the way to their cottages to pick up the makings of one of the Cape's favorite cocktail hour appetizers: smoked salmon on O'Donovan's home-baked Irish brown bread, spread with cream cheese and topped with a slice of O'Donovan's Swedish pickle with dill. The shop also makes a number of smoked fish pâtés and spreads and carries several unusual gourmet products, including many Moroccan spices and sauces. O'Donovan notes, "I have a food background, so I explain to customers how to use them."

Provincetown Portuguese Bakery, 299 Commercial St., Provincetown, MA 02657; (508) 487-1803. Even amid the crowds on Commercial Street, it's hard to miss this shop, where one of the bakers often stands in the window frying sweet dough in hot oil to make Portuguese *malassadas*. Step inside and you're transported to Portugal with the hefty white bread and rolls, the bakery's justly famous cakelike sweet bread called *massa cevada*, and *trutas*, a southern Portuguese pastry with a brandied filling of sweet potatoes, lemon, and sugar in a shell-shaped crust. Savory treats are also available, including croissants with *linguiça* and cheese and the Portuguese extravaganza sandwich of *linguiça* and cheese in a Portuguese roll, topped with a fried egg. One of Cape Cod's oldest bakeries, Provincetown Portuguese is open daily from Easter to late October.

Something Natural, 50 Cliff Rd., Nantucket, MA 02554; (508) 228-0504; www.somethingnatural.com. Some of Nantucket's best restaurants buy their breads from Something Natural, but you can get the whole wheat, pumpernickel, oatmeal, rye, six-grain, and Portuguese loaves straight from the source. The bakery also sells a wide variety of cookies and pastries and makes sandwiches and salads to eat on-premises or for takeout. Open daily May to mid-October.

Stage Stop Candy, 411 Main St. (Route 28), Dennisport, MA 02639; (508) 394-1791; www.stagestopcandy.com. When you enter this candy shop in the historic Jonathan P. Edward House, Raymond Hebert or his wife, Donna, might greet you at the door with a tray of chocolates to sample. Grandson of the founder of the Hebert candy empire in central Massachusetts, Raymond took his grandfather's recipe books when he moved to Cape Cod in the early 1980s to open his own candy shop. Following his grandfather's entrepreneurial example, he decided to add "a Cape Cod thing" and set out to perfect a cranberry cordial with whole berries. He picked berries in a wild bog, started experimenting, and "got lucky," as

French Breakfast Puffs

Affectionately called Dirt Bombs because the baker gets covered in sugar and spices making them—and so will you when you eat them—these confections are made like a muffin but taste like a doughnut. They were created by JoAnna Keeley, founder of the Cottage Street Bakery. You'll find them, along with dozens of other delights, in her excellent Cottage Street Bakery Cookbook, *available at the bakery.*

⅔ cup shortening or vegetable oil

1½ cups sugar, divided

2 eggs

3 cups all-purpose flour

3 tablespoons baking powder

1 teaspoon salt

½ teaspoon nutmeg

1 cup milk

1½ teaspoons cinnamon

½ cup melted butter or margarine

1. Preheat oven to 400°F. Grease muffin tins to hold 12 muffins.
2. Blend shortening and 1 cup of sugar in large bowl. Blend in the eggs.
3. Sift together the flour, baking powder, salt, and nutmeg.
4. Add flour mixture and milk, alternating, to shortening mixture. Pour batter into muffin tins. Bake until light brown in color (about 20 to 25 minutes).
5. While the muffins are baking, blend the remaining ½ cup sugar and the cinnamon thoroughly in a medium bowl. Set aside.
6. Roll muffins in melted butter, then in sugar-cinnamon mixture while still warm.

Makes 12 muffins

Cottage Street Bakery

5 Cottage St.
Orleans, MA 02653
(508) 255-2821
www.cottagestreetbakery.com

he puts it. "We got it right on the third try." The cordials, which resemble chocolate-covered cherries but are not as sweet, remain one of Stage Stop's leading sellers, along with Hebert's exquisitely smooth truffles. The Heberts recently introduced their Gold Coach line of chocolates, made from single-source cocoas from around the world.

Farmers' Markets

Falmouth Farmers' Market, Peg Noonan Park, Main St., Falmouth. Thursday from noon to 6:00 p.m., late June to late October.

Hyannis/Mid Cape Farmers' Market, Bank of Cape Cod parking lot, 232 Main St., Hyannis. Wednesday from 8:00 a.m. to noon, June to early September.

Nantucket Farmers' Market, corner of Main and Federal Streets, Nantucket. Monday through Saturday from 9:00 a.m. to 1:00 p.m., mid-June to mid-November.

Orleans Farmers' Market, Old Colony Way, Orleans Center. Saturday from 8:00 a.m. to noon, mid-May to mid-October.

Provincetown Farmers' Market, Ryder St. at Town Hall, Provincetown. Saturday from 11:00 a.m. to 4:00 p.m., mid-May to late October.

Sandwich Farmers' Market, Oak Crest Cove Field, Quaker Meetinghouse Rd., Sandwich. Tuesday from 2:00 to 6:00 p.m., mid-June to October.

West Tisbury Farmers' Markets, Grange Hall, State Rd., West Tisbury, Martha's Vineyard. Wednesday (June through August) and Saturday from 9:00 a.m. to noon, mid-June to mid-October.

Farm Stands

Bartlett's Ocean View Farm, 33 Bartlett Farm Rd., Nantucket, MA 02554; (508) 228-9403; www.bartlettsfarm.com. The Bartlett family has been farming these hundred acres since the early 1800s, when William Bartlett sailed over from Marblehead and started plowing the land. Dorothy and John Bartlett continue the tradition of growing flowers, vegetables, tomatoes, lettuces, and greenhouse plants. The Farm Market carries their own produce as well as fruit and dairy products, some from other local producers. You can pick up milk, cheese, and eggs, as well as farm-fresh salads, breakfast snacks, pies, and mostly meatless prepared entrees. The market is open daily from May through the first week of December.

Cape Abilities Farm, 458 Main St. (Route 6A), Dennis, MA 02638; (508) 778-5040; www.capeabilities.org. This highly productive farm employs fifty persons with disabilities to grow a wide variety of fruits and vegetables. The farm's greenhouses keep producing fresh tomatoes and lettuce well into October, when every other farm is reduced to selling just pumpkins and squash. (Cape Abilities has those too.) The stand is open from 10:00 a.m. to 5:00 p.m., July to late October.

Coonamessett Farm, 277 Hatchville Rd., East Falmouth, MA 02536; (508) 563-2560; www.coonamessettfarm.com. Ronald and Roxanna Smolowitz run this twenty-acre farm and "research enterprise," as Ron calls it. Coonamessett grows a panoply of vegetables and fruits in the fields (tomatoes, strawberries, raspberries, garden greens, etc.). What sets the operation apart are the greenhouse hydroponic systems, which produce salad vegetables and herbs throughout the year. Pick your own strawberries, vegetables, herbs, blueberries, raspberries, and pumpkins. The farm also has a small cafe, which usually offers salads, sandwiches, and baked goods, but also serves vegetarian buffet dinners on Friday and Saturday nights during the summer. For a small membership fee, you can get a reduced rate on produce and access to rental canoes to paddle on the abutting Coonamessett Pond. In addition to produce, the shop also sells the farm's own jams and salad dressing as well as alpaca yarn and knit items. Open daily throughout the year.

Eileen Blake's Pies, 515 State Rd., West Tisbury (Martha's Vineyard), MA 02575; (508) 693-0528. Old-fashioned baker Eileen Blake began selling pies from her front yard on Martha's Vineyard in the early 1970s, making up to 135 pies a day from scratch during the frenetic week leading up to Thanksgiving. Her daughter Mary Ellis now continues the tradition. One of the Blake specialties is burgundy pie, which is filled with a mixture of blueberries and cranberries sweetened with brown sugar and spiked with a teaspoon of nutmeg. Mary also makes apple, strawberry rhubarb, pumpkin, pecan, blueberry peach, blackberry peach, and lemon chess pies, as well as a Toll House pie full of chocolate and walnuts. Look for the gazebo along State Rd. near Cronig's Market and the Coop Bank. Open weekends April through June and mid-September through the week before Thanksgiving, daily July through mid-September, daily Friday through Wednesday before Thanksgiving. You can also special-order pies throughout the year. During the off-season, Ellis sells half- and full-size pies at Reliable Market (36 Circuit Ave., Oak Bluffs; 508-693-1102).

Morning Glory Farm, 290 West Tisbury Rd., Edgartown (Martha's Vineyard), MA 02539; (508) 627-9003; www.morninggloryfarm.com. Jim and Debbie Athearn operate Martha's Vineyard's largest and most comprehensive farm stand, selling their own vegetables and berries, baked goods, sweet corn, and huge heads of tender lettuce. The stand also carries fruit from other Massachusetts growers, as

Burgundy Pie

Martha's Vineyard pie maker extraordinaire, the late Eileen Blake, once cautioned that "a recipe is only a rough guide. You have to make it your own." This combination of fruits that are abundant on the Vineyard makes a rich, deeply colored pie. Her daughter Mary Ellis makes her crusts with all-purpose King Arthur flour and Crisco shortening but can't give an actual recipe. "It's all in the feel," she says.

Dough for a double-crust 9-inch pie

2 cups fresh or frozen blueberries

2 cups fresh or frozen cranberries (halved if using fresh)

1 cup firmly packed light brown sugar

¼ cup all-purpose flour

1 teaspoon freshly ground nutmeg

1 teaspoon salt

2–3 tablespoons unsalted butter

1 egg, beaten with 1 teaspoon water to form a glaze

1. Preheat the oven to 400°F. Have on hand a 9-inch pie pan.
2. In a bowl, combine the blueberries, cranberries, brown sugar, flour, nutmeg, and salt; toss until well combined.
3. Divide the pie dough into two parts, one slightly larger than the other. Using as little additional flour as possible, roll out the larger piece of dough and use it to line the pie pan.
4. Spoon the filling into the lined pan, then dot filling liberally with butter.
5. Roll out the remaining dough until it is large enough to cover the pie. Set it on the filling. Fold and crimp the overhang to seal it. Brush the surface with the egg mixture, and cut a few slashes to vent.
6. Bake the pie for about 50 minutes, or until the crust is golden. Let cool to room temperature before serving.

Makes 1 9-inch pie

Eileen Blake's Pies
515 State Rd.
West Tisbury (Martha's Vineyard), MA 02575
(508) 693-0528

well as cheese, peanut butter, crackers, and herbal remedies. Open daily July and August, otherwise Monday through Saturday from Memorial Day until Thanksgiving.

Tony Andrews Farm, 394 Old Meetinghouse Rd., East Falmouth, MA 02536; (508) 548-4717; www.tonyandrewsfarmstand.com. There are plenty of choices at this pick-your-own organic farm with twenty-three acres under cultivation. The season begins with strawberries and lettuce in June and progresses through spinach, peas, peppers, and tomatoes in summer before winding down with squashes and pumpkins in the fall. The farm stand also has other vegetables and cut flowers, as well as fruit from area orchards, local cider, eggs, jams, honey, and breads. In the course of the season you might find wax beans, lima beans, broccoli, cauliflower, lettuces, peppers, white zucchini, pumpkins, Silver Queen corn, tomatillos, Swiss chard, parsley, eggplant, Japanese eggplant, cucumber, shell beans, several kinds of squash, cabbage, kale, strawberries, and rhubarb. There's always a surprise, as owner Geoffrey Andrews likes to experiment with new crops and varieties each year. Farm stand open daily mid-June through October.

Fishmongers

Catch of the Day Seafood Market & Grill, 975 Route 6, Wellfleet, MA 02667; (508) 349-9090. Located across the highway from the entrance to Marconi Beach on the Cape Cod National

Seashore, Catch of the Day features little-neck clams and oysters from shellfish beds at Mayo Beach on Cape Cod Bay. Not only does the market have a breathtaking selection of perfect fish beautifully displayed, the staff will also cut and cook everything to order. Despite the casual feel—wooden picnic tables outside, wooden stools inside—this is definitely not your usual fish shack. Order sesame-seared tuna with a side of crème fraîche, a pan-seared fish of the day with a side of grilled vegetables, or a simple open-face clam roll (steamed littlenecks with spicy red or white garlic sauce). Of course, you don't have to have anything cooked: The owners will happily prepare sushi from the fish on hand. Open mid-April through mid-October.

Chatham Fish & Lobster, 1291 Main St., Chatham, MA 02633; (508) 945-1178; www.chathamfishandlobster.com. Chatham has one of the most dynamic small-boat fishing fleets on Cape Cod, and this fishmonger seems to always get pick of the catch, which means a real treat when the tuna harpooners are working in late summer and early fall. Lobsters range from the dainty one-pounders up to more than six pounds—enough to feed a family. You can buy fresh and prepared seafood, such as fish cakes, crab cakes, marinated mussels, and smoked bluefish, as well as bay and sea scallops, littlenecks, quahogs, and whatever finfish have come off

Cape Cod Crab Cakes

This spicy, colorful version of crab cakes comes from Chatham Fish & Lobster. If panko is not available, substitute unseasoned white bread crumbs.

3 tablespoons clarified butter
4 teaspoons olive oil
1 tablespoon finely diced onion
1 tablespoon finely diced red pepper
1 tablespoon finely diced yellow pepper
1 tablespoon finely diced celery
2 tablespoons chopped parsley
1 cup panko

¼ cup mayonnaise
1 egg, beaten
1½ teaspoons Dijon mustard
1 tablespoon lemon juice
1 teaspoon Creole seasoning
2 teaspoons Worcestershire sauce
1–2 dashes Tabasco sauce
1 pound shredded crabmeat
Salt and pepper to taste

1. Heat about 1 tablespoon clarified butter and 1 teaspoon of olive oil in a sauté pan. Sauté the onions, peppers, and celery until the onion is opaque.
2. Add the parsley and sauté for 30 seconds; remove from the heat.
3. In a large bowl, combine the panko, mayonnaise, egg, cooled vegetables, mustard, lemon juice, Creole seasoning, and Worcestershire and Tabasco sauces. Mix very well. Add the crabmeat and mix in gently.
4. Form into 8 cakes, each ¾ inch thick. Heat remaining 2 tablespoons butter and 3 teaspoons oil in a pan. Fry the crab cakes on each side until golden brown. Serve with additional Worcestershire and Tabasco sauces and lemon wedges.

Serves 4

Chatham Fish & Lobster
1291 Main St.
Chatham, MA 02633
(508) 945-1178
www.chathamfishandlobster.com

Ring Brothers Marketplace
485 Route 134
South Dennis, MA 02660
(508) 394-5004

the boat that day. Check out the wall of happy seafood-fed kitties, aka the Chatham Fish Wall of Cats. Just watch the little ones: A sign warns, KEEP YOUR CHILDREN UNDER CONTROL OR WE'LL SERVE THEM TO THE LOBSTERS. The adjacent **Marine Cuisine Restaurant** offers an even broader choice of prepared food for eating at the tables or taking home. Dishes range from fish tacos to lobster BLTs to a seafood lasagna with layers of scallops and shrimp. Marine Cuisine is open Wednesday through Monday for lunch and dinner; call (508) 945-1173 for winter hours. Chatham Fish & Lobster also has a second fish market at the **Ring Brothers Marketplace,** 485 Route 134, South Dennis, MA 02660; (508) 394-5004.

Cuttyhunk Shellfish Farms, Town Wharf, Gosnold, MA 02713; (508) 990-1317; www.cuttyhunkshellfish .com. Most of the oysters and clams that this aquaculture operation raises are sold to restaurants and wholesalers, but on summer afternoons there's also a floating raw bar on Cuttyhunk Pond, where you can purchase oysters and clams on the half shell, shrimp cocktail, crab spread, clam chowder, and stuffed quahogs (spicy or mild).

Green Pond Seafood, 366 Menauhant Rd., East Falmouth, MA 02536; (508) 540-1901; www.greenpondseafood.com. Located on the water at Green Pond Bridge, at the edge of a busy marina of pleasure boats, this small fish shack has been making locally famed stuffed quahogs since 1960. (The owners claim that Sara Lee and

Pillsbury have both tried without success to buy the recipe.) Stop by and decide for yourself whether they live up to their fame, but call one hour ahead if you want them to also cook you a lobster. Otherwise you can choose from fried fish, clams, scallops, calamari, shrimp, shrimp cocktail, lobster and seafood rolls, and clam chowder. The market case always has steamer clams and quahogs, a variety of finfish, and scallops in season. Live lobsters are always available.

Hatch's Fish Market, 310 Main St., Wellfleet, MA 02667; (508) 349-2810; www.hatchsfishmarket.com. Over the years, Hatch's has evolved from a simple stand behind the town hall into a lean-to and finally into an enclosed building. Whatever the local fishermen are catching or digging, Hatch's is selling. Hatch's also smokes fish and mussels and makes pâté. The lobster pool is always full of the Cape's favorite crustacean, and Hatch's will steam them on the spot. The biggest selection, however, is shellfish, including local bluepoint oysters, prized as some of the finest in the Northeast. During July and August a produce stand almost obscures the fish market as it overflows with local tomatoes, peppers, summer squash, and corn. Open late May through mid-September.

Larsen's Fish Market, Menemsha Harbor, Menemsha (Martha's Vineyard), MA 02552; (508) 645-2680. Although a few fishing boats venture from other ports, Menemsha remains the only true fishing village on Martha's Vineyard, and Larsen's is the place to go in the village for the fresh catch. In addition to the full array of finfish and shellfish, Larsen's also makes crab cakes (to take home or have heated on the spot), hors d'oeuvres, and specialty dips and will cook lobster, steamer clams, and mussels to order. The market also has a raw bar featuring oysters, littlenecks, and cherrystone clams. If you're on Martha's Vineyard but you can't get out to Menemsha, you can purchase the same fish (cooked or not) at **Edgartown Seafood Market** (138 Cooke St., Edgartown, MA 02539; 508-627-3791).

Nauset Fish Market & Lobster Pool, 38 Route 6A, Orleans, MA 02653; (508) 255-1019; and **Sir Cricket Fish & Chips;** (508) 255-4453. The market justifiably calls itself the "Home of the King-Size Lobster." Indeed, many of the crustaceans swimming in the icy water of its tanks are around eight pounds. (The largest ever sold was thirty-three pounds.) In addition to big lobsters, Nauset Fish has fresh finfish, clams, mussels, oysters, frozen dinners and chowders, cooked prepared lobster and crab meat, and shucked clams. Sir Cricket is the attached take-out fish shack, with just a few seats for indoor dining. English-style fish-and-chips, in honor of owner Ron Harrison's English grandfather, is the flagship of the menu, but you can also order fried clams, lobster rolls, fish sandwiches, and crab cakes. Open year-round.

Net Result, 79 Beach Rd., Vineyard Haven, MA 02568; (508) 693-6071 or (800) 394-6071; www.mvseafood.com. This operation is the largest distributor of seafood on Martha's Vineyard. Operated by the Larsen family, Net Result expanded recently with an on-premises cafe for steamed lobster, clams, sushi, and other briny delights. The cafe also packs up cooked fish for take-out and will ship fresh fish and shellfish overnight to anywhere in the continental United States.

Straight Wharf Fish Store, Straight Wharf, Harbor Square, Nantucket, MA 02584; (508) 228-1095; www.straightwharfrestaurant.com. Nantucket's fishing fleet is small, but the offshore location and the nearby shoals guarantee an incredible range of fish. This shop carries all varieties of finfish, as well as clams, oysters, lobsters, and crab and its own bluefish pâté and

Net Result Baked Cod

Codfish baked in milk is a classic New England dish, but Beth Larsen of Net Result has developed a twist on tradition that produces an elegant main course— a good dish for company or special occasions. Since cod is a juicy fish and the mushrooms give up their juices, you may have to drain off a little liquid before serving.

1½ pounds fresh codfish fillets
1 cup sliced mushrooms
1 pound small shrimp, shelled
½ teaspoon minced garlic
2 tablespoons butter

1½ cups shredded cheddar cheese
Salt and pepper to taste
¼ cup milk

1. Preheat oven to 350°F.
2. Lay fish in a greased baking dish. Layer mushrooms and shrimp over fish and sprinkle on the garlic. Dot with pats of butter.
3. Cover fish with cheese, season with salt and pepper to taste, and pour milk over top.
4. Bake at 350°F for 30 to 40 minutes, until fish is firm to touch.

Serves 6

Net Result
79 Beach Rd.
Vineyard Haven, MA 02568
(508) 693-6071 or
(800) 394-6071
www.mvseafood.com

DIG YOUR OWN

Shellfish don't come any fresher than those you've just plucked from the sand. Each coastal town has its own regulations and licensing procedure (always more expensive for visitors than residents), but with a little care and a copy of the tide tables, especially for Cape Cod Bay, you can assemble your own feast. Note that Wellfleet, in particular, has set aside specially seeded oyster and clam beds for recreational shellfishing. If you just want to give clam digging a try, Harwich is one of the few towns offering a one-day license for nonresident families. The following are the main shellfish taken on Cape Cod.

Bay scallop (*Argopecten irradiens*): Also called the Cape scallop. Most people eat only the hinge muscle, saving the body for bait. Scallops live about two years and develop a pronounced growth line the second year. Only second-year scallops can be legally harvested. They are found on the bottom in shallow flats and protected bays, often in eelgrass beds. Harvest with a dip net from a boat or wearing waders.

Blue mussel (*Mytilus edulis*): This mussel with a dark blue shell grows in clumps on rocks, pilings, and flats. Gather by hand or with a rake. Scrub well to remove external mud and tiny anchor threads. They open when steamed. (Mussels that don't open should not be eaten.)

Oyster (*Crassostrea virginica*): Oysters live on hard, sandy bottoms or attach themselves to rocks and piers. They must be at least 3 inches long for legal harvest.

Quahog (*Mercenaria mercenaria*): Also known as the hard clam or round clam, quahogs are harvested by digging just below the surface between low and high tide. Clams less than an inch thick at the hinge must be carefully replanted. Small quahogs are often called little-necks; medium-size ones, cherrystones. Those larger than 3 inches are good for chowder, clam pie, or fritters.

Razor clam (*Ensis directus*): Sometimes called the jacknife clam, this strong digger is usually found near the low-water mark. Dig as for soft-shell clams, but deeper and faster.

Sea clam (*Spisula solidissima*): Also known as surf or bar clams, these are the biggest clams found in Massachusetts waters. At 5 to 9 inches, they're good for clam pie or chowder. They're easily dug by hand, as they sit just below the surface of flats exposed at low tide.

Soft-shell clam (*Mya arenaria*): Found 4 to 12 inches below the surface between tide lines, these clams must be dug carefully to avoid breaking their fragile shells. Clams under 2 inches long are seed clams and must be replanted quickly with necks up under a very thin sand layer. Served steamed, fried, or stewed, they are also called steamer, longneck, or long clams.

various marinades. You can also order sandwiches, swordfish and tuna steak, lobster rolls, crab cakes, seafood gumbo, and raw-bar items (clams, scallops, and oysters) to go from late morning until about 7:00 p.m. The dining room at the adjacent **Straight Wharf Restaurant** (508-228-4499) has fancy preparations at fancy prices, but the attached bar/cafe does simpler, less expensive versions. Open in season for dinner only.

Swan River Fish Market, 5 Lower County Rd., Dennisport, MA 02639; (508) 398-2340. "This is where the fishermen unload their catch," explains one of the cheerful young men behind the counter as he trims a large bluefish into fillets. The market offers a complete seafood line from its own day boats. It will also steam lobsters (caught locally, of course) at no extra charge. The fish market, which has a stunning spot on marshlands at the mouth of the Swan River, is open year-round. At the back of the parking lot is one of the Cape's most famed fish restaurants, **Swan River Restaurant** (508-394-4466), serving the complete range of broiled, fried, and sautéed seafood, which comes straight from the boats to the kitchen daily. The dining room's big windows overlook the marsh and river. The restaurant is open for lunch and dinner daily from late May through mid-September.

Mid-May: **Nantucket Wine Festival,** 'Sconset Casino, Nantucket, MA 02554; (508) 228-1128. More than a hundred wineries and restaurants participate in tastings at Nantucket homes, as well as special wine dinners and seminars. The capper is a grand tasting at the 'Sconset Casino.

Mid-June: **A Taste of the Vineyard,** Martha's Vineyard Preservation Trust, 99 Main St., Edgartown, MA 02539; (508) 627-4440. The top restaurants and caterers of Martha's Vineyard turn out to offer samples of their cuisine and beverages to benefit the Preservation Trust.

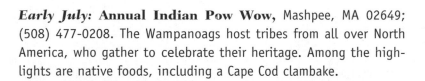

Early July: **Annual Indian Pow Wow,** Mashpee, MA 02649; (508) 477-0208. The Wampanoags host tribes from all over North America, who gather to celebrate their heritage. Among the highlights are native foods, including a Cape Cod clambake.

Mid-August: **Martha's Vineyard Agricultural Livestock Show & Fair,** West Tisbury Fairgrounds, West Tisbury, MA 02575; (508) 693-9549. Sample the baked goods, admire the prize fruits and vegetables, and purchase some of the preserves at this old-fashioned country fair.

***Mid-October:* Wellfleet Oysterfest,** various locations in Wellfleet; www.wellfleetoyster.org. The Atlantic bluepoint oysters of Wellfleet are famed throughout the Northeast as some of the finest cold-water oysters of the region. This festival brings out restaurateurs to show off their oyster dishes, lets champion shuckers compete against one another to separate the bivalves from their shells, and even pits local restaurants against one another. Whatever else happens, you won't leave hungry.

Learn to Cook

Green Briar Nature Center and Jam Kitchen, 6 Discovery Hill Rd., East Sandwich, MA 02537; (508) 888-6870; www.thornton burgess.org. Back in 1903, Ida Putnam began making jams and jellies and operated a tearoom here, turning over the operation to Martha Blake in the early 1950s. Now owned by the Thornton Burgess Society, the building is a "living museum of how Cape Cod used to be," says executive director Jeanne Johnson. Its existing jam kitchen, with twenty propane burners on a long table, dates from 1917. Burgess, the prolific author of such children's books as *The Mother West Wind Stories,* lived in Sandwich until age 18 and often visited the jam kitchen in his youth. Recalling those days, he wrote to Ida Putnam in 1939, "It is a wonderful thing to sweeten the world which is in a jam and needs preserving." The Thornton W. Burgess Museum is open May through October, but the jam kitchen runs two-hour Wednesday evening (for adults) and Saturday morning (for families) jam-making workshops between September and April. All supplies for making jams and preserves are supplied and participants take home four to six full jars. The gift shop also sells the jam kitchen products—chutneys, relishes, salsas, marmalades, jams, and jellies, including (of course) the classic jelly of Cape Cod, beach plum.

Highfield Hall, 56 Highfield Hall, Falmouth, MA 02541; (508) 495-1878; www.highfieldhall.org. This Italianate mansion is an arts and cultural center for Falmouth, and its programs include an extensive list of one-day workshops in everything from knife skills for Asian cooking and stew making to dipping chocolates and decorating tables. The Kids Culinary Academy is a sneaky way to get children involved in the kitchen, with a series of six ninety-minute classes for ages three to five, six two-hour sessions for ages six to ten, and five three-hour sessions for ages twelve to sixteen. Maybe they'll cook for you when they get home!

Landmark Eateries

Black Dog Tavern, Coastwise Wharf, Beach St. Extension, Vineyard Haven (Martha's Vineyard), MA 02568; (508) 693-9223; $$. Also **Black Dog Bakery,** 11 Water St., Vineyard Haven; (508) 693-4786 and **Black Dog Cafe,** 509 State Rd., Vineyard Haven;

(508) 696-8190; www.theblackdog.com; $. This tavern, dating all the way back to 1971, has evolved into a Martha's Vineyard landmark, as much for its unrelenting marketing as for its cozy quarters. The Black Dog logo is emblazoned on everything on- and off-island, it seems. Yet the tavern remains a good place for soups and stews, hearty sandwiches, and a friendly pint of root beer in this dry town. The Black Dog Cafe serves soups and sandwiches on house-made bread. The Black Dog Bakery is more snack-oriented, with muffins, doughnuts, hearth breads, soups, and sandwiches. Tavern open daily for lunch and dinner.

Bookstore & Restaurant, 50 Kendrick Ave., Wellfleet, MA 02667; (508) 349-3154; www.wellfleetoyster.com; $$. The name of this peculiar business should also include "& Shellfish Beds," for the clams and oysters raised a short distance away are the main reasons for seeking out this casual beachside restaurant. The best bet is always the raw bar—especially the clams and Wellfleet bluepoint oysters on the half shell—but the kitchen also makes a stirring Portuguese stew of shellfish and *linguiça* as well as a satisfying plate of baked cod, scallops, and shrimp. In the summer the sun sets over the water behind Great Island—the best views are from the second-floor dining room. Serious imbibers will enjoy the pub atmosphere of the Bombshelter, the basement bar. The bookstore at the back of the building contains a bewildering array of used books and magazines, many of which seem to be the sort left behind in summer rental cottages. Open mid-February through December for breakfast, lunch, and dinner.

Brazilian Grill, 680 Main St., Hyannis, MA 02601; (508) 771-0109; $–$$. Brazilian immigrants flood onto Cape Cod to take many of the seasonal service jobs. Sensing a critical mass, in 2000 Walter Witt and Maximiliano De Paula opened this authentic *churrascaria,* where waiters circulate with long skewers of meat and diners help themselves from a buffet salad table. The barbecue includes several cuts of beef and pork as well as chicken, *linguiça,* lamb, quail, and chicken hearts. If you're not quite ready for the full-press carnivore treatment, you can also order Brazilian specialties from the menu, including *moqueca* (fish and shrimp sautéed in a tomato-cilantro sauce and served in a clay casserole) or *bife à cavalo* (steak and eggs with rice and veg-etables). Open daily for lunch and dinner.

Cape Sea Grille, 31 Sea St., Harwichport, MA 02646; (508) 432-4745; www.capeseagrille.com; $$$. Set on the marshy shores of Harwichport, the Cape Sea Grille has the grace and gentility of a fine country home with the whole bottom floor opened up to provide elegant dining. Douglas and Jennifer Ramler took over the well-established restaurant in 2002 and transformed a fine-dining restaurant into a gourmet destination for creative American cuisine with an emphasis on fresh local shellfish and produce. Doug worked in one of Boston's best French provincial kitchens (Hamersley's Bistro), and the down-home Burgundian touch shows in such appetizers as crispy duck confit in a Swiss chard purse and the house-made country pâté. With such dishes as lobster, shrimp, and scallops tossed with pasta, peas, asparagus, and Pernod cream sauce, his entrees bring Mediterranean style to Cape foodstuffs. A few tables look out the back to gorgeous summer sunsets over the marshes, but that time slot must be reserved far in advance. Open for dinner April through mid-December.

Chillingsworth, 2449 Route 6A, Brewster, MA 02631; (508) 896-3640; bistro $$, restaurant $$$$; www.chillingsworth.com. For more than three decades, Chillingsworth has led the pack as Cape Cod's top haute cuisine dining room, although current management has added a more casual bistro where the a la carte menu features imaginative New American cooking in simpler dishes than those offered in the restaurant's seven-course fixed-price repast. Dine in shirtsleeves with an open collar on seared tuna steak with a salad of Asian vegetables, New York steak frites with grilled onions, or roasted pork loin with polenta. Or opt for the dress-up formal service and culinary complexity of the dining room and start with such treats as oysters in puff pastry and asparagus with morel mushrooms before applying the silverware to a seared duck breast and duck confit salad graced with blackberries and a balsamic vinegar sauce. Chillingsworth has been credited with raising the gastronomic bar all over the Cape. There are even a few rooms upstairs for overnight stays. Bistro open daily for lunch, dinner, and Sunday brunch Mother's Day through Thanksgiving, restaurant for dinner only.

Coonamessett Inn, 311 Gifford St., Falmouth, MA 02540; (508) 548-2300; www.capecodrestaurants .com/coonamessett. Talk about local! Except for six weeks in the dead of winter, all the produce and herbs for fine dining are grown specifically for the 200-year-old Coonamessett Inn. Much comes from nearby Coonamessett Farm (see Farm Stands), some from the inn's own gardens. Local seafood features prominently on the dinner menu and can include such treats as a lobster-and-shrimp-studded "seafood macaroni." Locals come to feast on the weekend prime rib dinners, which always include a popover garnish. Open daily for lunch and dinner and Sunday for brunch.

Home Port Restaurant, 512 North Rd., Menemsha (Martha's Vineyard), MA 02552; (508) 645-2679; www.homeportmv.com; $$$. When owner Will Holtham threatened to close a few years ago, locals panicked. After all, the Home Port has been a Menemsha tradition since 1931, and the large dining room is almost always packed. Fortunately, Holtham relented, and the fishing port's classic dining room, with its wall of mounted fish and weathered wood trim, continues to serve some of the Vineyard's finest fish meals. All prices are for full meals, which include salad, appetizer, entree, and dessert. One of the most popular is the shore dinner of appetizer, corn, lobster, mussels, stuffed clams, and dessert. If you're so foolish as to show up without a reservation (the phone starts ringing in the spring for July tables), you can go to the take-out window and carry your repast to nearby Menemsha Beach for glorious alfresco sunset dining. Open nightly for dinner from late May through mid-October.

Menemsha Galley, Menemsha Harbor, Menemsha (Martha's Vineyard), MA 02552; (508) 645-9819; $. Nestled amid the fishermen's shacks at the end of the harbor, the Galley is the low-cost alternative for waterfront food. The take-out menu is fairly standard, but the Galley is famous for its lobster rolls, which consist of big servings of shredded lobster meat barely held together with a dab of mayonnaise and served on a grilled hot dog bun. Open daily for lunch and dinner Memorial Day weekend through Labor Day.

The Regatta, Route 28, Cotuit, MA 02635; (508) 428-5715; www .regattarestaurant.com; $$–$$$$. It's hard to choose between elegant candlelit dining in the small dining rooms of this landmark circa-1790 mansion or the warm and cozy confines of the newly expanded tap room. Chef-owner Weldon Fizell maintains something of a split personality in the kitchen, producing an elegant New American and French a la carte menu for one of Cape Cod's most sumptuous dining experiences—while producing inventive yet simpler fare for the tap room. On the fine dining side, you might start with local Cotuit oysters before trusting Fizell for the entree trio of local fish and shellfish that changes nightly. But if you're merely ordering a microbrew or a glass of white Sancerre in the tap room, you might find pan-seared scallops with an Asiago risotto and sau-

THE DINNER TRAIN

One of Cape Cod's most moving dining experiences, the **Elegant Dinner Train** of the Cape Cod Central Railroad offers a five-course meal served on crisp white linen tablecloths. It's a taste of a bygone era, and proper dress and advance reservations are essential. The dinner train operates from May through October. The kids aren't left out either. During July and August, the railroad runs a more casual **Family Supper Train.** Adults choose from fare similar to that of the Elegant train, while children have a choice of items such as macaroni and cheese or chicken finger dinners. All trains board at the Hyannis station and travel to the Cape Cod Canal and back.

Cape Cod Central Railroad
252 Main St.
Hyannis, MA 02601
(508) 771-3800 or
(888) 797-7245
www.capetrain.com

téed snow peas a better match. Open Tuesday through Saturday for dinner, nightly in summer.

Toppers, Wauwinet Inn, 120 Wauwinet Rd., Nantucket, MA 02584; (508) 228-8768; www.wauwinet.com; $$$. Back in the mid-1800s, the Wauwinet Inn's predecessor, Wauwinet House, was a shore-front restaurant where patrons arrived by boat. The gastronomy at Toppers is a far cry from the simple shore dinner, but guests who aren't staying at the inn can still arrive on *The Wauwinet Lady,* an open launch that cruises across Nantucket Harbor between the village wharves and the inn. There's even cocktail service on board. Toppers offers elegant New American dining, with a focus on fish and shellfish that hardly seems out of place some 30 miles from the mainland. There are two sophisticated dining rooms, but lunch and brunch guests can also dine on the west-facing terrace (a great spot for sunset drinks). Open daily for lunch, dinner, and Sunday brunch from early May through late October.

THIRSTY NANTUCKET

People always ask what Nantucketers do in the off-season. Well, some of them make beer, wine, and distilled spirits. (They brew, vint, and distill in the summer, too.) You'll find the products of **Cisco Brewery, Nantucket Vineyard,** and **Triple Eight Distillery** at most bars in Nantucket and many on the mainland, but to sample and get a feel for their origins, visit the brewery, winery, and distillery on Bartlett Farm Rd.

Cisco Brewers launched in 1993 as a barrel-at-a-time brewery. Having stepped up to a much larger brewing operation, the company has perfected a line of distinctive craft brews dressed by some of the best-designed labels in the business. The Sankaty Light golden ale is an easy-drinking light beer (3.8 percent alcohol and 128 calories) well suited to a summer beach barbecue. The amber Whale's Tail is a gently balanced English-style ale with just a kiss of Kent Golding hops (perfect with bluefish), while Bailey's Ale is the Nantucket salute to Pacific Northwest pale ales. Master brewer Randy Hudson likes his own ales darker, brewing the Moor Porter so strong and chocolatey that it resembles a stout. The true stout—Captain

Offshore Ale Company, 30 Kennebec Ave., Oak Bluffs (Martha's Vineyard), MA 02557; (508) 693-2626; www.offshoreale.com. This breezy island brewpub is open year-round for lunch and dinner (seafood gumbo, steaks, burgers, pizza). The beers are as amiable as the bar, with the pale and amber ales flowing the most freely. Live entertainment is also on tap most evenings from late spring into the fall.

Swain's Extra Stout—is darker yet, but is dry-hopped with Chinook hops, resulting in a faint pine aftertaste that cuts through the murkiness of the robust malts. Cisco also produces several seasonal ales.

Dean and Melissa Long tried their hands at growing *vinifera* grapes on Nantucket for sixteen years, but conceded that Nature wasn't cooperating. In 1997 they turned instead to vinting fine varietal wines from premium grapes grown in Washington's Yakima Valley, on Long Island, and in California's Central Valley. Nantucket Vineyard now produces Riesling, Chardonnay, Merlot, and Zinfandel wines and has opened a sister operation, Triple Eight Distillery, to make grain spirits, including flavored vodkas.

Tasting rooms open Monday through Saturday 10:00 a.m. to 6:00 p.m., Sunday noon to 5:00 p.m.

**Cisco Brewers, Nantucket Vineyard,
and Triple Eight Distillery**

5 Bartlett Farm Rd.
Nantucket, MA 02584
(508) 228-9235
www.ackwine.com or www.ciscobrewers.com

Cape Cod Winery, 681 Sandwich Rd., East Falmouth, MA 02536; (508) 457-5592; www.capecodwinery.com. Founded in 1994, this ambitious winery is already producing an extensive list of soft, early-drinking wines from its own plantings of French-American hybrid varietals Seyval and Vidal Blanc. The winery has its own mature plantings of Cabernet Sauvignon, Cabernet Franc, Merlot, Chardonnay, and Pinot Grigio that it uses for varietal wines and blends with a splash of cranberry juice. You can visit the winery for tastings and purchases from 11 a.m. to 4:00 p.m. on weekends in spring and fall, Thursday through Sunday during July and August.

Truro Vineyards of Cape Cod, Route 6A (Shore Rd.), North Truro, MA 02652; (508) 487-6200; www .trurovineyardsofcapecod.com. This small winemaking operation is a pioneer in the art of growing European wine grapes in the sandy soils of the outer peninsula. Boasting Cape Cod's first successful *vinifera* plantings, the winery grows its own Cabernet Franc, Chardonnay, Merlot, Cabernet Sauvignon, and Vignoles grapes for its varietal wines, as well as some proprietal blends. The grounds are a real show-case, and visitors are encouraged to stroll through the vineyards, taste the grapes, and peek in on activities in the state-of-the-art winery that opened in 2008. Guided tours are offered Memorial Day weekend through Columbus Day weekend. Open April through

December. The winery also hosts an Annual Grape Stomp and Wine Festival in late September. Open for tasting and sales April through Memorial Day, Friday through Sunday, noon to 5:00 p.m. Also open for sales Memorial Day through October, noon to 5:00 p.m. daily; November through mid-December, Friday through Sunday, noon to 4:00 p.m.

Appendix A: Food Happenings

January

Boston Wine Expo (Boston), 188

Dinner in a Country Village
(Sturbridge), 101

Super Hunger Brunch (Boston), 188

February

Dinner in a Country Village
(Sturbridge), 101

March

Dinner in a Country Village
(Sturbridge), 101

Winter Restaurant Week (Boston), 188

May

Nantucket Wine Festival
(Nantucket), 289

Quaboag Valley Asparagus & Flower
Festival (West Brookfield), 101

Taste of Essex (Essex), 144

World's Largest Pancake Breakfast
(Springfield), 64

June

Lavender Festival (Buckland), 64

New Fish Festival (Gloucester), 144

Scooper Bowl (Boston), 189

Strawberry Festival (Ipswich), 145

Summertime Polish Feast (New
Bedford), 240

Taste of the Vineyard, A
(Edgartown), 289

July

Annual Clambake (Dartmouth), 241

Annual Indian Pow Wow (Mashpee),
289

Boston Harborfest (Boston), 189

Festival Betances (Boston), 189

Pilgrim Breakfast (Plymouth), 240,
242

Religious festivals (Boston), 189

August

Adams Agricultural Fair (Adams), 26

Agricultural Exhibition/Old Sturbridge Village Fair (Sturbridge), 105

Caribbean-American Festival (Boston), 189

Feast of the Blessed Sacrament (New Bedford), 241

Gloucester Waterfront Festival (Gloucester), 145

Martha's Vineyard Agricultural Livestock Show & Fair (West Tisbury), 289

Religious festivals (Boston), 189

Summer Restaurant Week (Boston), 190

Tanglewood Wine & Food Classic (Lenox), 26

Three-County Fair (Northampton), 64

Ware Grange Fair (Ware), 101

September

Bourne Scallop Fest (Buzzards Bay), 244

Deluxe Chocolate Bar opens for season (Boston), 190

Eastern States Exposition (West Springfield), 65

Essex Clamfest (Essex), 146

Fall Festival (Marblehead), 145

Hancock Shaker Village Country Fair & Crafts Festival (Pittsfield), 26

Mahrajan Lebanese Festival (Lawrence), 145

North Quabbin Garlic and Arts Festival (Orange), 65

What's the Fluff? Festival (Somerville), 190

October

Annual Applefest (Princeton), 102

Boston Vegetarian Food Festival (Boston), 191

Brookfield Apple Country Fair (Brookfield), 102

Church bazaars (Boston), 191

Topsfield Fair (Topsfield), 146

Wellfleet Oysterfest (Wellfleet), 290

November

Chocolate Dessert Buffet and Silent Auction (Northampton), 66

Cider Days (Franklin County), 65

Church bazaars (Boston), 191

Thanksgiving Dinner at Plimoth Plantation (Plymouth), 244

December

Cambridge School of Culinary Arts Holiday Bake Sale (Cambridge), 191

Appendix B: Specialty Foods and Produce

The following shops and businesses are especially known for these items, which they produce or grow.

Cheese and Dairy Products

Chocolate and Candy Specialties

Mimo Restaurant, 248
New Bedford Linguiça Company, 225
Provincetown Portuguese Bakery,
270

Russian Specialties
Berezka (market), 165

Sausage
Chicopee Provision Company, 40
Gaspar's Sausage Company Factory
Outlet, 216
Lionette's Market, 173
New Bedford Linguiça Company, 225
Pekarski's Sausage, 48
Wohrle's Food Warehouse, 15

Smoked Fish and Shellfish
Chatham Fish & Lobster, 279, 280
Hatch's Fish Market, 282
Ipswich Shellfish Fish Market, 142
Nantucket Wild Gourmet &
Smokehouse, 269
Net Result, 284
Westport Lobster Co., 238

Spices, Herbs, and Flavorings
Almaeedeh International Market, 221
Atlantic Spice Company, 262
Charles H. Baldwin & Sons (vanilla
extract), 8, 9
Christina's Spices and Specialty
Foods, 168
Ed Hyder's Mediterranean
Marketplace, 84
Oakdale Farm (herbs), 233
Shalimar India Food & Spices, 178
Syrian Grocery Importing Company,
180

Teas
Dunbar Tea Shop, 265, 266, 267
Hong Kong Supermarket (Chinese
herbal teas), 171
Plymouth Tea Co., 261
Tealuxe, 181

Vegetarian Specialties
Coonamessett Farm (buffet), 275
Paul & Elizabeth's (restaurant), 70
Vegetarian Food Festival, 191

Massachusetts Eateries Index

Recipes Index

General Index

M

Mahrajan Lebanese Festival, 145
Malden, 142
Mansfield, 229
Mansfield Farmers' Market, 229
Maple syrup, grading, 42
Marblehead, 129, 134, 145
Marblehead Farmers' Market, 134
Maria & Ricardo's Tortilla Factory, 218
Marine Cuisine Restaurant, 281
Marion, 216, 223
Marion's Pie Shop, 268
Martha's Vineyard, 257–58, 269, 274, 276, 277, 283, 291, 296, 299
Martha's Vineyard Agricultural Livestock Show & Fair, 289
Mashpee, 289
Mattapoisett, 224, 234
Maurizio's, 204
Maynard, 134
Maynard Farmers' Market, 134
McCusker's Market, 48
Melrose, 135
Melrose Farmers' Market, 135
Menemsha, 283, 295, 296
Menemsha Galley, 296
Mercury Brewing Company, 153
Middleboro, 229

Middleboro Farmers' Market, 229
Mike and Tony's Pizzeria at Green Emporium, 68, 69
Millie's Pierogi, 41
Milton, 229
Milton Farmers' Market, 229
Mimo Restaurant, 248
Miss Florence Diner, 68
Miss Worcester Diner, 104
Misty Brook Farm, 99
Mix Bakery, 174
Modern Homebrew Emporium, 174
Montague, 43
Monterey, 6, 10, 28
Monterey Store, 10
Morning Glory Farm, 276
Morse Fish Company, 187
Mountain View Farm, 22
Mrs. Nelson's Candy House, 127
Murdick's Fudge, 269

N

Nantucket, 257–58, 259, 271, 273, 274, 284, 289, 297, 298
Nantucket Farmers' Market, 273
Nantucket Roasters, 259
Nantucket Vineyard, 298
Nantucket Wild Gourmet & Smokehouse, 269

Lemon Tree goods

325 N. Main St
Natick
508-655-2600

Renew

19 S. Main St
Natick
508-318-4892

FRAMINGHAM DOWNTOWN RENAISSANCE
METROWEST REGIONAL TRANSIT AUTHORITY
PRESENT

OCTOBER FEST (ON FARM POND

El domingo, 4 de octubre de 2015
11:00-3:00 pm, llueve o truene
Dudley Road en Framingham

¡Traiga a su familia para muchas actividades divertidas al aire libre para niños y adultos! Entrada gratuita y estacionamiento disponible en el sitio.

ASPECTOS INTERESANTES INCLUYEN
Música en vivo
Arte local
Lanchas para alquiler
Capoeira con Cais da Bahia USA
Actividades divertidas para niños
Comida
Danza de vientre
Organizaciones locales sin fines de lucro
Camiones de varios departamentos del municipio

Facebook.com/DowntownFramingham

Framingham
DOWNTOWN
Renaissance

Metro West
Regional
Transit
Authority

Diseño: Estudiantes del departamento de arte y música, Framingham State University

About the Authors

Patricia Harris and David Lyon met over ratatouille made from fresh garden vegetables and courted over fudge-topped brownies. Decades later, they're still cooking. They are co-authors of *The Meaning of Food* and *Boston Off the Beaten Path* (both Globe Pequot Press) and are authors of the Hungry Travelers Web site (hungrytravelers .com). They have written about Spanish cheese, Belgian beer, Tahitian *poisson cru*, and Neapolitan pizza for such publications as the *Boston Globe, The Robb Report,* and *Cooking Light.* They live in Cambridge, Massachusetts.